Heideggerian Theologies

Heideggerian Theologies

The Pathmarks of John Macquarrie, Rudolf Bultmann,
Paul Tillich, and Karl Rahner

HUE WOODSON

WIPF & STOCK · Eugene, Oregon

HEIDEGGERIAN THEOLOGIES
The Pathmarks of John Macquarrie, Rudolf Bultmann, Paul Tillich, and Karl Rahner

Wipf & Stock
An Imprint of Wipf and Stock Publishers
199 W. 8th Ave., Suite 3
Eugene, OR 97401

www.wipfandstock.com

PAPERBACK ISBN: 978-1-5326-4775-8
HARDCOVER ISBN: 978-1-5326-4776-5
EBOOK ISBN: 978-1-5326-4777-2

Manufactured in the U.S.A.   11/09/18

Contents

PREFACE

The Heideggerian Pathmark

In its previous life, this book existed as *Ventures in Existential Theology: The Wesleyan Quadrilateral and the Heideggerian Lenses of John Macquarrie, Rudolf Bultmann, Paul Tillich, and Karl Rahner*, having been oriented towards the 2015 completion of my Th.M. in History and Theology from Brite Divinity School at Texas Christian University. At that time, the concern was to demonstrate the ventures that Macquarrie, Bultmann, Tillich, and Rahner take through existential theology and the individual influences Heidegger has exerted on them. More importantly, each theologian contributed to a larger structure of the work that was tied to scripture, tradition, reason, and experience under the theological umbrella of the Wesleyan Quadrilateral. The intent, then, was to presuppose each theologian's "Heideggerian" concerns, by first, denoting the relationships each of them had with Heidegger as the origins of the development of these theologies. What remains, even in its prior life, is ascertaining the pathmarks each theologian assumes—within the Wesleyan Quadrilateral, as it were—as their Heideggerian influence takes them towards αλεθεια.

Existential theology remains a concern in this book's new life, which is all the more reason why the introductory section has been maintained. The difference, however, is with expressing how existential theology can trace its philosophical origins in the relationships each theologian has had with Heidegger, and the extent to which that origin fundamentally changes the way each theologian does theology. As with *Ventures in Existential Theology*, this revised edition searches for the meaning of being in each theologian's existential theology, positions their respective existential theology as an extension of Heidegger, and assumes a stance that is directed towards an unconcealment of scripture (Macquarrie), tradition (Bultmann), reason (Tillich), and experience (Rahner). While each of these are representations of the meaning of being, through existential theology, the task of each theologian is to sort out the question of the meaning of being beyond its representation in the world and towards an attunement of αλεθεια.

Now, in its current life, *Heideggerian Theologies: The Pathmarks* of John *Macquarrie, Rudolf Bultmann, Paul Tillich, and Karl Rahner* significantly expands on *Ventures in Existential Theology*, by explaining the tasks of each theologian as contributing to four Heideggeerian theologies. Though there remains a structural importance in directedness of the four theologians towards the Wesleyan Quadrilateral of the prior work, this book prioritizes the "pathmark" as guiding each theologian to αλεθεια. In this shift in focus—though not necessarily out of the view of the previous work—the intent, here, is to further expound on the nature of rhe relationship Heidegger has with each theologian, especially from a historical context as it influences the philosophical contexts of each. Through this, the Heideggerian theologies of each theologian, as they each trace αλεθεια, uses Heidegger as their guide.

Acknowledgments

First and foremost, I want to give special thanks to Dr. James O. Duke and Dr. David J. Gouwens, who served as advisors for the first-life of this project. Both have been tremendous mentors for me. I am grateful for the wonderful talks I have had with both, and the wisdom they have shared with me. They are intellectual giants and amazing men, and I hope to carry the baton forward for them. In this project's second-life, they have both served as guiding angels.

I would also like to give thanks Dr. Keri Day, Dr. Warren Carter, Dr. Namsoon Kang, and Dr. Toni Craven, all of whom I have had courses with along the way while attending Brite Divinity School at Texas Christian University and still owe a debt of gratitude.

Also, I want to give thanks for Dr. Stacy Alaimo, Dr. James Warren, Dr. Penelope Ingram, Dr. Tim Richardson, Dr. Cedrick May, Dr. Amy Tigner, Dr. Kathryn Warren, and Dr. Kevin Porter for all serving as mentors for me during my current journey through dissertating at the University of Texas at Arlington. I would be remised, of course, to not mention Dr. Luanne Frank, who has strengthened my understanding of Heidegger.

Additionally, I would like to thank Linda Dabney, Dr. Valerie Forstman, Reina Rodriguez, Sandra Brandon, Dr. Joretta Marshall, Dr. Jeffery Williams, and Dr. Newell Williams for always extending me boundless kindness while I attended Brite Divinity School, especially when I needed it the most.

I would like to thank my mom for always giving me her support, for believing in me, and for consistently recognizing my potential to succeed.

I want to thank Jeanne and Craig McKinnis, my in-laws, for their support.

Acknowledgments

And, I am thankful for my wife, Samantha, for her love and support, during many long days and nights, listening to my philosophical conversations, and supplying loving feedback.

Task and Method
of Existential Theology

What is Existential Theology?

Existential theology is not simply a synthesis of theology and existential philosophy. Such a synthesis is an important place to begin, but it is certainly only a superficial understanding of what existential theology is and does. Rather, existential theology is chiefly concerned with expressing theology by way of existential errands.[1] This term "existential errands" does two kinds of work, which must be explained straight away. First, suggesting that *existential theology expresses theology by way of existential errands* means that existential theology is preoccupied with meaning-making. This meaning-making is "existential," since it is a process of stripping away superficial meaning to uncover a meaning that is more intrinsic, pure, and innate. Existential theology's mission, then, is to uncover a theological meaning—it is an "errand" that must venture beyond traditional theological frameworks and conventional thinking. For this reason, an "errand" does a second kind of work—it denotes the extent to which meaning-making, as a process, is not straightforward, but requires venturing off the beaten track.[2]

---

1. I have taken this term from the title of a 1972 collection of essays by Norman Mailer.

2. I have borrowed "off the beaten track" from the English translation to the German title of Heidegger's collection of essays entitled *Holzwege*. Heidegger uses "holzwege" to describe a path that both leads somewhere and nowhere—in effect, Heidegger is essentially describing a "cul-de-sac" path that leads somewhere but has the potential to lead

Together, the "existential errands" of existential theology attempt to work out the problem of *being* through the meaning-making of existence and theologically pursuing what I will call "pathmarks."[3] In other words, existential theology, at its most fundamental, must pursue existence wherever existence is—it must trace existence as *being*. To do so, existential theology's task is to establish two very important duties: it centers itself upon a theological stance oriented towards "the existential," while it constructively critiques *being* as a teleological *'grundlage.'*[4] That is to say, it means theologizing with issues of existence in mind—it is about taking a theological stance oriented towards "the existential" and looking to decidedly existential concepts to conceive, grasp, and explain the way that theology can work epistemologically.

The way that existential theology works epistemologically is by an episteme—that episteme is deliberately fashioned for and around issues of existence. From that distinct system of knowing, existential theology speaks existential language, and that language, at its core, focuses on existence in terms of *being*. Through this kind of language, though undeniably theological in its ends, *being* becomes the ultimate concern of existential theology's underlying philosophy. When speaking of existential theology's concern with *being*, existence is viewed as containing both ontical being and *primordial being*—for anything to exist, be existing, or have existence, its ontics and primordiality are two sides of the same proverbial coin.[5] These two sides are respectively expressed in appearance and actuality of being itself—to this end, *being* that, on one hand, reveals itself, while, on the other, hides itself. It is through these two manners of *being*—which can

---

back to the path's beginning. Heidegger, *Off the Beaten Track*, ix.

3. I have also borrowed "pathmarks" from the English translation of another collection of essays by Heidegger entitled, *Wegmarken*. In the preface to the German edition of *Wegmarken*, Heidegger describes the term as "marks" in a path that "seek to bring to attention something of the path that shows itself to thinking only on the way: shows itself and withdraws." Heidegger, *Pathmarks*, xiii.

4. I have used this German word for "groundwork," or "foundational ground."

5. "Two sides of the same proverbial coin" has an important connotation worth mentioning for clarity. It is rooted in Ferdinand de Saussure's "signifier" and "signified" as "the sign." In this sense, the "signifier" is about primordiality and the "signified" is about ontics. If I take the signifier-signified relationship to mean the relatedness between primordiality and ontics respectively, then the concept of "the sign" is a concept about *being*. Saussure, *Course on General Linguistics*, 65.

also be called modes[6]—between which existential theology, in the general sense, seeks to make a firm distinction.

To be clear, up to this point, existential theology has only been discussed in a general sense. The intent has been to lay down the foundational structure where theory and practice will intersect in a prolegomena. At that intersection, any discussion of existential theology must be accomplished—if it is to be pure, practical, and aesthetic—by not just defining what existential theology is as a qualifier, but what it does quantitatively.[7] This means it is important to take an approach which expresses existential theology's praxis, in order to effectively quantify what existential theology can look like, rather than simply objectifying it and assigning a body of knowledge to it.[8] But, such praxis is only the beginning of the two-part task of this thesis.

That task, in its preliminary part, involves establishing a theoretical understanding of existential theology so that the intention proceeding from that basic understanding moves beyond denoting what existential theology is in the general sense. What arises from these preliminaries is the possibility of outlining a more specialized approach that is not limited to the synthesis that the term "existential theology" implies. Though this is a very important place to begin, remaining there will prove to be only a one-dimensional understanding of existential theology itself. Speaking about it in the general sense—as in purporting the existential-theological dialogue explicit in its nomenclature—only qualifies "what it is" as something that

---

6. I use the term "modes" to consider that "being," like Heidegger, can be represented in different forms. These "modes" are, essentially, manners in which "being" chooses to disclose itself. In other words, the "modes of being" are often manners in which "being" conceals and hides itself to prevent itself from "unconcealment." For Heidegger, "being," particularly through "modes," likes to hide and prefers to conceal itself. This is the problem pf metaphysics, as Heidegger argues. Any attempt at overcoming metaphysics must be founded on overcoming the "modes" of "being" to disclose "being" in a state of "unconcealment." See Heidegger, *Kant and the Problem of Metaphysics.*

7. By saying "pure, practical, and aesthetic," I am thinking specially of Kant's Three *Critiques* that examine reason respectively as "pure reason," "practical reason," and "aesthetic judgment." I offer this to suggest, then, that existential theology should—and must—follow "reason," especially as an Kantian analytic, so to speak.

8. In other words, rather that objectifying "existential theology" as a term, my intent is to examine what it actually looks like in "praxis." In other words, I want to examine how it works in action, or its performativity. Objectification only gets to what it is qualitatively, in the general sense—I wish to explain what it can do quantitatively, in the narrow sense.

requires, by necessity, to describe "what makes it there" in quantitative terms.[9]

The second, and most important part of the task of this thesis is to discuss and explain existential theology in a narrow sense, which means expressing only a specific kind of existential theology. What that means, then, is that there is not one, monolithic existential theology, but various existential theologies. There are many ways to do existential theology, since, just as there are various views of existential philosophies, there are many theological stances. To recognize this is to make certain disclaimers up front for clarity—these disclaimers must be specific and specialized if for no other reason than to prevent us from being limited to simple prelimi- naries, or qualifying existential theology in only a general sense.

With this in mind, this thesis seeks to quantify what existential the- ology can be in a narrow sense. In effect, this thesis will offer *a kind of existential theology* construed through a specific kind of "theology" and a certain type of "existential" philosophy—what I will call *ventures in exis- tential theology*. To do so, let us consider these two parts separately—first, the "theology" and then the adjectival "existential" part—in order to define what kind of existential theology this thesis intends to present.

"The Wesleyan Quadrilateral" as a Theological Stance

The "theology" offered in this thesis is based on the Wesleyan Quadrilateral, which is named for the Anglican theologian John Wesley (1703–1791). As coined by Albert Outler (1908–1989), the Wesleyan Quadrilateral is a con- ceptual framework used to construct John Wesley's theology around the four tenets of scripture, tradition, reason, and experience—this theologi- cal "quadrilateral" forms an important "marrow of Christian truth" for the evangelical movement known as Methodism.[10] Not only has the Wesleyan Quadrilateral become an essentialist way to categorize Methodist theologi- cal thinking into a relationship between scripture, tradition, reason, and experience, but Outler's contribution of this framework has had cross-

---

9. See note 8.

10. This is taken from the *2012 Book of Discipline*, which states the following: "...there is a marrow of Christian truth that can be identified and that must be conserved. This living core, as [Methodists] believed, stands in revealed Scripture, illumined by tradition, vivified in personal and corporate experience, and confirmed by reason." *2012 Book of Discipline of the United Methodist Church*, 55.

denominational influence, specifically as a traditional way to conceive of, grasp, and explain what theology is and what it does.

To some extent, there is "a crucial methodological question as to whether in the sprawling array of [Wesley's] writings and editings there are consistent interests that amount to a coherent self-understanding."[11] The "crucial methodological question," then, is if a framework can be applied to Wesley's theology—in particular, is there a "coherent self-understanding" or any "consistent interests" to the way Wesley worked as a theologian? Outler suggests that there is a "coherent" framework. It becomes "instructive," according to Outler, "to notice the reiterative pattern in [Wesley's] doctrinal formulations [where] basic themes appear repeatedly"[12] So, as further explained by Outler, "[Wesley's] thought was consciously organized around a stable core of basic coordinated motifs."[13] From these "basic coordinated motifs," in Outler's view:

> We can see in Wesley's a distinctive theological method, with Scripture as its preeminent norm but interfaced with tradition, reason and Christian experience as dynamic and interactive aids in the interpretation of the Word of God in Scripture.[14]

Clearly, for Outler, Wesley's thought incorporates "basic coordinated motifs" that have scripture at their core. Scripture, then, becomes not just the basis for Wesley's sense of a theological norm, but is pivotal to Wesley's theological method itself.[15] That method, as Outler argues, revolves mainly around what is "interfaced" between scripture and "tradition, reason, and Christian experience." By way of this "interface" or what I would call intersectionality, Outler believes that Wesley's understanding of tradition, reason and Christian experience become "dynamic and interactive aids in the interpretation of the Word of God in Scripture." Consequently, Outler suggests that, though there are four elements to Wesley's theological method:

> This complex method, with its four-fold reference, is a good deal more sophisticated than it appears, and could be more fruitful for contemporary theologizing than has yet been realized. It preserves the primacy of Scripture, it profits from the wisdom of tradition, it

---

11. Outler, ed., *The Works of John Wesley: Volume 1: Sermons I, 1–33*, 5.

12. Outler, ed. *John Wesley*, 26.

13. Ibid., 27.

14. Outler, "The Wesleyan Quadrilateral—In John Wesley," 9.

15. Jones, *John Wesley's Conception and Use of Scripture*, 11–16.

accepts the disciplines of critical reason and its stress on the Christian experience of grace gives it existential force.[16]

To be sure, Outler describes Wesley's "complex method" as a "four-fold reference," which, ultimately, exudes an "existential force." The key to Outler's conception of Wesley's theological method is through that conception's "existential force." This "existential force," if attending to Outler's understanding of the "Quadrilateral," means that the "four-fold reference" of scripture, tradition, reason, and experience contain—both as four individualized concepts and through their conceptual, four-fold intersectionality—the possibility of meaning-making.

Outler presents the Wesleyan Quadrilateral as a framework of four essentialist parts that should not be situated as equivalents, as the geometric dimensions of the "quadrilateral" would suggest. With this in mind, as a disclaimer, Outler offers the "quadrilateral" as something that should not be "taken too literally."[17] Instead, Outler proposes that the "quadrilateral" is "intended as a metaphor for a four element syndrome, including the four-fold guidelines of authority in Wesley's theological method."[18] The "quadrilateral," as Outler understands it, is simply a way to conceptualize Wesley's theological method. Granted, Outler views scripture, tradition, reason, and experience working in conjunction with one another in a "quaternity"[19] However, he is careful to emphasize that scripture is at the center of the "quadrilateral," since, as Outler puts it, "Holy Scripture is clearly unique."[20] This uniqueness of scripture, when taken within the confines of the quadrilateral, leads directly to what Outler denotes as the "primacy of scripture" over tradition, reason, and experience.[21]

What becomes particularly essential about Outler's framework is that it provides an important episteme about theology, one that adds issues of history, logic, and phenomenology to *sola scriptura* and the ever-evolving discourse between doctrine, humanity, and God.

---

16. Outler, "The Wesleyan Quadrilateral—In John Wesley," 10.

17. Ibid., 11.

18. Ibid.

19. Ibid.

20. Ibid.

21. Ibid., 16.

"Heideggerian Being" as an Existential Lens

While Outler's Wesleyan Quadrilateral framework provides the theological stance for this thesis, its lens will be existential in genre. More specifically, that existential lens will be Heideggerian in its approach —it is a lens based on the "existential-ontological"[22] concepts of Martin Heidegger (1889–1976) first introduced in *Sein und Zeit* in 1927, and first translated into English in 1962 as *Being and Time*.

However, before going any further, there are two prefaces that must be made up front. The first is this: Heidegger never completed *Being and Time*. In its current form, *Being and Time* is only a fraction of the work that Heidegger initially conceived—as inarguably a fragment, the work does not completely represent what Heidegger envisioned the work would be. This fact is evident by the outline Heidegger offers at the end of the work's "Second Introduction," and, in turn, is noted by the 1962 translators.[23] In my view, what this preface poses is an important, first problem when discussing "Heideggerian Being" in reference to *Being and Time*. The question that must be asked is this: *where would Heidegger's argument about being have ultimately gone, if he had finished Being and Time as planned?* I do not intend to answer that question, but to simply ask it, for now. Not only does this question require that Heidegger's unfinished argument be worked out in a fashion adequate enough to call anything a "Heideggerian lens" or "Heideggerian Being," but another question must be asked in conjunction. That second question is related to the years shortly after the original publication of *Being and Time*, when it has been argued that Heidegger makes a change in his thinking—it is a shift known in a sector of Heideggerian scholarship as the *die kehre*, or "the turn."[24] This second preface leads to

---

22. This term denotes the kind of philosophy Heidegger was engaged in, particularly in *Being and Time*. Though Heidegger's task can be (and is often) described as existential philosophy, it is, in fact, "existential-ontological," meaning that the ultimate task is to make meaning out of "the ontological." To be more specific, this means making meaning out of ontics, with the intent of deconstructing all of metaphysics and arriving at an "existential" understanding of the meaning of *Being*.

23. Heidegger, *Being and Time*, 64.

24. This "turn," as it has been called, was first argued by William J. Richardson. For Richardson, this "turn" in Heidegger's understanding of the problem of being is best exemplified in Heidegger's most important work after the 1927 publication of *Being and Time* entitled *Beiträge zur Philosophie (Vom Ereignis)*, which was written from 1936 to 1938, but not published until 1989 as *Contributions to Philosophy (From Enowning)*. Though, in the decade or so before *Beiträge zur Philosophie*, Heidegger produces three

a second question that can be expressed as the following: *does Heidegger's understanding of the problem of being truly change at all?* I do not intend to answer this question either, since such an answer, as with a possible answer to the first, will only prove to take the definitions of *Heideggerian lens* and *Heideggerian Being* too far afield.

In lieu of an answer to either preface's question, I propose that there is little doubt that *being* is Heidegger's main, overarching preoccupation. In effect, I believe that there is no "turn" in Heidegger's thought. To say that there is a "turn" supposes that there is a fundamental change in Heidegger's philosophizing. I do not think this is so. Instead, if there is any "turn" in Heidegger, it is towards a more primordial understanding of *being*—and inevitably towards the ground of *primordial being* in ἀλήθεια. Any *die kehre*, so to speak, is not so much about Heidegger's concern with redefining "what being is"—or, "turning" away from the fundamental conceptualization of *Being and Time*—but, rather, with refining the very essence of the language used to describe *what being is*. In Heidegger's view, to determine *what being is* means thinking a new kind of thought about *what being is*, which would be based on learning *what being is*.[25] Such thinking requires a *Heideggerian lens*. To this end, a *Heideggerian lens* will be chiefly concerned with disclosing *what being is*, adequately working out *Dasein* through deconstructing *being-in-the-world*, and understanding human existence beyond the ontical.

This lens utilizes a Heideggerian form of existentialism—considering, of course, that this is merely a categorization, of which Heidegger himself would question and refute. Nevertheless, I feel it is important to denote a "Heidegger's existentialism" as a distinct brand of existential philosophy from those of Kierkegaard, Nietzsche and Sartre.[26] This Heideggerian kind

---

other works that recapitulate his understanding of the problem of being—*Kant und das Problem der Metaphysik*, (1929), *Was ist Metaphysik?* (1929), and *Einführung in die Metaphysik* (1935)—it is especially with *Beiträge*, as Richardson argues, that Heidegger's "turn" is the most apparent. See Richardson, *Heidegger: Through Phenomenology to Thought*.

25. Heidegger makes this argument at the outset of his lecture entitled "What is Called Thinking?" In it, he begins by drawing a connection between learning and thinking, suggesting that the former must precede the latter. Heidegger, *What is Called Thinking?*, 3.

26. Kierkegaard and Nietzsche are considered as "founders" or "fathers" of existentialism that were mainly reacting to the philosophical systemization of Hegel, while Heidegger and Sartre develop existential philosophy into different modernized brands. Setting aside the fact that Heidegger resisted the "existentialist" label and Sartre embraced that moniker, I have presented a relatively broad survey of the roles of Kierkegaard,

of existentialism has, within itself, two strains of thought directly related to *die kehre*: they have been referred to as "early Heidegger" and "later Heidegger."[27] This thesis will mostly employ "later Heidegger," but it will also refer to the "early" period frequently, particularly as a foundational starting point to what *Heideggerian Being* is in that "early" period and what it becomes in "later Heidegger." Moreover, it is by way of that "early" period that I will ground my interpretation of a *Heideggerian lens*. Though Heidegger's "early" period is mainly argued in *Being and Time*, essential echoes of this seminal text reverberate throughout the corpus of Heideggerian thought as re-articulations and recapitulations up to and including the later period: *Heideggerian Being* has primordial significance reaching beyond superficial ontics and the whole of metaphysics itself.

By taking up the thought of *Heideggerian Being*, this thesis intends to apply that thought to theological thinking about the Wesleyan Quadrilateral. The assertion is that existential theology can be focused on the possibility that *being* can be recovered, discovered, or uncovered—or, as later Heidegger calls it, "unconcealed"—respectively from the four tenets of scripture, tradition, reason, and experience. In effect, each tenet contains *being* at their primordial cores. At those primordial cores, truth, or ἀλήθεια, must be *unconcealed*, since scripture, tradition, reason, and experience are all "concealments" of ἀλήθεια.[28]

To do theology through a *Heideggerian lens* means, first and foremost, adhering to a theological stance—that stance, as previously defined, is with Outler's Wesleyan Quadrilateral. From that theological situatedness, one

---

Nietzsche, Heidegger, and Sartre within a rather fractured field of existentialism. There is some consensus in this matter, which can be found in the following eight sources: William Barrett, *Irrational Man: A Study in Existential Philosophy* (Garden City, NY: Doubleday and Company, 1958); William Barrett, *What is Existentialism?* (New York, NY: Grove Press, Inc., 1964); H.J. Blackham, ed., *Reality, Man, and Existence: Essential Works of Existentialism* (New York, NY: Bantam, 1965); H. J. Blackham, *Six Existentialist Thinkers* (New York, NY: Harper and Brothers, 1959); Ernst Breisach, *Introduction to Modern Existentialism* (New York, NY: Grove Press, Inc., 1962); James Collins, *The Existentialists: A Critical Study* (Chicago, IL: Henry Regnery Company, 1952); John Macquarrie, *Existentialism* (New York, NY: World Publishing Company, 1972); and Mary Warnock, *Existentialism* (New York, NY: Oxford University Press, 1970).

27. See note 22.

28. The term "truth" is a very crude, albeit problematic, translation of the Greek term ἀλήθεια. As a term, "truth" carries a lot of unnecessary hermeneutical baggage and that baggage diminishes or reduces any essentialist meaning of the original Greek term. In order to follow in a Heideggerian approach, it is important to utilize ἀλήθεια as the better, more accurate term.

must engage in thinking a thought focused on excavating ἀλήθεια from the ontics of scripture, tradition, reason, and experience, in order to essentialize existential meaning inherent, but suppressed within them. This means carefully stripping away the ontical structures in each and, subsequently, deconstructing the metaphysics of those ontics to allow *being* to reveal itself as it already is.

Once disclosed, *being*, as it respectively exists in scripture, tradition, reason, and experience, opens the possibility to examine existence along two lines of inquiry: primordially and ontically. Though both embark on a study of *being*, the former is concerned with *being* in the narrow sense, while the latter is devoted to *being* in the general sense. In other words, perhaps that difference can be respectively explained as *being* at the micro-level and *being* at the macro-level. In the former, *being* is expressed in an innate, inherent fashion, with the intent of interpreting *being* as the most fundamental groundwork from which an object of understanding exists at its lowest denominator. To be sure, what *being* is at this primordial level is analogous to Gottfried Leibniz's "monad."[29] In another sense, primordiality can be likened to Aristotle's "unmoved mover."[30] In other words, similarly to the "monad" and "the unmoved mover," *primordial being* is the most indivisible entity that all objects of understanding share as Kantian things-in-themselves, representing what I will henceforth denote as "is-ness."[31]

This *is-ness* must be encased in what I will call "there-ness," or something that can be objectified beyond perception or justified belief, but as something that can be explained with a rational account.[32] To explain with

29. As Gottfried Leibniz describes in an essay entitled "The Principles of Philosophy, or the Monadology" in 1714, "monads" are the "true atoms of nature" and "the element of all things." The "monad" is critical to how Leibniz conceives of the truth as being either one of "reasoning" or one of "fact." In either case, truth is contingent on the monad, as a "simple substance, which goes to make up composites." Leibniz, *Discourse on Metaphysics*, 251; Leibniz, *Philosophical Essays*, 213.

30. Aristotle's concept of "the unmoved mover" occurs in two texts: *Metaphysics* and *Physics*. In the latter, *Physics*—the text that scholars believe predates *Metaphysics*—Aristotle describes "the unmoved mover" as "the first mover" which is "eternal," in Book Theta, Lines 258b-259a. In the former, *Metaphysics*, Aristotle suggests that "the unmoved mover" is "changeless" while it affects change in other beings, in Book Lambda in 1071b. See Aristotle, *Physics*, and Aristotle, *Metaphysics*.

31. To be clear, my term "is-ness" utilizes the same conceptualization of the primordial as Leibniz's "monad." My notion of what is "is" is formulated, in part, through "monadology." See note 29.

32. Though "there-ness" is operating in the Heideggerian sense of "Dasein," I must note that my understanding of "there-ness" and "being-there" derives from the Platonic

a rational account involves formulating *being* at an ontical level. In this way, ontical *being* is *there-ness* at this ontical level—*there-ness* is how *being* expresses itself through the temporality of its everydayness.[33] In this sense, what makes this level different from the primordial level is that *being* is materialized as Frege's "reference," or bracketed with Husserl's "phenomenological epoche."[34]

"Is-ness" and "There-ness"

At an ontical level, the four theological tenets of scripture, tradition, reason, and experience are tangible representations of *there-ness* that are connected to primordial *is-ness*. That *is-ness* is analogous to Heidegger's notion of the constant presence of "what-ness."[35] Through either case, *is-ness* is translated into *there-ness* as a referent and *there-ness* points back to *is-ness*. Or, in other words, if continuing for just a moment through a Platonic framework, *is-ness* is "the whole," while "the parts" of the whole are delineated into four kinds of *there-ness*.[36] To be sure, as far as scripture, tradition, reason, and experience are concerned, they are four different forms of construed *is-ness* translated as four representations of *there-ness*. Each has "being-in-the-world" in what can be described as authentic existence.[37]

For now, I will use *authentic existence* rather loosely, since it will prove to be problematic as I proceed. At this point, what must be said about *authentic existence* is that it is our main focus, particularly if that focus should be on *being* at the primordial level. However, at present, let us continue with

---

understanding of knowledge. See Line 210B from Plato, *Theaetetus*, 92.

33. Heidegger, *Being and Time*, 421.

34. I use Frege's "reference" and Husserl's "phenomenological epoche" as complementary concepts, when materializing "being" from its primordial level. Both are constituted by "sense" or an "idea." But, in keeping in mind the continuity in the thinking between Husserl and Heidegger, the Husserl's "phenomenological epoche" and the necessity of bracketing contains a more important relationship between the primordial level and the ontical level. Husserl, *Ideas: General Introduction to Pure Phenomenology*, 107–111

35. Heidegger, *Basic Questions of Philosophy: Selected "Problems" of "Logic,"* 66–67.

36. Through Socrates, Plato describes the relationship between "the whole" and "the parts" in *The Republic*. One example of this is in Lines 434d-441c with the explanation Socrates provides of the composition of the soul, as a whole, which is delineated between the rational, spirited, and desiring parts. Plato, *The Republic*, 101–110.

37. That is, "being-in-the-world" that is superficially authenticated in the everydayness of being and its explication in the world.

authentic existence loosely before deconstructing it. *Authentic existence,* rather loosely, is a way of understanding what existence is—in another sense, *what existence is* equates to *what being is.* To say *what existence is* means differentiating existence as either primordial *is-ness* or ontical *there-ness.* The latter is a manifestation of the former. If *there-ness* at the ontical level is only translation of *is-ness* at the primordial level, it becomes possible to recognize that *there-ness* is not *authentic existence,* especially if a focus on *being* should occur at the primordial level.

First, an explanation of *authentic existence* must be given. In brief, what I mean by the term is that each of the four theological tenets has real meaning in the world, is shaped by time and space, and authentically engages with human understanding for the sole purpose of concretizing *is-ness* into *there-ness.* For instance, when suggesting that scripture has *authentic existence,* its *there-ness* can be referenced as a single biblical text, or even the collection of biblical texts canonized as the Bible. In turning to tradition as another example, when asserting that tradition has an *authentic existence,* its *there-ness* can be referenced in the history of Christianity, the historical Jesus, or even the historical development of the Church up to the present day. Similarly, reason and experience have *authentic existence* since they allow human faculties to think rationally and experientially about the authenticity of scripture and tradition and then, by extension, position human epistemology by thinking theologically.

But, when using the term *authentic existence,* what is authenticated is only at the ontical level with *there-ness.* I believe that this is a very important way to define *authentic existence*—it is only an ontical representation of being as *there-ness.* When considering scripture, tradition, reason, and experience as having *authentic existence,* each of them and their respective *there-ness* merely conceals the *primordial being* in each of them, and that concealed being is truly *authentic existence.*

Such a claim does not mean to imply that *there-ness* is inauthentic existence. Any claim in that fashion is misunderstanding what *there-ness* is, and assuming that *there-ness* is not true existence. Rather, *there-ness* is only ontical *being* and, as such, is only the most superficial level of inquiry about *being.* To be sure, there is nothing inauthentic about *there-ness,* since the human capacity to reference "being-there" is an essential part of the human epistemological process.[38] *There-ness* is *being* as it is most readily disclosed in the world to us, through what Heidegger refers to as "being-

---

38. "Being-there" is a reference to Heidegger's "Dasein."

in-the-world" and "ready-to-hand"—it is referenced, or referential *being* in everydayness.[39] Nevertheless, to examine *being* through an existential lens means examining *is-ness*. This sort of inquiry allows for a primordial assessment of each of our four theological tenets by first presupposing that they are each comprised of *primordial being*, or an *is-ness*, and then acknowledging that an existential lens—a *Heideggerian lens*, to be exact—must deconstruct any assumptions about *there-ness* as *authentic existence*. *There-ness* may be what is there, but *there-ness* is not *what being is*. On the contrary, *is-ness* is *what being is*. But, again, *there-ness* must be deconstructed so that, by way of that deconstruction, *is-ness* yields itself "as it already is."[40] To do this, as Heidegger argues in the introduction to *Being and Time*, it means fundamentally changing the way we currently think in order to learn how to think a new kind of thought[41] about *there-ness*, *is-ness*, and the categorical, existential difference between them. In short, what this means, first and foremost, is resigning to the notion that *there-ness* is not *being* in the *authentic sense*.

Essentially, if *there-ness* is not *authentic existence*, then it is only what I would describe as *concealed* existence.[42] In other words, *there-ness* is existence that is "being-in-the-world." Simply put, *there-ness* is a way through which *being* chooses to reveal itself in the world—that choice is based, as Heidegger posits, on *being* preferring to hide itself, instead of showing itself as it already is.[43] When *being* situates itself as *there-ness*, it becomes essentially a stand-in *is-ness*—if the ultimate concern for being is to disclose

---

39. Heidegger, *Ontology—The Hermeneutics of Facticity*, 65–67

40. "As it already is" is drawn from Heidegger's notion that "being," as such, must disclose, unmask, or reveal itself as it already is. To be clear, when "being" unconceals itself "as it already is," this kind of unconcealment in invested the essence of freedom and "letting beings be." Martin Heidegger, "On the Essence of Truth," In *Basic Writings*, Edited by David F. Krell, 111–138 (San Francisco, CA: Harper San Francisco, 1992), 125.

41. Though Heidegger argues for a new way of thinking about the concept of being in *Being and Time*, he speaks more specifically about the task of thinking in the lecture entitled "*Was Heisst Denken?*" Thinking a new kind of thought requires fundamentally restructuring how thinking happens. In that lecture, Heidegger states that "in order to be capable of thinking, we need to learn it first." That is, of course, assuming that we do not know how to learn which, in turn, has affected what we call thinking. Heidegger, *What is Called Thinking?*, 4.

42. "Concealed existence," as I have called it, is a kind of existence that is not authentic, since it conceals "is-ness." In other words, "concealed existence" is "there-ness," or "what is there" at only the most superficial understanding of "being."

43. See Note 38.

what being is "as it already is," then that concern is with authentic existence, which can only occur, as such, as *is-ness*.

For Heidegger, *is-ness* is "ek-sistence"—it is nothing more than an existential manner in which *being* allows itself to be perceived, grasped, and explained through what Heidegger denotes as "standing out."[44] This manner is ecstatic, since *being* discloses its *is-ness* through an ecstatic essence.[45] *Is-ness*, then, is "the dimension of the ecstasis of ek-sistence."[46] As Heidegger coins it, "ek-sistence" expresses not only the extent to which "there-ness" is different from "is-ness"—an explicit distinction made in the term from the implied term—but the extent to which the latter embodies a "dwelling in the nearness of Being."[47] To this end, "is-ness," as the ek-sistence of humanity's *being*, has a "nearness of Being" because it "stands ek-sistingly in the destiny of Being."[48] What Heidegger is arguing, then, is that "ek-sistence"—what I have referred to as *authentic existence*, or even what might be furthered with my Heidegger-hypnenated "*being*-authenticated-in-the-destiny-of-*Being*"—is an analytic possibility of *Dasein*,[49] which leads *being* towards "the destiny" of becoming "as it already is." The *authentic existence* of *being*—"ek-sistence," or "is-ness"—becomes critical to how Heidegger wishes to examine *being* itself, especially as what I would like to henceforth refer to exclusively as "primordial being."

"Primordial Being," the Existential Theologian, and ἀλήθεια

As with Heidegger's examination of *primordial being* as an analytic possibility of *Dasein*, the same examination preoccupies the philosophical thought of the existential theologian. If such a theologian views their existentialism through a *Heideggerian lens*, the main concern is with differentiating *is-ness*

---

44. "Stand out" refers to Heidegger's assertion that the "ek-sistence" is based on "standing in the clearing of Being." In this regard, then, "the clearing," as Heidegger describes it, allows *Being* to "stand out" as something that can be disclosed "out of" what is "there." This "out of," particularly for Heidegger, utilizes the Greek prefix of "ἐξ-"—this can be translated as "out of." Heidegger, "Letter on Humanism," 228.

45. Ibid., 235.

46. Ibid., 237.

47. Heidegger, "Letter on Humanism," 245.

48. Ibid., 239.

49. Heidegger, *Being and Time*, 36–40.

from *there-ness*. This differentiation is made in order to uncover and isolate *primordial being* from the "concealedness" of its everydayness.[50]

Though Heidegger's stance is not explicitly theological, it is possible to tease out what might be referred to as a "Heideggerian theology."[51] *Being and Time*, for example, begins on philosophical footing, but proceeds in a theological manner. Clearly, Heidegger begins his examination of *being* by situating his philosophical argument as an extension of Plato's *Sophist*.[52] What follows, essentially, is a careful, albeit tedious, deconstruction of how the history of philosophy after Plato has incorrectly conceptualized *what being is*.[53] This deconstruction, or what Heidegger denotes as '*destruktion*,' is the task ('*aufgabe*') of *Being of Time*, particularly the work's Part II.[54] But, I as mentioned earlier, Heidegger never completed *Being and Time*, and only approximations can be made about what Heidegger's '*destruktion*' would have looked like. However, what *Being and Time* makes clear is this: there is a distinction that Heidegger creates between ontical *there-ness* and primordial *is-ness*. In my view, this distinction moves from the philosophical (issues of ontics) to the theological (issues of primordiality).

The incomplete sections of *Being and Time*—though they can, again, only be approximated from the outline offered and reconstructing claims made subsequently in *Kant and the Problem of Metaphysics*, *An Introduction to Metaphysics*, and *The Basic Problems of Phenomenology*, not to mention from other works such as *Contribution to Philosophy (From Enowning)*, *Logic: The Question of Truth*, *Being and Truth* and *The Event*—would have likely forged into theological territory about *primordial being*.[55] What I

50. This sort of differentiation, as I have argued, can be linked to one of the first two directives Heidegger outlines in his *Parmenides* lecture. The first directive, as such, involves approaching the terms "unconcealedness" and "concealedness" as respectively "aletheia" and "lethe." Heidegger, *Parmenides*, 15–16.

51. I must be careful with this term, since, at face value, it seems nonsensical. However, if we are looking at what Heidegger's investigation in the meaning of Being is—that is, what the primary goal of that investigation is—then Being does carry a divine quality to it that requires interpretation and meaning-making. Theology, then, is about the study of the divine. Sure, theology can be referred to as "the study of God," but "theos" is also something divine. Heidegger's *Being* is something divine, something that is like "theos."

52. Heidegger, *Being and Time*, 1.

53. Ibid.

54. Schalow and Denker, eds, *Historical Dictionary of Heidegger's Philosophy*, 94.

55. The lectures/notes that were eventually published as *Kant and the Problem of Metaphysics*, *An Introduction to Metaphysics*, *The Basic Problems of Phenomenology*, *Contribution to Philosophy (From Enowning)*, *Logic: The Question of Truth*, *Being and Truth*,

mean, then, is that the argument in Part II of *Being and Time* is point-ing towards a concept of *primordial being* which can only be theologically explained, especially if the theological influences upon Heidegger's *primor-dial being* are rooted in medieval theology and scholasticism of the High Middle Ages.[56]

Nevertheless, it is important to be careful about suggesting that Heidegger intends to theologize about *primordial being*. When I offer "theologize," I do so in a very narrow sense. Any such "theologizing," for Heidegger's *Being and Time*, would involve a kind of thinking that ques-tions and attempts to "overcome" the categorizations of Christian theol-ogy, by "following Nietzsche."[57] Though Heidegger is inarguably "following Nietzsche," it is, in fact, unfair to suggest that Heidegger's approach to "overcoming metaphysics"[58] and, by extension, an understanding of the influence of Neoplatonism upon Christian thought,[59] is based on an athe-istic perspective. Certainly, that perspective is manifested "in the wake of Nietzsche's declaration of the death of God,"[60] but, rather than labelling Heidegger an atheist, he simply refuses to assume a theological voice. That refusal, as Laurence Hemming proposes, is "a way of taking up a position with regard to the whole of the history of Western philosophy and the way in which it has articulated God."[61] As a result, Heidegger's "position" is not necessarily based on a view of faith, but, instead, "springs from a strictly

and *The Event* are all considered as drafts of the incomplete Part II of *Being and Time*. In each of these "lectures/notes," Heidegger is concerned with "primordial being"—this is a path towards primordiality and "what being is."

56. To be clear, my term "primordial being" is equivalent to Heidegger's "Being." To this end, like Heidegger, the Scholastics of the High Middle Ages—such as Duns Scotus, William of Ockham, Thomas Aquinas, and Bonaventure—consider "Being," as Judith Wolfe notes in *Heidegger and Theology*, as ". . .nothing less than another name for God himself." Wolfe, *Heidegger and Theology*, 81,

57. Gall, *Beyond Theism and Atheism: Heidegger's Significance for Religious Thinking*, 27.

58. Though, on one hand, I am referring to the task Heidegger sets forth in the Intro-duction of *Being and Time*, which is the necessity of the question of Being in relation to a history of inadequately asking that question that begins with Plato, on the other, I am pointing to Heidegger's more explicit notion of "overcoming metaphysics" in the aptly titled essay that appears in *The End of Philosophy*. In this essay, Heidegger traces the His-tory of Being to, among others, Nietzsche, to which Heidegger ascribes a kind of meta-physics by which "philosophy is completed." Heidegger, "Overcoming Metaphysics," 95.

59. O'Meara, "Introduction," in *Neoplatonism and Christian Thought*, ix-xi.

60. Hemming, *Heidegger's Atheism: The Refusal of a Theological Voice*, 44.

61. Ibid.

philosophical motive."[62] Yet, Heidegger is deeply invested in the problem of God, however implicit that investment may be in *Being and Time*.

Even if he approaches the problem of God by way of the necessity of "the question of the meaning of *Being*" (*'die Frage nach dem Sinn von Sein'*),[63] Heidegger's *Dasein*, in my view, gestures towards understanding *being* theologically. This is the task of the incomplete Part II of *Being and Time*—the necessity (*'die Notwendigkeit'*) of the question of the meaning of *Being* through overcoming metaphysics, adequately working out the problem of *being*, and forming a theological-like doctrine on primordiality.[64] Absent from this task, as Hemming has rightly pointed out, is a theological voice—to be sure, there is a refusal to use a theological voice in *Being and Time*. Because of this, *Dasein* is a stand-in for speaking theologically, without actually speaking theologically—and yet it is based on Heidegger's belief in theology as a positive science.[65] The concept of *Dasein*, as Heidegger presents it, becomes the means by which Heidegger brings us to the problem of God by placing us in the role of an "interlocutor" to the problem.[66] What undergirds this, then, with *Dasein* always in the backdrop, is an "unclarified" relationship that Heidegger makes between his notion of *Being* and the problem of God.[67] This becomes especially apparent, as Robert Gall seems to agree in the following:

> [. . .]if we understand the description of Dasein in *Sein und Zeit* as pointing to some greater reality, a ground of beings, beyond the thrownness, contingency, and conditionedness of beings as a whole, a creator who is author of man's being. Such an

---

62. Ibid.

63. Heidegger, *Sein und Zeit*, 1.

64. I believe Heidegger operates from an implied "theological doctrine of primordiality," since he explains, early in the First Introduction to *Being and Time*, the following: "Theology is seeking a more primordial interpretation of man's Being towards God, prescribed by the meaning of faith itself and remaining within it." What Heidegger recognizes, of course, is what theology is and how theology operates "by the meaning of faith and remaining within it." Heidegger does not wish to "remain" within faith, particularly if his concern is theological and that concern is focused on "a more primordial interpretation of man's Being towards God." So, I believe that part of the task Heidegger set for *Being and Time*'s incomplete Part II was to find a way to speak about primordiality and *Being* (in the sense of something more primordial to humanity's *being*) without "remaining within" faith. Heidegger, *Being and Time*, 30.

65. Heidegger, "Phenomenology and Theology," 7.

66. Hemming, *Heidegger's Atheism: The Refusal of a Theological Voice*, 45.

67. Kovacs, *The Question of God in Heidegger's Phenomenology*, 22.

understanding is usually coupled with the criticism that Heidegger needs to go farther than he does in *Sein und Zeit* in order to avoid pessimism and nihilism.[68]

Heidegger's "description of Dasein" does, indeed, point "to some greater reality, a ground of beings." That "greater reality" is more theological than it is philosophical. Since *Dasein* points to "a creator who is the author of man's being" on the way towards overcoming metaphysics and isolating *what being is*, the incomplete Part II would have been the most theological part of *Being and Time*—this seems especially so, particularly given what Heidegger's *die kehre* becomes chiefly focused on.[69]

I am making this sort of argument about *Being and Time* in order to make clear what *Being and Time* does and what it does not do. That is to say, what must be addressed is where the argument of *Being and Time* begins and where that argument ends—Heidegger begins his argument about *primordial being*, but that argument falls short. Even if, as Gall argues, "[he] needs to go farther than he does," Heidegger's argument ends with a stance. Though it may be an incomplete argument, Heidegger has developed a stance, just the same. My concern, then, is to suggest that this stance—even if being derived from an incomplete argument—must function through theological dispositions about the *concealment* of *primordial being*. If Heidegger's intent in the incomplete section of *Being and Time* is for a phenomenological "destruktion" of the history of ontology, certain theological dispositions are necessary and critical.[70]

With these theological dispositions in mind, there are four representative existential theologians that theologize from a Heideggerian stance that fundamentally seeks to "unconceal" *primordial being* from the *concealment* of everydayness.[71] These theologians are John Macquarrie (1919–2007), Rudolf Bultmann (1884–1976), Paul Tillich (1886–1965), and Karl Rahner (1904–1984), all of which are deeply influenced by Heidegger. This

68. Gall, *Beyond Theism and Atheism: Heidegger's Significance for Religious Thinking*, 25.

69. If we are to argue that '*die kehre*' is focused not just on "what being is," but on the "unconcealment" of being as "aletheia," then it is perhaps possible to suggest that Heidegger's preoccupation with "aletheia" is devoted to a theological understanding of it. That is, to say that the only way to know "what being is" is through an unconcealment of it, as well as being exposed to the openness of the clearing, so that "what being is" can be as it already is.

70. Heidegger, *Being and Time*, 41–49.

71. Heidegger, *Parmenides*, 15–16.

Heideggerian influence serves two purposes. First, each of these existential theologians has set for themselves the task of searching for *primordial being* by completing the incomplete Part II of Heidegger's *Being and Time*—each chiefly accomplishes this through a respective systematic theology that assumes Heideggerian existential categories. Moreover, though each existential theologian's corpus of writings is extensive, each ultimately centralizes the argumentative hub of their theological approach to *primordial being* in a respective magnum opus. Now, the second purpose, as each presents a different systematic theology expressed in a respective magnum opus meant to complete and extend *Being and Time*, is to radicalize how each approaches an understanding of *primordial being* as theological deconstructionists pushing back against their respective traditional theological lineages.

Despite these lineages, each theologian is overwhelmingly indebted to Heidegger's existentialism in their distinct brands of existential theology. As decidedly "existential" theologians, Macquarrie's Anglicanism, Bultmann and Tillich's Lutheran-Protestantism, and Rahner's Jesuit-Catholicism utilize Heidegger's two-fold task in working out the question of *being* in the "Second Introduction" to *Being and Time*. Consequently, the existential theologies of Macquarrie, Bultmann, Tillich, and Rahner embody four theological stances using *Heideggerian lenses*. Their respective dedication to uncovering and isolating *primordial being* from its everydayness can be best investigated by the Wesleyan Quadrilateral, with the respective relationships between *being* and scripture, *being* and tradition, *being* and reason, and *being* and experience explicated separately.

For each of the aforementioned existential theologians, the primordiality of *being* is respectively situated in nominative constructions of λογος (logos), κηρυγμα (kerygma), καιρος (kairos), and χάρις (charis).[72] These nominative constructions, rather than how they appear in other cases, provide a much more existentially-accessible meaning, especially when using

---

72. I am using the nominative constructions of each since, in themselves, I believe they represent a primordial understanding of their respective meanings. When each assumes the genitive, the dative, or the accusative case, they are ontically construed in reference to other words within a given sentence. Only in the nominative case do these words present meanings that are at their most primordial. In the nominative case, these words have stand-alone meanings. Since I am concerned with "primordial being," or "being" in primordiality, I find that nominative constructions are more helpful than the other cases—in my view, the nominative cases of each word more accurately discloses their individual meanings, which are oriented more exclusively towards ἀλήθεια, or "unconcealment."

that meaning to point towards the primordiality of *being*.[73] From each of their nominative constructions, their individual primordialities lead towards ἀλήθεια. In other words, to focus on these nominative conceptions means focusing on the primordiality of *being* and the extent to which that *primordial being* leads to the "unconcealment" of *being*, or ἀλήθεια.

Like later Heidegger's focus on the etymological roots of the original Greek meaning of "unconcealment,"[74] each existential aforementioned theologian conceptualizes *primordial being* in an individualized, existential way, but ties each conception to ἀλήθεια. To do so, I would like to define the term ἀλήθεια through a *Heideggerian lens*.

For Heidegger, ἀλήθεια is defined as "that which has already come forward into appearance and has left concealment behind."[75] What this stands to suggest, then, is that, when *being* is in a state of *unconcealment*—or a condition in which *primordial being* is *unconcealed* in primordiality—that state is an existential mode in which *being* already exists as it is, despite "that which" has been in *concealment* (ʼληθεʼ).[76] More importantly, it is essential to describe ἀλήθεια as "that which" has been constituted on the *unconcealment* of previously *concealed* (ʼληθεʼ) *primordial being*—ἀλήθεια is what *primordial being* looks like when it is unhidden, empowered, and allowed to be original and teleological.[77] In other words, *primordial being* is what Heidegger calls "the truth of Being," and this "truth of Being" is inevitably oriented towards ἀλήθεια as an object of "sovereign knowledge."[78] *Pri-*

73. As I have stated in the previous note, I consider nominative cases as the primordiality of being in λόγος (logos), κήρυγμα (kerygma), καιρός (kairos), and χάρις (charis).

74. In a 1943 lecture course entitled "Aletheia," Heidegger traces the etymological roots of ἀλήθεια to the Fragment B-16 of Heraclitus. Heidegger traces ἀλήθεια back to ἀλήθεσια and, then, to another form λάθοι, both of which contain a relatedness to the term "conceal," or "hide." Heidegger, *Early Greek Thinking: The Dawn of Western Philosophy*, 103.

75. Ibid., 104

76. From here forward, I will simply use ληθε to refer to "conceal," "concealment," "concealed," and "concealedness." For Heidegger, there are subtle variations to ληθε, with respect to the different versions of the aforementioned words. I have presented some of Heidegger's variations in Note 69.

77. This is drawn from Heidegger's lecture "The Essence of Truth" where he discusses, in one of two parts, Plato's Allegory of the Cave. At one point in that discussion, Heidegger looks at Book VI of Plato's *Republic*, before Plato's presentation of The Cave allegory, suggesting that Plato's "Idea of the Good" is focused on the empowerment of being and unhiddenness. Heidegger, *The Essence of Truth: On Plato's Cave Allegory and Theaetetus*, 69–72.

78. Heidegger begins the lecture course entitled *Basic Questions* by questioning "the

mordial being is based on having "sovereign knowledge" about *what being is*. This can only occur when the everydayness of *being* is unhidden—that is to say, *being* must be unhidden as it already is in primordiality. When *being* is unhidden, ἀλήθεια can be accessed in the openness of clearing.[79]

In order to conceive of and grasp λογος, κηρυγμα, καιρος, and χάρις as conceptions of *primordial being* that have each been unhidden in the openness of clearing, each embody what Heidegger describes as "the correctness of representation."[80] This philosophical notion, then, becomes the grounding question (what is *being*?) and the guiding question (what is *Being*?)[81] of the existential theologian—each respectively takes what I would describe as a "Heideggerian pathmark," in order to explain what ἀλήθεια is in Greek correlations of scripture (λογος), tradition (κηρυγμα), reason (καιρος), and experience (χάρις). Along this Heideggerian pathmark,[82] each theologian uses their respective Greek correlations of scripture, tradition, reason, and experience to locate *primordial being—being* as it exists in primordiality— to arrive at ἀλήθεια.

Chapter 1 will discuss Macquarrie's existential theology as devoting itself to *primordial being* in the *concealment* ('λήθε') of scripture. This "existential theology of scripture," as I will label it, is culminated in *Principles of Christian Theology* (1966), not to mention in lectures and essays collected in *Studies in Christian Existentialism* (1965) and *God-Talk: An Examination of the Language and Logic of Theology* (1967), and the aptly titled *An Existentialist Theology: A Comparison of Heidegger and Bultmann* (1955). In Macquarrie's existential theology, λογος is a stand-in for *being*. Through a *Heideggerian lens*, Macquarrie conceives of scripture as λογος, or "word," since it reveals ἀλήθεια. As a result, the "Heideggerian pathmark" Macquarrie takes is what I will refer to as a "linguistical-existential" venture, on the way towards *unconcealment*, or ἀλήθεια.

---

truth of Being," which involves, as he explains, "not of this or that being or even of all beings, but of Being itself." This sort of questioning is about seeking "sovereign knowledge"—or knowing the sovereignty—about "the truth of Being." Heidegger, *Basic Questions of Philosophy: Selected "Problems" of "Logic,"* 6–7.

79. The relationship between "openness" and "the clearing" is situated on what Heidegger describes as the "vacillating self-concealment" of Being itself. Ibid., 177–180.

80. Heidegger, *Nietzsche: Volume 3: The Will to Power as Knowledge and as Metaphysics*, 34.

81. Heidegger, *Nietzsche: Volume 1: The Will to Power as Art*, 67–68.

82. See note 3.

Chapter 2 will take a look at Bultmann's existential theology which concerns itself with *primordial being* in the *concealment* ('λη̄θε') of tradition. This "existential theology of tradition," as it will be denoted, in the 2-volume *Theologie des Neuen Testaments* (1948–1953), translated as *Theology of the New Testament* (1951–1955), but is further recapitulated in lectures and essays collected, such as in *History and Eschatology* (1955) and *Jesus Christ and Mythology* (1958). In Bultmann's existential theology, κηρυγμα is a representation of *being*. Through his "demythologization" process, Bultmann's *Heideggerian lens* seeks excavate κηρυγμα, or "proclamation," from Christian mythology, in order to find ἀλήθεια. To this end, Bultmann's "Heideggerian pathmark" is what I refer to as a "historical-existential" venture, on the way towards *unconcealment*, or ἀλήθεια.

Chapter 3 will consider Tillich's existential theology as oriented towards *primordial being* in the *concealment* ('λη̄θε') of reason. This "existential theology of reason," as I have named it, is rooted in his 3-volume *Systematic Theology* (1951–1963), as well as several shorter works, especially those written after the publication of his *Systematic Theology*. In Tillich's existential theology, καιρος is a manifestation of *being*. Tillich's *Heideggerian lens* places emphasis on καιρος, or "event," in relation to humanity's issue of thrownness, so that all empirical facts are ultimately concerned with ἀλήθεια. Because of this, Tillich's "Heideggerian pathmark" is what I will refer to as a "rational-existential" venture, on the way towards *unconcealment*, or ἀλήθεια.

Chapter 4 will appraise Rahner's existential theology through a consideration for *primordial being* in the *concealment* ('λη̄θε') of experience. This "existential theology of experience," as I intend to call it, is expressed in Rahner's systematic work *Grundkurs des Glaubens: Einführung in den Begriff des Christentums* (1976), translated as *Foundations of Christian Faith* in 1978, and further elucidated in several volumes of his 23-volume *Theological Investigations* (1961–1992) and his rejected philosophy dissertation *Geist in Welt*. In Rahner's existential theology, χάρις is an expression of *being*. Rahner's transcendental slant is a *Heideggerian lens* that envisions χάρις, or "grace," as a representation of ἀλήθεια. In this regard, Rahner's "Heideggerian pathmark" is what I refer to as an "experiential-existential" venture, on the way towards *unconcealment*, or ἀλήθεια.

CHAPTER 1

"Being" in Scripture and Macquarrie's "λογος"

John Macquarrie's existential theology is devoted to *primordial being* in scripture, which is expressed as "logos." With a *Heideggerian lens*, Macquarrie conceptualizes *being* in scripture as λογος, or "word,"[1] since, at a primordial level, it reveals ἀλήθεια. The primordiality of λογος suggests, first and foremost, that λογος in an articulation of *being*—in other words, λογος is what being looks like when it is unhidden, or *unconcealed*. In order to address what λογος is at its primordial level, it is essential to confront what λογος is at an ontical level: scripture.[2] In this regard, scripture adheres to the interrelationships between words and how, in the context of a sentence or a proposition, a string of words expresses a multiplicity of meaning. The extent to which any one sentence, statement, or proposition can be interpreted a variety of ways underscores the Heideggerian problem of language: a problem that is taken up by Macquarrie. The problem arises from the understanding that what is interpreted from any given sentence, statement, or proposition is not only the best approximation of what that sentence, statement, or proposition might mean to any given interpreter, but the best possible approach an interpreter can take to truly grappling with the λογος within. To be clear, especially if applying a Heideggerian understanding to language, it is a hermeneutical problem—it is a problem

---

1. Balz and Schneider, eds., *Exegetical Dictionary of the New Testament: Volume 2*, 356.

2. I use the term "scripture" in a monolithic fashion, and even as a generalization. I am referring to any text that requires hermeneutical cultivation, in order to conceive of, grasp, and explain ἀλήθεια.

that strives for unhiddenness, when that *unconcealment* is surrounded by layers of *concealment* ('λη θε').

For Macquarrie, scripture is the ontical representation of λογος—the ontology of scripture hides and conceals λογος in a language that requires constant primordially-oriented interpretation.[3] Through *concealment* ('λη θε') of λογος, any hermeneutical activity seeks to venture beyond the technical or grammatical layers of the way language works in order to get to the metaphysics of language.[4] With Macquarrie's *Heideggerian lens*, language, at its most primordial, contains λογος—furthermore, such a claim stands to suggest that scripture, or written language, is only ontical language. That is to say, the ontics of language is represented by scripture and, accordingly, making-meaning from scripture is an act that involves the roles of two horizons: a "fusion" between a horizon of the text and a horizon of the reader.[5] Essentially, the goal of the meaning-making process—the hermeneutical act, or any active, existential engagement in the systematic interpretation of a text for the purposes of uncovering hidden meaning in it—is to excavate λογος as ἀληθεια from ontical scripture's *concealedness* ('λη θε').

Macquarrie and Heidegger

Macquarrie was never a student of Heidegger's at the University of Marburg, nor the University of Freiburg, nor did he ever hold a professorship at either university during Heidegger's periods there—the two universities at which Heidegger held teaching positions during his career.[6] Because of

3. To this end, I am referring to the task of hermeneutics, particularly as an activity that calls for the breaking down of language from its ontical representation (words and sentences) into something more primordial (the meaning behind the word and sentences).

4. I am using the terms "technical" and "grammatical" as Friedrich Schleiermacher does. Schleiermacher, *Hermeneutics: The Handwritten Manuscripts*, 69.

5. Gadamer uses the term "fusion of horizons" when discussing the horizon of the text, the horizon of the reader, and the meaning-making between these two horizons. See Gadamer, *Truth and Method*, 273. In addition, Anthony Thiselton provides an excellent explication of Gadamer's "fusion of horizons." Thiselton, *Two Horizons: New Testament Hermeneutics and Philosophical Description with Special Reference to Heidegger, Bultmann, Gadamer, and Wittgenstein*, 12.

6. This is in contrast to Bultmann, Rahner, and Tillich, all of which established academic relationships with Heidegger, to some extent, as either a student (Rahner) or a colleague (Bultmann and Tillich) at either Marburg or Freiburg.

this, Macquarrie's Heideggerian influence is not as direct or first-hand as Bultmann's, Rahner's, or Tillich's. It is, in fact, a different kind of influence, which makes it instantly difficult to ascertain what exactly Macquarrie is influenced by and what meaning we precisely can make out of that influence itself when we speaking about a Macquarrie-Heidegger relationship—that is to say, if Macquarrie's influence is not first-hand, as either a colleague or student of Heidegger's, we must investigate the potency of Macquarrie's second-hand Heideggerian influence. I do not mean to minimize the nature of that influence upon Macquarrie, but to be sure that we place that influence in its proper context. This is required, if we are interested in the Macquarrie-Heidegger relationship as such, and the lack of personal contact between the two.

Rather than having personally encountered Heidegger's thought, Macquarrie's "encounter" with Heideggerian thought can be traced generally to the 1950s, during a time of philosophical resurgence for Heidegger. This is a different "Heidegger" from what Bultmann, Tillich, or even Rahner experienced in the 1920s and 1930s at Marburg and Freiburg, before end of World War II and the fall of the Third Reich in Germany. For Macquarrie, this "Heidegger" is overwhelmingly a post-World War II version of the thinker, which was rehabilitated by and through the existentialist work of Jean Paul Sartre (1905–1980). A word or two on Sartre is necessary before contextualizing Macquarrie's "Heidegger" any further. To be clear, it is Sartre's development of "existentialism" and the explicit indebtedness of his thinking to Heidegger that brings Heidegger to not just the consciousness of France, but to the global stage. That is not to say that Heidegger was totally unknown before Sartre's use of him, since *Sein und Zeit*, at the time of its publication in 1927, was an immensely significant book, both in and outside of Germany. Rather, Sartre can be best described—though this is only one of many possible arguments—as a vehicle through which Heidegger could be applied to existentialist concerns, even if we know, in hindsight, that Heidegger thoroughly disapproved of this. It is widely known that Sartre read Heidegger's *Sein und Zeit* while Sartre was a prisoner of war from 1940 to 1941. Through the influence of having read this work and becoming deeply influenced by it—and the Husserlian phenomenology within Heidegger's work—Sartre would write and eventually publish *L'Être et le néant* in 1943. In this origin story, Sartre has often been criticized for fundamentally misreading *Sein und Zeit* for the purposes of *L'Être et le néant*, to the extent that his misinterpretation of Heidegger is erroneously carried forward more broadly into existentialism. What Sartre did for or did to Heidegger—depending on the perspective taken—is provide an interpretation of Heidegger's thinking about the meaning of being that was ultimately filtered falsely into Sartre's attempt to tie existentialism to a brand of humanism in *L'existentialisme est un humanisme* in 1946. Heidegger's *Brief über den Humanismus*, written in December 1946 and published in 1947, directly confronts, challenges, and refutes Sartre's reading of *Sein und Zeit*. Nevertheless, due to the popularity of Sartre's work, the damage had, essentially, been done to Heidegger's thought—. What arose, then, was a sort of divide between the "Heidegger" of existentialism and Sartre's existentialism –though Macquarrie is aware of this divide between schools of existentialism, his Heideggerian influence is undoubtedly translated through Sartre, if we can remember that Macquarrie's "Heidegger" is a representation of the thinker after Sartre.

Macquarrie's "Heidegger," as tempered as it is through Sartre and what can be best described as a "later Heidegger," comes to Macquarrie shortly after the Heidegger-Sartre debate about existentialism. Strictly in terms of chronology, this is immensely important, because this historical context shapes what Macquarrie thinks about Heidegger, as much as it molds his determination of existentialism itself. There is a larger body of work for Macquarrie to judge Heidegger by the very early 1940s, to which we can trace Macquarrie's entrance into the conversation about the importance of Heidegger. We do, indeed, see Macquarrie encountering a rehabilitated "Heidegger," a "Heidegger" that could speak to the concerns of both philosophy and theology. The latter, of course, was what grounded Macquarrie's contribution to the *Makers of Contemporary Theology* series with a slim volume on Heidegger in 1968. Starting here, not only do we see Macquarrie making a case for Heidegger's importance to theology, but he is precisely concerned, more importantly, with justifying how Heidegger's thought is generally important. In this work, Macquarrie immediately asserts in its short "Preface" that:

> It may seem strange to include Martin Heidegger in a series of books dealing with "Makers of Contemporary Theology," for Heidegger is no theologian but a philosopher, and he is often reckoned to be a thoroughly secular philosopher at that. Yet I think it would be true to say that one could hardly hope to advance very

far in the understanding of contemporary theology without some knowledge of Heidegger's thought.[7]

In admitting that "it may seem strange to include" the thought of Heidegger with theological reflection and discussion, we find that Macquarrie is aware of the audience with which he is speaking: the theologian. In these circles, as was evident during Heidegger's time at Marburg, there was often resistance to Heidegger's contribution to theology, even though Bultmann, in particular, made a conscious effort to include Heidegger in "talks" within the Theology Department at Marburg. That inclusion was partly due to Bultmann's own interests in how philosophy could speak to theology, for the sake of his research into Paul and eventually the Gospel of John, but it was also part of Heidegger's own concerns with how phenomenology could be applied to various facets of thought, including theology. Both of the interests converged at Marburg through both professional and personal collaborations. Still, even though Bultmann brought Heidegger to the table of theological reflection at Marburg, Bultmann was relatively alone in this effort, which was not helped by Heidegger leaving Marburg for Freiburg and, ostensibly fracturing his relationship with Bultmann. Though Bultmann and Tillich, both from Heidegger's Marburg period, carried Heideggerian thought through their approaches to theology, and later, Rahner would do the same, though from the perspective of a former student of Heidegger's at Freiburg, Heidegger's involvement of Nazism from the 1930s up to the end of World War II significantly tainted the Heidegger's relationship with theology. In fact, we can see, even by the time Macquarrie makes this case in the *Makers of Contemporary Theology* series, Heidegger has become a controversial figure, particularly in the field of contemporary theology, or what we can refer to as postmodern theology. Macquarrie is correctly aware that, by 1968, Heidegger is a key contributor to this kind of theology, spearheaded through the theologies of Bultmann, Tillich, and Rahner, just to name a few—each of them embodying a theology that purposely kept Heidegger in the loop theologically, regardless of his being, as Macquarrie writes, a "thoroughly secular philosopher." By implicitly referring to Bultmann, Tillich, and Rahner, Macquarrie acknowledges that:

> [Heideggger's] influence seems to appear everywhere—in demythologizing and problem of hermeneutics; in the doctrine of man; in theories of revelation; in the debate about God; and in other matters besides. Though not himself a theologian, he is a maker of

7. Macquarrie, *Martin Heidegger*, ix.

theology, in the same way in which Plato and Aristotle and Kant have been makers of theology.[8]

As veiled as this reference is, Macquarrie is not so veiled about his assertion that Heidegger is "a maker of theology," even if, to be sure, Macquarrie recognizes that Heidegger was "not himself a theologian." Within this, there is the subtle notion that being a maker of theology means being a theologian, to which Macquarrie obviously disagrees. For Macquarrie, Heidegger, though a "secular philosopher," can be "a maker of theology"—this is so, especially when we are speaking of the shifting boundaries and the shaking of foundations[9] of postmodernized theology, understanding the discourse that is necessary between theology and philosophy, and situating Heidegger in that discourse. When contextualizing Heidegger in this manner—as he notes, in "the same way" as Plato, Aristotle, and Kant—Macquarrie knows that this requires a thorough-going explanation of what makes Heidegger "a maker of theology," and how Heidegger actually speaks to the concerns of theology. Such an explanation, then, asks for a specific task and scope, so that Heidegger and theology speak to one another effectively. If we say that Heidegger is "a maker of theology," what Heidegger "makes" in and of theology is an understandings about existence and the nature of being. Here, we locate Macquarrie's approach: the relationship between Heidegger and theology towards what either can tell the other about "existence" and "being." Even when positioning Heidegger this way, as Macquarrie undoubtedly does, there will needs to be a figure on the theology-side that can be an interlocutor for Heidegger—a theological interlocutor capable of leaning philosophically enough to effectively engage Heidegger's notions of "existence" and "being," while grounding an understanding of both as fundamentally theological. These conditions can be assessed in the following assertion from the close of Macquarrie's "Preface" to *Martin Heidegger*:

> Heidegger's philosophy is no substitute for Christian theology, and certainly it should not be allowed to dominate the work of the theologian, but it does provide the kind of conceptual framework that the theologian needs if he is to state the Christian faith in terms intelligible to today's world.[10]

8. Ibid.

9. I am using this specific term from Paul Tillich, but my concern is with how this term can be generally comported to apply to all postmodern concerns in theology.

10. Macquarrie, *Martin Heidegger*, ix.

Even though this is dated to 1967, it revisits Macquarrie's preoccupations of the mid-1950s, during the time Macquarrie was dissertating at the University of Glasgow. It is there that Heidegger's influence on Macquarrie can be traced. As much as Sartre's reading of Heidegger is in the immediate background of Macquarrie's doctoral work, it is largely unclear if Macquarrie had directly read any Heidegger or Sartre's "Heidegger," not just before his first Glasgow period, but in the interim before his second Glasgow period. To the best of my knowledge, neither of these periods in Macquarrie early academic career have ever been mined for Heideggerian or Sartrean evidence. Because of this, we can only speculate to what extent an early 1940s reading of Heidegger or Sartre's "Heidegger" actually influenced Macquarrie's experience of Heidegger on the forefront of his doctoral work at Glasgow, when returning there after serving as a parish minister in the Church of Scotland up to 1953.

In his "Pilgrimage in Theology," appearing in 1980, Macquarrie writes of the transition from graduate studies in theology at Westminster to being a parish minister to committing to doctoral work in theology as a return that "was almost accidental."[11] What also seems "almost accidental" is Macquarrie's introduction to Bultmann as a tangential introduction to Heidegger. Macquarrie makes it clear that he had initially heard about Bultmann's work from J. G. Riddell, Macquarrie's theology professor at Glasgow, who, in turn, "mentioned that he had a brilliant colleague, Professor Ian Henderson, working on Bultmann, and thought that my parish duties were light enough to allow me to do research and to travel occasionally to Glasgow for supervision [under Henderson]."[12] Judging from this, it seems that Macquarrie had some prior knowledge about Bultmann during this graduate philosophy work—though it is impossible to be exact here—and entered into his doctoral work in theology at Glasgow under the supervision of Henderson with an interest, through the facilitating of Henderson, tracing the roots of Bultmann's thought. In other words, Henderson became an important intermediary through which Macquarrie came to understand Bultmann's relationship to Heidegger and how Heidegger exerted a significant influence on Bultmann's thought—this sort of connection was important for Macquarrie's synthesis of theology and philosophy more generally and, more specifically, the hand that Bultmann and Heidegger respectively play

11. Macquarrie, "Pilgrimage in Theology," in *Being and Truth: Essays in Honor of John Macquarrie*, xiii.

12. Ibid.

in that overarching synthesis. Macquarrie does point this out, considering that, under Henderson's supervision, "the upshot was that I began working for a PhD, the thesis topic being the influence of Heidegger's philosophy upon Bultmann's theology."[13] However, it was not Henderson alone at Glasgow that aided Macquarrie's approach to Bultmann and Heidegger—also at Glasgow, Macquarrie's experience of Heidegger was influenced by Macquarrie's relationship with Charles Campbell.

To be sure, Macquarrie's experience of Heidegger comes by way of two important academic intermediaries at Glasgow: Charles Arthur Campbell (1897–1974) and Ian Henderson (1910–1969). Charles Campbell was Glasgow's Professor of Logic and Rhetoric, and served as a mentor to Macquarrie during Macquarrie's graduate philosophy studies at Glasgow. This is the first academic period to which I have already referred. Leading up to his M.A. degree in philosophy in 1940, Macquarrie studied, especially from Campbell, "the roles of philosophy and theology in relation to the centrality of experience in religion."[14] Campbell exposed Macquarrie to the work of Bultmann and Heidegger, as examples of the intersectionality of philosophy and theology. As a result, Campbell provided "a receptive yet critical framework for Macquarrie's reading of Bultmann and Heidegger," which are the two major influences on Macquarrie's existential theology.[15]

Following his philosophical studies, Macquarrie pursued theological studies at Glasgow, which eventually led to the completion of a B.D. degree in 1943. Nearly a decade later, after a seven-year stint as a parish minister, Macquarrie began serving as a lecturer in systematic theology at Trinity College at Glasgow. This is the beginning of Macquarrie's second academic period, when Macquarrie studied for a Ph.D. degree under the direction of Ian Henderson. Like Campbell, Henderson became a conduit through which Macquarrie could read Bultmann's Heideggerian approach to New Testament exegesis—at the time that Macquarrie began working with Henderson, Henderson had already published *Myth in the New Testament* in 1952, as the first introduction to the English-speaking world to the controversy over Bultmann's program of demythologizing.[16] This played a part in Macquarrie's 1954 dissertation, which was subsequently published

13. Ibid.

14. Long, *Existence, Being, and God: An Introduction to the Philosophical Theology of John Macquarrie*, 3.

15. Ibid.

16. Ibid.

in 1955 as *An Existentialist Theology: A Comparison of Heidegger and Bult-mann.* The primary goal of Macquarrie's *An Existentialist Theology* was, as assessed by Eugene Long, "to contribute to the understanding of the influence of existentialist philosophy on contemporary theological thought."[17] Macquarrie himself explains the work as something that "sought to show how Bultmann's interpretation of the New Testament as a way of life had drawn upon the analysis of human existence given by Heidegger."[18] From here, Macquarrie adds, almost as an aside, but as a point of affirmation, "Bultmann himself was kind enough to commend the work [in *An Existentialist Theology*] as an accurate presentation of his thought."[19] Not only was this, as Macquarrie writes, "importan[t] for my own pilgrimage" due to the work being no "uncritical," he suggests that "it did seem to me to bring me much closer to reconciling religious faith with intellectual integrity."[20] Though this was already a preoccupation of his, Macquarrie's positioning of Bultmann and Heidegger as seminal figures in *An Existentialist Theology* was presented more explicitly. More importantly, rather than just a straight-forward comparative study of Bultmann and Heidegger, Macquarrie respectively offers criticisms of Bultmann and presents his own Heideggerian analysis of human existence. Macquarrie's analysis, then, is based on a Heideggerian understanding of a "range of human or existential possibilities."[21] For Macquarrie, this is the task of philosophy—his Heideggerian task, to be clear—and, in particular, a task that Macquarrie describes as ontical or pre-theological.[22] This task, through its criticism of Bultmann, is equally critical of Tillich and Rahner, and how, like Bultmann, they have assumed Heideggerian stances towards their theologies. What this means, if we see Macquarrie's critical approach to Bultmann through critical approaches to Tillich and Rahner, as a way of positioning himself in his own theology as more authentic to his Heideggerian approach in *An Existentialist Theology*, Macquarrie's assessment of the following in its proper context:

---

17. Ibid., 4.

18. Macquarrie, "Pilgrimage in Theology," in *Being and Truth: Essays in Honor of John Macquarrie*, xiii.

19. Ibid.

20. Ibid.

21. Long, *Existence, Being, and God: An Introduction to the Philosophical Theology of John Macquarrie*, 4.

22. Ibid.

I was never, however, quite happy with Bultmann's almost pure existentialism. It seems to me in danger of becoming quite subjective. I noted too that although Bultmann relied heavily on the earlier Heidegger, he took no notice of the later ontological work. I felt that I had to broaden the base of my theology. Tillich's *Systematic Theology*, which had begun to appear in 1953, attracted me, though I think that most of what is of value in its philosophical structure has been better said by Heidegger. But more important than Tillich was my discover of Rahner, who at that time was untranslated and virtually unknown in Britain. The first thing of his that I read was his little work on death. He had been a student of Heidegger, but he takes up the study of death where Heidegger leaves off, and the result seemed to me to be that synthesis of [C]atholic faith and philosophical thought for which I had been searching.[23]

Here, not only does Macquarrie provide specific critiques of Bultmann, Tillich, and Rahner that are, essentially, critiques of how they have each used Heidegger for their respective theologies, but Macquarrie provides a framework, through each of their attempts to do so, for "which [he] had been searching." This is accomplished, as Macquarrie suggests, through a "comparison" between Bultmann and Heidegger.

Though the subtitle of *An Existentialist Theology* denotes a "comparison" between Bultmann and Heidegger, the term can be a bit misleading. That is to say, *An Existentialist Theology* is not necessarily a comparison, in the strictest sense of the word. Macquarrie seems more interested in staking a Heideggerian position that differs from Bultmann's, rather than offering an even-handed, objective study of Bultmann and Heidegger. In other words, *An Existentialist Theology* is quite frankly more about Heidegger than it is about Bultmann—just as Macquarrie used Campbell and Henderson as intermediaries to Heidegger, Bultmann is used in the same regard. This is evident, too, in the "Preface" to the work, when Macquarrie writes, "the aim of this work is to make some contribution towards understanding the influence of existentialist philosophy upon contemporary theological thought."[24] Because that contribution is concentrated on Bultmann and Heidegger especially, Macquarrie is careful to note that this relationship is

23. Macquarrie, "Pilgrimage in Theology," in *Being and Truth: Essays in Honor of John Macquarrie*, xiv.

24. Macquarrie, *An Existentialist Theology: A Comparison of Heidegger and Bultmann* xi.

not just a "very close one," but it is "a very interesting one, for both of these men—even if we disagree with their teaching sometimes—appear to me to be, in their own fields, really original and outstanding thinkers."[25] The care that is necessary to assert this is predicated on the influence that Heidegger has on Bultmann, yes, but it is grounded, nonetheless, in the originality of Heidegger to philosophy and Bultmann to theology. Furthermore, what must be maintained, nevertheless, is how Macquarrie uses Bultmann's demythologizing program to construct his own existentialist program.

While not explicit in *An Existentialist Theology*, Macquarrie's own theological-philosophical program is more explicit in his second book, *The Scope of Demythologizing*, published in 1960, as what Macquarrie himself concedes is a "companion" to the former book. However, unlike the former book, *The Scope of Demythologizing* did not arise out of dissertation research, but, instead, as Macquarrie notes in the "Preface" to the book, "is a revised and much expanded version of a series of lectures given in March, 1957, at Union Theological Seminary, New York."[26] These lectures, just as Macquarrie admits, were given at the "invitation" of the President and Faculty of Union,[27] since Macquarrie, as we know, was still serving as a lecturer at Glasgow. An invitation of this sort informs of a couple of important contextual notes—first, it is clear that this "invitation" arose from Union's recognition of the importance of Macquarrie's work in *An Existentialist Theology*, and secondly, Union was certainly interested in giving Macquarrie a receptive forum for his understanding of the Bultmann-Heidegger relationship. It would seem, too, that this invitation was welcomed by Macquarrie, since it would provide him with a larger audience beyond Glasgow. More importantly, if we think more closely about the mid-1950s, as the elevation of Heidegger's stature not only through, in the previous decade, Sartre's use of Heidegger for the purposes of existentialism, but through Heidegger's active participation in the philosophical scene in France as a result of Heidegger's ban rom teaching from 1945–1951. But also, Macquarrie's invitation to Union was in reaction to Heidegger's own re-emergence after his ban from teaching was lifted, when Heidegger delivered the *Was Heißt Denken?* lecture (translated as *What is Called Thinking?*) at Freiburg in the Winter 1951/1952 (GA 8). Throughout the 1950s, especially, Heidegger was actively publishing articles (some of which are included in GA 7

---

25. Ibid.

26. Macquarrie, *The Scope of Demythologizing: Bultmann and his Critics*, 9

27. Ibid.

and GA 12) and had delivered the lecture, *Der Satz vom Grund* (translated as *On the Essence of Ground*) in Winter 1955/1956 (GA 10). This up-tick in Heidegger's activity and the rehabilitation of his professional persona in academia was undoubtedly integral in the situation in which Macquarrie found himself, especially after writing *An Existentialist Theology*. Clearly, though Bultmann had certainly utilized Heidegger unapologetically, we can see Macquarrie's work on Bultmann and Heidegger as unique, since it was more than just a comparative study of both figures, but intended to consider more thoughtfully how Heidegger could engage with theology. For Macquarrie, this was expressed more narrowly in the context of Bultmann's work, particularly when we recognize, of course, that Macquarrie is concerned with Bultmann's theology and the need to give Bultmann a wider exposure. To be sure, giving Bultmann this wider audience means giving Heidegger a wider audience too—still, there is a balance here, of which Macquarrie was surely aware. If we can say, then, that Macquarrie's approach to Bultmann is an approach towards understanding not just the theological limits of Bultmann's demythologizing, but the extent to which that program, for Bultmann, is a philosophical limitation of Bultmann's employment of Heidegger, it becomes all the more clear what the goals were for Macquarrie in 1957.

As a direct extension of his study of Bultmann's demythologizing program in *An Existentialist Theology*, Macquarrie explains, in the "Preface," that the work "takes up what I regard as the central problem presented by Bultmann's theology—what I have called 'the limit of demythologizing.'"[28] Macquarrie further explains that this "problem," as he has approached it, "is discussed in relation to the main points of criticism to which Bultmann's views have been subjected in the course of the demythologizing controversy." In an effort to address these points with care, Macquarrie confronts Bultmnann's critics—with himself seemingly notwithstanding, perhaps—by showing the limits of Bultmann's program through a demonstration of its scope. In effect, such an approach to Bultmann assumes a positive stance, instead of negative one, which is particularly poignant since Macquarrie takes into account his own correspondence with Bultmann and Bultmann's "detailed comments on [*An Existentialist Theology* which have] proved most useful to me, and have, I hope, led me to a much clearer understanding of his views on many topics.[29] As a result, not only

28. Ibid.
29. Ibid.

do these "detailed comments" help Macquarrie finely-tune his "Bultmann" from *An Existentialist Theology* to what eventually becomes *The Scope of Demythologizing*, but it allows, more importantly, for the latter work to be an engagement with both Bultmann and Heidegger—Bultmann becomes more of an intermediary than in *An Existentialist Theology*, so that, when Bultmann is evaluating the scope of Bultmann's program, that evaluation, in turn, is ultimately directed towards Heidegger.

The Scope of Demythologizing, according to Eugene Long, "evaluates what [Macquarrie] takes to be the central problem in Bultmann's theology, the limits inherent in the program of demythologizing."[30] These "limits," in Macquarrie's view, are weaknesses in Bultmann's program, especially in Long's assessment. Even if we know that Macquarrie considered Bultmann's "detailed comments," what we see, through Long's assertion, is that the "weaknesses" Macquarrie reads, interprets, and understands in the scope and limits of demythology itself are structural problems, which are certainly contingent on how Bultmann reads, interprets, and understands Heidegger. What this means, then, is that for there to be "weaknesses" in Bultmann's program, these "weaknesses" are in how Bultmann synthesizes Heideggerian philosophy and theology. That is not to say that Bultmann's program, for Macquarrie, exercises an inherent incompatibility between the concerns of philosophy and the concerns of theology, at which demythology is at the juncture of these concerns—instead, whatever "weaknesses" exist in Bultmann's demythology, as argued by Macquarrie, arise directly from how Bultmann uses Heidegger for a specific purpose, while assuming a decidedly theological stance. With this keenly in mind, I do not wish to suggest that Bultmann's stance is entirely inflexible—I do not believe that Macquarrie is making this assertion either, considering that he does, to some degree, take into account Bultmann's own comments of Macquarrie's characterization of Bultmann's program—but Macquarrie is, rather, adequately working out his own theological stance. If it is safe to say that Macquarrie and Bultmann do not share the same theological stance, any more than they share the same fundamental reading and application of Heidegger towards their respective stances, Macquarrie's critique of what Bultmann does or does not do (what is accomplished or left uncomplished) seems interested in authentically representing Heidegger's philosophy outside of Bultmann, as a means of ensuring, when used by

---

30. Long, *Existence, Being, and God: An Introduction to the Philosophical Theology of John Macquarrie*, 5–6.

Macquarrie, it is used correctly. To whatever degree that "correctly" is, it is clearly contingent on how Heidegger is read, and how Heidegger is applied to theological reflection. It is also that very theological reflection that concerns Macquarrie, when ascertaining Bultmann's theological stance— Macquarrie is focused on a correctness in Bultmann's theological reflection too. The Bultmann-Heidegger and Macquarrie-Bultmann relationships are contextualized by Long in the following assertion:

> In his discussion of Bultmann's program of demythologizing, Macquarrie also insists, in a way that Bultmann does not, that there must be a 'minimum core of factuality' in the Christian faith. Faith as authentic understanding must be supplemented by an appeal to the historical Jesus. . .Macquarrie, however, does not intend to make theology dependent on historical research or to argue that historical research may provide a proof of faith.[31]

Long's point is well made. However, there are problems that must be pointed out. What Long asserts is about what Macquarrie insists upon in relation to what Bultmann does not—as Long quotes, Macquarrie insists "that there must be a 'minimum core of factuality' in the Christian faith." But, unfortunately, Long omits a very important part of what Macquarrie insists upon over Bultmann. If we to be more precise in the matter, we find, too, that Long is reading Bultmann through Macquarrie, but he is not directly engaging the same "Bultmann" that Macquarrie is. As a result, Long misquotes and misunderstands Macquarrie's "Bultmann" altogether, such that Long's mishandling of Macquarrie's "Bultmann" misrepresents not just Macquarrie's actual words, but greatly distorts Bultmann.

To be clear, in *The Scope of Demythologizing*, Macquarrie suggests that Christian faith contains "a minimum core of *historical* factuality"[32] With emphasis added, there is a big difference between this quote, and what Long has misquoted. I feel it is imperative that this distinction be made and settled, before moving on, if our intent remains to understand the Macquarrie-Bultmann relationship as viewed by Long. The "historical" aspect to Macquarrie's quote offers further insight not just into an existential connection Macquarrie makes between history and "factuality," but it is precisely contingent on the degree to which Macquarrie's connection is Heidegger-influenced—and to whatever extent Macquarrie believed that Bultmann was not . Macquarrie's understanding of "historical" and "fac-

---

31. Ibid.

32. Macquarrie, *The Scope of Demythologizing: Bultmann and his Critics*, 93.

tuality" are grounded Macquarrie's definitions of Heideggerian terms: 1.) "temporality," which involves dimensions of the past, present, and future, as "the most basic characteristic of human existence," and 2.) "facticity," which denotes all the elements that are simply given, not chosen, in a human existence.[33] Yet, through these two terms, what remains "a minimum core of *historical* factuality" (emphasis added on my part) is language and existence. We can find that both are concerns in the theological reflections of Bultmann and Macquarrie, but it is especially pivotal and crucial to Macquarrie's approach to Heidegger. Long agrees with this, suggesting that:

> [Macquarrie] is primarily concerned with outlining Heidegger's analysis of the relation between language and existence. With [*The Scope of Demythologizing*], Macquarrie also begins a dialogue with analytical philosophers and lays the groundwork for his later efforts to develop a logic of the language of religion.[34]

The relation between language and existence, for Macquarrie, is at the forefront of his critique of Bultmann's demythologizing. This can be viewed as how Macquarrie sees demythology itself as a juncture between language and existence, more so than Bultmann's own recognition of that juncture. Long is correct, then, in suggesting that Macquarrie's concern is "with outlining Heidegger's analysis of the relation between language and existence," if that concern is pointedly directed towards how Bultmann makes use of or misuses Heidegger. We do see, of course, that Macquarrie's critique of Bultmann is critical of what Bultmann has used Heidegger for, but, since language and existence are central to the very fundamental business of theological reflection, it seems that Macquarrie expects, in his findings of the scope and limits of demythology, Bultmann to use Heidegger for the purposes of unconcealing theological language and theological existence through Heidegger's understanding of philosophical language and philosophical existence. Essentially, Macquarrie sees that Bultmann's chief task—the task that is not just foundational to demythology specifically, but foundational to what it means to do theology at all—should be to allow Heidegger's philosophy to make language and existence clearer theologically. Macquarrie makes this point clearer later in *Martin Heidegger*, positing that the theological task of Bultmann's demythology towards the use of philosophy, language, and existence—though, by this time in 1968, Macquarrie

33. Macquarrie, *Martin Heidegger*, 62.

34. Long, *Existence, Being, and God: An Introduction to the Philosophical Theology of John Macquarrie*, 7.

is speaking more generally about the relations of theology-philosophy—is about trying "to understand language as the expression of existence [and] to allow for possibilities of interpretation which are ruled out where empirical referring is taken to be the standard function of language."[35] In other words, in order "to allow for possibilities of interpretation," any hermeneutical activity must move beyond "empirical referring"—that is, it must transcend the referent facts of what is being interpreted. This "empirical referring" becomes inaccurately defined as "the standard function of language," because it involves simply taking a superficial approach to interpretation. That is to say, superficially-interpreting from either a technical or a grammatical level, if reminding ourselves of Schleiermacher, only takes interpretation so far.[36] Because of this, Macquarrie recognizes that any true hermeneutical activity is a negotiation of a language's existence and an existence's language, such that the fundamental relationship between language and existence is predicated on "allow[ing] for possibilities of interpretation." We can see this as part of the limitations that Macquarrie finds in Bultmann's demythologizing itself, but it is also, more importantly, pointing to a much larger concern with the limitations that Macquarrie finds in Bultmann's use of Heidegger for demythologizing, in particular, and theology, more generally. Macquarrie views this, through his *Heideggerian lens*, as the problems of language and hermeneutics—this is one of the four topics into which Macquarrie organizes Heidegger's *Sein und Zeit*.[37]

If we place Macquarrie in this context, it is possible to see Macquarrie's citing of the limitations of Bultmann's demythology and the limitations of Bultmann "Heidegger" as best positioning Macquarrie for a more direct confrontation with Heidegger's thought. In other words, in critiquing Bultmann's "Heidegger," Macquarrie's "Heidegger" becomes all the more apparent by necessity. This is, for sure, explicitly evident in Macquarrie's approach to *The Scope of Demythologizing*, even though the earlier *An Existentialist Theology* is more explicit in this regard. What arises from Macquarrie's progression from *An Existentialist Theology* to *The Scope of Demythologizing* is a directedness towards understanding the scope and limits of theology itself in relation to philosophy—it is the sense that theology, through a call for more postmodern theological reflection, need not be diminished for the

---

35. Macquarrie, *Martin Heidegger*, 54–55.

36. I am using the terms "technical" and "grammatical" as Friedrich Schleiermacher does. Schleiermacher, *Hermeneutics: The Handwritten Manuscripts*, 69.

37. Macquarrie, *Martin Heidegger*, 52.

sake of philosophical inquiry. Towards the end of *The Scope of Demytholo-gizing*, in the "Concluding Remarks" of the lecture, though he believes that "demythologizing looks like being one of the most promising ways forward for theology in our time,"[38] Macquarrie is clearly searching for another "promising way." This way, in an effort to move "forward for theology in our time," must more adequately address, for Macquarrie, what Heidegger can say (and cannot say) to and/or for theology—especially, Christianity itself. As important as this is, Macquarrie believes "there is always the danger that Christianity may be represented not as a religion in which God addresses man but as just another possibility of human existence to be set alongside those held out to us by Heidegger [. . .]."[39] This is Macquarrie's final word on Heidegger in *The Scope of Demythologizing* and, as a final word, it, in itself, is an interesting and poignant final thought: the sense that using Heidegger for theological purposes makes Christianity into "just another possibility for human existence." It is precisely this danger that most worries Macquar-rie, especially if we see this preoccupation as being at the heart of critique of Bultmann. Not only does Macquarrie see Bultmann as "hav[ing] come pretty close to this danger," we can see Macquarrie telegraphing his own "scope" and "limitations." Since, as Macquarrie suggests, "the limit to demy-thologizing is nothing other than the recognition of the difference between philosophy of human existence and a religion of divine grace," Macquarrie seems poised to employ a "Heidegger" that achieves something that is not limited by/through demythologizing. To do this, Macquarrie undoubtedly turns away from Bultmann to Heidegger—by 1957, this turn attempts to do more than just become a "recognition of the difference" between Hei-degger's "philosophy of human existence" and his own sense of the nature of the "religion of divine grace."

In an attempt to do a more thorough-going assessment of Heidegger—in a manner that is more rigorous than a very small section in the brief conclusion to *An Existentialist Theology* and not so narrowly focused to Bultmann in *The Scope of Demythologizing*—Macquarrie's turn toward Hei-degger seemingly coincides, in the same year as his delivering the lectures that became *The Scope of Demythologizing*, with the appearance of an eighth German edition of Heidegger's *Sein und Zeit* in 1957. What this pointed out to the original German publishers was that—in light of Sartre's use of Hei-degger and Heidegger's active involvement in French philosophical circles,

---

38. Macquarrie, *The Scope of Demythologizing: Bultmann and his Critics*, 244.
39. Ibid.

evidence of Heidegger's expanding importance at Glasgow while Macquarrie worked on his dissertation there, and how Macquarrie's invitation to Union signaled a further expansion of Heidegger's philosophical reputation into the United States—there needed to be an English translation of *Sein und Zeit*. The British publisher SCM Press acquired the translation rights *Sein und Zeit*, but scholarship into how this occurs is extremely scarce—if we are speaking about the chronology of events or the accounts of the period—not to mention the circumstances into how Macquarrie and Edward Robinson were selected as the translators. of the German edition by Max Niemeyer Publishing House. We can speculate, of course, that Macquarrie's previous work on Heidegger in his 1955 dissertation at Glasgow and the 1957 lectures that followed at Union displayed an attractive understanding of the contextualization of Heidegger's thought necessary to translate *Sein und Zeit*. Also, something can definitely be said about Macquarrie's 1957 lectures appearing as *The Scope of Demythologizing* in 1960 by SCM Press, and the possibility that Macquarrie was viewed, especially by his publisher, as an English-speaking advocate for Heidegger.

To the best of my knowledge, Macquarrie's *On Being a Theologian* provides the only account of the events that led to Macquarrie's participation in the translation of *Sein und Zeit*. In it, what we have speculated finds special credence. Macquarrie writes that, as a project, the translation "was completed at Glasgow, and occupied much of my time there. It was a kind of spin-off from my doctoral thesis, but a spin-off which was no less onerous than the thesis itself."[40] The translation of *Sein und Zeit* arose out of Macquarrie's dissertating work on An Existentialist Theology, whereby, doing the process of working, he cites having "had made a fairly detailed synopsis in English of *Being and Time*."[41] Purely on its face, this admission is interesting, not so much for the fact such a claim does not exist in any other scholarship into the genesis of the translation of *Sein und Zeit*, but because it confirms the unavoidably of the translated Heidegger—even if it is nothing more than a "detailed synopsis," as Macquarrie concedes—towards Macquarrie's need to accurately represent Heidegger against Bultmann. It is by way of this "detailed synopsis" that Macquarrie goes on to write that, at his publisher's suggestion, it was requested that "[he] should go on to make a complete translation."[42] Though Macquarrie forthrightly provides

---

40. Macquarrie, On Being a Theologian, 21.

41. Ibid.

42. Ibid.

misgiving he had had at the time about undertaking a translation of *Sein und Zeit*—due to the number of attempts that had been made at a translation since the book's original 1927 publication, and the sense that Heidegger was "untranslatable, because it relies so much on the idiosyncrasies of the German language"—his initial hesitation was thwarted by Macquarrie's publisher "obtain[ing] the translation rights from the German publisher."[43] Coupled with the discovery that Edward Robinson, an American philosopher, from the University of Kansas was also at work on a translation of *Sein und Zeit*, and the suggestion "that the two of us might co-operatre, to lessen the burden" of the translation work, Macquarrie relented and, of course, by 1962, the first English translation of *Sein und Zeit* was published as *Being and Time*.

With special reverence to this work on Heidegger, the previous work on Bultmann, and his overall commitment to outlining a theology-philosophy synthesis, Macquarrie was approached by, as he admits in his *Twentieth-Century Religious Thought*, "some members of the editorial staff of Messrs Harper and Brothers. . . [to] write the story of religious thought in the [20th] century, with special reference to the relations of philosophy and theology."[44] Macquarrie asserts that this happened four years before, which would date this account of the genesis of *Twentieth-Century Religious Thought* to 1957—the same year as Macquarrie's delivery of the lectures at Union. In a short timeframe, after the 1962 translation of *Sein und Zeit*, especially by 1968, Macquarrie published in relatively quick succession *Twentieth-Century Religious Thought* in 1963, *Studies in Christian Existentialism* in 1965 (a collection of essays and lectures, which includes, most notably, two chapters revised from the "Some Heideggerian Themes and their Theological Significance" lectures given at McGill University in Montreal in 1963), *Principles in Christian Theology* in 1966, *God-Talk: An Examination of the Language and Logic of Theology* in 1967, *God and Secularity* in 1967 (which is Volume III of the *New Directions in Theology Today* series), and then *Martin Heidegger* in 1968. Still, if we consider all of this with respect to his participation in the co-translating of *Sein und Zeit*, which appeared in 1962 as *Being and Time*—as the first English translation—Macquarrie's stature as a premier Heidegger scholar further established him as an important postmodern theologian with a bent for philosophical inquiry.

43. Ibid.

44. Macquarrie, *Twentieth Century Religious Thought: The Frontiers of Philosophy and Theology, 1900–1970*, 13.

To this end, it is through his use of Heidegger and an overarching preoc-cupation with how theology can speak to theology and vice versa that Mac-quarrie arrives at the notion that theological hermeneutics, which, as he asserts in Martin Heidegger, "should be about "understand[ing] language as the expression of existence."[45] It is not by accident that such a sentiment appears in his slim biography of Heidegger. We know, to be sure, that Mac-quarrie viewed Heidegger as a "maker" of contemporary theology and that means, in turn, a "maker" of what it means to do theological hermeneutics in a contemporary setting. But, what we find in a statement as the relation-ship between language and existence—to the understanding of the former, and to the expression of the latter, we must note—is that Macquarrie sees what is tangible as pointing to what is understood. That is to say, when we speak of scripture as an understanding of language and an expression of ex-istence, what we are really equating is scripture with λόγος. For Macquarrie, through his Heideggerian lens, scripture is undoubtedly an understanding of language couched in the interrelationship between words, but scripture itself points to λόγος as something that is understood before understand-ing the language that us necessarily infused in scripture. Viewed this way, λόγος becomes the understanding of language, and scripture is more of an expression of the existence of λόγος —in other words, λόγος is too much of an abstraction to be anything more than an understanding of language, so λόγος must be concretized in scripture as the expression of its existence. The sort of balance between "understand[ing] language" and the "expres-sion of existence" is essential to Macquarrie's theological hermeneutics. To accomplish this kind of theological hermeneutics, Macquarrie follows Heidegger's correlation between language analysis and existential analysis to construct an existential theology of scripture.

Macquarrie's Existential Theology of Scripture

Macquarrie's "existential theology of scripture," as I have called it, begins with a clear understanding of how existential theology works in Macquar-rie's thinking. Interestingly enough, there are only two books that explicitly discuss a relationship between existential theology and Macquarrie: Eugene Long's *Existence, Being, and God: An Introduction to the Philosophical Theol-ogy of John Macquarrie* published in 1985 and David Jenkin's *The Scope and Limits of John Macquarrie's Existential Theology* published, as a dissertation,

45. Macquarrie, *Martin Heidegger*, 54.

in 1987. Though Long and Jenkins both fundamentally tie Macquarrie to existential theology through Heidegger as a grounding point for Macquarrie's theology, what we see in their respective books are different directions they take in the matter. If we are to be true to what it means to do existential theology, and what it means, in particular, for Macquarrie to engage in existential theology, we need to discuss, at least in a controlled manner, the assertions made by Long and Jenkins—on one hand, while Long proposes a "new style" of natural theology in Macquarrie as effectively centered on the interconnected of human existence and God's Being towards a concept of truth, while, on the other hand, Jenkins denotes Macquarrie's existential methodology as being inherently problematic towards issues of epistemology through Macquarrie's concept of truth. Because both have their respective focus on the concept of truth and how grasping truth, as such, requires phenomenology, we see, first and foremost, that there is a common thread between Long and Jenkins. We can even recognize, too, that both Long and Jenkins are deeply concerned with how to explicate Macquarrie's meanings of "existence" and "being" as essential to what it means to do theology from a philosophical perspective, and the extent at which Heidegger plays a role in how both view Macquarrie's existential tendencies. What separates the two is how they read, understand, and interpret Macquarrie's starting point after employing Heidegger's philosophy.

Let us consider Long's argument for a moment. Towards the end of the first chapter—or what is clearly an introductory section, though it is not expressly referred to as this—in his *Existence, Being, and God*, Long makes the suggestion that Macquarrie, through his directedness towards existential theology, proposes a "new style of natural theology."[46] This, of course, is an interesting argument, since, as Long is right to point out, if our concern is with how "religious faith is to have any relevance to modern culture," traditional natural theology falls far short in making this possible. Long considers, and rightly so, the "significant criticisms leveled at [natural theology]" and how natural theology does not provide the best foundation to grounding the meanings of religious faith and modern culture, yes, and does not do any favors for philosophical issues of "existence" and "being." So, for Long, this means that Macquarrie is engaged in a "new style of natural theology," since it does not resemble any traditional understanding of the term. Rather, for Long's reading of Macquarrie, "Macquarrie's new

---

46. Long, *Existence, Being, and God: An Introduction to the Philosophical Theology of John Macquarrie*, 11.

style of natral theology is founded on Heidegger's analysis of the experience of existence and Being."[47] Here, Long outlines what it means to do
natural theology for Macquarrie—it means unconventionally doing "natural theology" philosophically and not theologically, and it means, more
importantly, filtering what is to be done philosophically through Heidegger
under the scope and limits of what is to be done from the stance of natural
theology. With this in mind, Long continues: "Indeed, Macquarrie refers
to Heidegger's philosophy as offering a natural religion or theology that
can be considered in its own right and that might be satisfying to those not
attracted to institutional religion."[48] At this point, Long cites Macquarrie's
Principles of Christian Theology in conjunction with a reference to the Wil-
helm Dilthey (1833–1911), as seemingly as means of explaining the notion
of "institutional religion," particularly, when referring back to Macquarrie,
any interpretation is necessarily based on an initial understanding of what
is being interpreted and not on an institutionalized representation of that
interpretation. What this means, for Long, is that natural theology, as such,
in a traditional sense, has become institutionalized to the point that it does
not lend itself to meaningful interpretations, if we want to tease out of it
the meanings of human existence and God's Being. The concern, here, is
with locating our initialunderstandings of human existence and God's Being, without both becoming overly-institutionalized by the institution of
religion, as such—natural theology, in the traditional sense, limits what we
can initially understand, when, for Long, it offers the best chance at truly
grasping what we already know about human existence and God's Being.
Macquarrie's "new style of natural theology," then, according to Long, "is
thus a bridge between our ordinary ways of understanding ourselves in the
world and faith's understanding of human existence in relation to Being or
God."[49] Even though this assertion about Macquarrie's "new style of natural
theology" is certainly debatable, Long is correct, nonetheless, in arguing
that "the central problem for Macquarrie, again, is how one can talk of
God within an existentialist framework, how one can make the transition
from statements about human existence to statements about God, we can
certainly understand Long contextualizing this "problem" through "a new
style of natural theology." Yet, if, as Long makes clear, "for theology to begin
with the experience of existence and Being [. . .] Macquarrie finds this in

47. Ibid.
48. Ibid.
49. Ibid., 12.

phenomenology," natural theology, however "new" of a "style" it is, seems to be only one of many possible means of assuming a phenomenological lens rooted in theology. As Heideggerian as this "lens" undoubtedly is, Long's pointing to natural theology inevitably undercuts the extent to which Macquarrie uses Heidegger to sort out and sort through Macquarrie's "central problem," as such.

Let us turn our attention, now, to Jenkins. Like Long, Jenkins' approach also contextualizes Macquarrie's "central problem," but does so, as Jenkins asserts in the abstract to his work, by "applying Macquarrie's existential methodology to issues of theology." Jenkins accomplishes this through an epistemological lens, though Jenkins equates this as a form of existential phenomenology that, as a more specialized lens, "reduces knowledge to knowledge about the universal structures of Being, which do not themselves give information about the factual conditions of the world or about history." Of course, we do not see this in Long, though it is clear that Long's working through natural theology offers a certain set of factual conditions that, in the end, still reduces knowledge, even if Long recognizes that Macquarrie is embarking on a "new style of natural theology." As "new" as that "style" is, it must be reiterated that the factual conditions remains just as factual—and the underlying phenomenology, then, exerts limitations on what we can know about the meaning of human existence, God's Being, and the relationship between the two. In other words, even a "new style of natural theology" still reduces what can be known about "the universal structures of Being," since it "does not [itself] give information about the factual conditions of the world." For Jenkins, science and history have the same limits, when they are viewed through existential phenomenology. Jenkins considers Macquarrie's understandings of science, history, demythology, interpretation, The Resurrection, Christology, and language as all examples embodying respective sets of "factual conditions" that are not wholly given informationally from the systems to which they belong—in each of these separate understandings, Jenkins locates difficulties in Macquarrie's existential phenomenology. In the title itself, by referencing Macquarrie's 1955 dissertation, Jenkins finds a "scope" to Macquarrie's existential phenomenology that contains "limits" within it, such that Macquarrie's "system," as it were, "ends up making it impossible for a theologian to refer meaningfully to the empirical, factual aspect of knowledge." In this, Jenkins is concerned with how this adversely affects the concept of truth—it is the notion that, through Jenkins' understanding of Macquarrie, truth is always-already reduced by existential phenomenology.

What we find in both Long and Jenkins there is a focus on the concept truth, though the avenues both take have different points of origin—both of which themselves are fraught with problems. But, the problem with what Long suggests and what Jenkins suggests is that both cite language in some fashion, and yet, neither focuses exclusively enough on language, when language is imperative to how Long argues for Macquarrie's "new style of natural theology," language is equally vital to Jenkins' understandings of science and history. Language is primordial to all else, since, it must be noted, that nothing exists outside of language. The same can be said about the concept of truth, which, as a concept, it is so limited by either Long's notion of Macquarrie's new style of natural theology or Jenkins' understandings of Macquarrie's notion of science and history that truth is not truly "truth" at all. For us to be able to confront language at its most primordial—not reduced by what we can know of it—and truth at its most primordial within the parameters of existential theology means allowing existential theology itself to be confronted at its most primordial. To even speak of a thing called language this way, and speak of a thing called truth as another way, we always-already trap what we speak of and greatly hinder the possibility of ever authentically knowing either as they are in themselves and not strictly in the contexts of "a new style of natural theology" for Long nor an existential phenomenology for Jenkins. To do existential theology this way, if we are to better understand Macquarrie outside of Long and Jenkins, it means bringing together two strands of thought that are deeply and inevitably dependent on one antoher—the meaning of language and the meaning of truth—by the relationship between human existence and God's Being.

Conducting existential theology, through Macquarrie, means not cleaving ourselves to the meaning of language as such nor the meaning of truth as such, but orienting ourselves to what is primordial to both: λόγος and αλεθεια. To do this, and effectively confront the coming-together of human existence and God's Being, we must think of Macquarrie as offering an existential theology of scripture, by which λόγος is the ultimate object of Macquarrie's Heideggerian lens.

If λόγος is the object of Macquarrie's *Heideggerian lens*, then his accompanying existential theology of scripture is centralized on the problem of the relationship between theology and language. That juncture, as such, contains the existential situatedness of λόγος, as a stand-in for God.[50] In other words, Macquarrie views this problem of conceiving, grasping and explaining λόγος by how it is grounded in the theology-language relationship. To be clear, this problem is not just with how theology can be expressed through language, but how language can accurately express what theology is—or, the issue at hand is with what might be referred to as theological language.[51] Such language, when decidedly theological, arises out of the need to apprehend God to a certain degree, to make affirmations about God, and suggest "that God must be such and such, if he is a reality at all."[52] This is precisely where the problem with theological language lies—it lies in using language to explain who God is, what God does, and how God functions, within an overarching framework of a conceptual, interpretative reality about God.

However, even when suggesting that there is a "reality about God," Macquarrie contends, and appropriately, that "human language invariably objectifies God [since God's] reality lies beyond the objectification."[53] This sort of objectification poses a problem. In this regard, Macquarrie notes the following:

> We cannot discuss the question of the reality of God by asking whether there exists an entity corresponding to the concept. The method must rather be as follows. The concept of God is an interpretative concept, meant to give us a way of understanding and relating to reality as a whole.[54]

To "discuss the question of the reality of God" means, as Macquarrie proposes, attempting to provide a language that "can articulate and bring into intelligible relations the swirling chaos of experiences only because there is some order there to be discovered. . ."[55] In doing this, it becomes possible to develop a working, conceptual understanding of "the reality of God."

50. Macquarrie suggests that "it was not God himself who had spoken to Moses at the burning bush, as explained in Exodus, but the "Logos." Macquarrie, *In Search of Deity: An Essay in Dialectical Theism*, 24.

51. Macquarrie, *God-talk: An Examination of the Language and Logic of Theology*, 33.

52. Macquarrie, *In Search of Deity: An Essay in Dialectical Theism*, 25.

53. Ibid., 161.

54. Ibid., 29.

55. Macquarrie, *In Search of Humanity: A Theological and Philosophical Approach*, 104.

That conceptualization must develop without resorting to "asking where there exists an entity corresponding to the concept" itself. In effect, when discussing "the reality of God," as such, that reality is being discussed in juxtaposition to humanity's reality. From this, the role of human language is to place not only humanity's reality in order, but to project "some order" upon God's reality, since any interpretative understanding of the latter concretizes—or, even, what I might call "existentializes"[56]—the former.

Language about "the reality of God," then, is meant, first and foremost, to "bring what we talk about out of its hiddenness into light."[57] According to Macquarrie, once "what we talk about" is "into light," language "isolates and brings to notice that about which the speaker wishes to say."[58] This is an unmasking. It allows what is isolated and brought to notice to be unhidden as ἀλήθεια. Furthermore, when connecting "what we talk about" to what is brought into the light as ἀλήθεια, Macquarrie explains the following:

> [. . .]at least one characteristic of saying anything, and perhaps even the fundamental characteristic, is that what is talked about is brought into the light. That is to say, what is talked about is made to stand out from the undifferentiated background of all that may be vaguely present to our minds at any given time, or even what may be in our memory or our anticipation. It is brought into the focus of attention and is shown for what it is. To put it in another way, that which is talked about is manifested and made unhidden; and, as Heidegger never tires of pointing out, 'unhiddenness' or aletheia is precisely the expression which the Greeks used to express the notion of 'truth.' We speak truly if we make what we are talking about unhidden.[59]

In this respect, "what we talk about" is always focused on bringing something into the light. In other words, "what we talk about" is "made to stand out" from an "undifferentiated background" of *concealment*. The task of saying anything, then, is edified by "speak truly" in order to "make what we

---

56. Even though this is my term, I think it captures the extent to which the meaning-making process is an existential endeavor. I see "concretizes" and "existentializes" as analogous terms. However, in moving forward, I will chiefly use the latter.

57. Macquarrie, *In Search of Humanity: A Theological and Philosophical Approach*, 103.

58. Ibid.

59. Macquarrie, *God-talk: An Examination of the Language and Logic of Theology*, 64.

talking about unhidden"—for Macquarrie, "what we talk about," or the way of language itself, is a process based on ἀλήθεια.

When discussing "what we talk about" in this manner, Macquarrie carefully notes how important language is to the theologian's ability to talk about the reality of God. What Macquarrie suggests is that:

> [The theologian] must have some idea, explicit or implicit, of what language is. If [the theologian] is wise, [the theologian] will pay attention to what has been said on the subject by those who have made language the specific theme of their researches.[60]

As a theologian, there is no doubt that Macquarrie has "some idea" about "what language is." However explicit or implicit that idea may be, Macquarrie has a presupposition about language and carries that presupposition forward in his task as a theologian—in fact, as a theologian, Macquarrie does indeed make "language the specific theme of [his] researches." To be sure, Macquarrie's "researches" into "what language is" is attached to an existential understanding of what theology is in reference to what language is, and vice versa. The intersectionality of theology and language is evident in what theological language is. What Macquarrie is concerned with is the scope and limits of theological language, particularly, as he suggests, if "we can acknowledge that theology is rather a strange kind of language [and] is a special form of God-talk."[61] In the aptly titled work *God-Talk: An Examination of the Language and Logic of Theology*, Macquarrie defines God-talk as "a form of discourse professing to speak about God."[62] With this in mind, Macquarrie contends that God-talk is fundamentally different from common discourse about everydayness.[63] Because of this, God-talk presents a unique problem that is not especially evident in the common discourse of everydayness—Macquarrie proposes that "this problem is to show how in a human language one can talk intelligibly about a divine subject-matter."[64] Yet, what underlies this problem and this existential theology of scripture, as Macquarrie rightly references, is more than just asking what theological language is—it is about a more fundamental question: what is language?

60. Ibid., 54.

61. Ibid., 11.

62. Ibid.

63. Ibid.

64. Ibid., 33.

For Macquarrie, when approaching the scope and limits of theological language—a relationship between "what theology is/does" and "what language is/does"—it is important to ask the question *what is language*, as a highly peculiar question, since:

> [. . .]in order to ask the question, we have to use of the very language about which we are asking. This implies that before we ask the question, we must already have some understanding of language in order to be able to ask the question at all. So perhaps the answering of the question consists in no more than making explicit and clarifying as far as possible the understanding of language which we already have. To ask the question of language is possible only for one who, so to speak, exists linguistically. This question about language might be compared with Heidegger's question, "What is the meaning of being?". . .[65]

If, as Macquarrie argues, the question about language "might be compared" with Heidegger's question about the meaning of being, then this comparison is associated with the relatedness between language and being. This comparison must be explicitly made. Like Heidegger, Macquarrie seems to view this relatedness as the extent to which the former is "the house" of the latter.[66] Though Macquarrie is operating from a *Heideggerian lens* and positioning himself with a Heideggerian-like question, his intellectual duty is not solely about thinking the thoughts of Heidegger.[67] In other words, it can be argued that Macquarrie is not a staunch Heideggerian, or "even a thoroughgoing existentialist [since] his intellectual integrity holds him back from any uncritical or superficial identification with Heidegger's position."[68] Nevertheless, Macquarrie grounds his intellectual duty as a philosophical theologian, by using a *Heideggerian lens* to construct a style of philosophizing[69] about the relationship between language and being.

Macquarrie's "style" is that of an existentialist, operating within the framework of a kind of existential theology—a theology that takes an existential approach. That point must be clearly made. Though Macquarrie

---

65. It must be noted that Macquarrie continues with comparing the question of language to Frege's question of the number one. Ibid., 55.

66. I am referring to Heidegger's assertion that "language is the house of being." Heidegger, *On the Way to Language*, 63.

67. Brown, *The Self in Time: Retrieving Existential Theology and Freud*, 12.

68. Ibid.

69. Ibid.

might disagree and resist such a label, because, as Charles Brown argues, Macquarrie "seeks on many occasions to distinguish his theology from what he calls existential theology," the kind of work Macquarrie is doing ventures into existential theology nonetheless.[70] While it may be possible to justify that Macquarrie philosophizes in a "style" that is "existential without labeling it as such, or even denoting it as existentialist,"[71] Macquarrie's style requires such a label and denotation. Sure, we may justify against applying the terms "existential" and "existentialist" to Macquarrie,[72] but any justification in this direction would prove unhelpful and ultimately do a great disservice to Macquarrie's *Heideggerian lens.* Just as Brown points out, Macquarrie's "style" is decidedly existential, since it involves philosophizing in a way that "is directed towards analyzing human existence in terms of a secular language accessible to everyman."[73] Brown rightly proposes, then, that this "secular language [that is] accessible to everyman" is what Macquarrie calls "existential-ontological"—a language capable of describing the universality of structures and experiences.[74] This, of course, is based on Macquarrie's belief that:

> Language has to be understood as both an existential and an ontical phenomenon; interpretation demands both questioning and listening, a sense of direction and a willingness to be directed.[75]

If language is "both an existential and an ontical phenomenon," then interpretation is more than just about overcoming the ontology of language. When adhering to the existential requirements of understanding what

---

70. Ibid.

71. Ibid.

72. Charles Brown seems to suggest that a justification can be made against Macquarrie's role as an existential theologian. Brown conceives of the work of existential theology as something that is in contrast to Macquarrie's work. I do not agree with this. If Macquarrie's "style" is devoted to human existence—even if it is predicated on issues of theology and human language—and that devotion is theologically-oriented towards what is existential. Essentially, I believe that Macquarrie is concerned with what meaning can be made from theology through language, and from language through theology. Nevertheless, Brown does seem to agree with this, especially since Brown does not shrink from aligning Macquarrie with Heidegger, and, in turn, calling Macquarrie a "Heideggerian." Ibid.

73. Ibid.

74. Ibid.

75. Macquarrie, *God-talk: An Examination of the Language and Logic of Theology,* 167.

language means, interpretation also makes it possible to uncover "what language is." The interpretation of language—as a demand of both questioning and listening—is a task oriented towards λόγος and ἀλήθεια.

Macquarrie's task of interpretation becomes more than just the interpretation of language as "statements about human existence," but transitions to theological language as "statements about God"—this is what Eugene Long calls Macquarrie's "central problem."[76] That problem is with finding "how one can talk about God within an existentialist framework,"[77] when finding meaning in talking about God is about finding existential meaning in scripture. That is, the being in scripture at being's most primordial. In order to approach scripture as a kind of language capable of lending existential meaning and pointing towards the primordiality of being, Long suggests that Macquarrie develops "a theory of the truth of religious language," which is dependent on Heidegger's definition of truth—it is a notion that scripture, as a religious language, "may be said to be true to the extent that it lights up or discloses reality as it is given."[78] I agree with Long's assertion. Clearly, Macquarrie's "theory of the truth of religious language" is based on the degree to which the ontics of language (physical descriptions of reality), once lighted-up or disclosed as the *primordial being* in scripture, or λόγος (existential descriptions of reality), can point to ἀλήθεια.

Λογος in Scripture and the "Linguistical-Existential" Pathmark

Macquarrie's pathmark in existential theology searches for λόγος in scripture—this venture pursues a *Heideggerian pathmark* of "logos" as an object of primordiality. Through Macquarrie's existential theology of scripture, *what we talk about* must be translated from its ontic state into what it already is[79] as *primordial being*—that is, *what language is*. Macquarrie's λόγος is "linguistical-existential," since *what language is* gets to *what being is*, at its most primordial.

---

76. Long, *Existence, Being, and God: An Introduction to the Philosophical Theology of John Macquarrie*, 15.

77. Ibid.

78. Ibid., 100.

79. "What it already is" is what primordial being is when it is disclosed, unmasked, or unhidden in a state of unconcealment. It is, in fact, a state where "beings" are allowed "to be as they are." See Note 40.

What I mean by "linguistical-existential" is that λόγος, as a *Dasein*-like analytical possibility,[80] makes meaning out of *what we talk about* in order to *unconceal* what language is as ἀλήθεια. To be clear, the *linguistical-existential* is predicated on the meaning-making of linguistics—the extent to which meaning must be made out of *what we talk about*, through a foundational, grounding knowledge of *what language is*. For Macquarrie, λόγος is a linguistical entity[81] that differentiates *what we talk about* in its *concealedness* (ληθε), from the primordiality of *what language is* as ἀλήθεια. In using a *Heideggerian lens* and an understanding of λόγος in scripture, Macquarrie excavates the ontics of scripture (*what we talk about*) in order to unmask *primordial being* (*what language is*) on the way toward ἀλήθεια.

The *linguistical-existential* pathmark Macquarrie takes is a specific approach to language on the way towards ἀλήθεια.[82] Macquarrie's approach does not come by way of an analytic philosophy, but more accurately through Continental philosophy—the latter, in particular, is where he situates his *Heideggerian lens*, his "theological inquiry," and how he understands language in a theological setting with respect to the question of human existence.[83] Though Macquarrie is a philosophically-oriented theologian concerned with the philosophy of language, he is more concerned with a specific kind of language, or discourse: theological language, or scripture. From this, Macquarrie's existential theology of scripture is based on the abiding idea that scripture, which he refers to as Christian vocabulary:

> [. . .]stands in continual need of being reinterpreted if it is to remain meaningful, but at any given time there may be several ways of doing this. At the present time, however, it may be claimed that

80. See note 46.

81. In other words, λόγος is a "Dasein-like" entity, but it is narrowly devoted to working out issues of "linguistical" existence—where language and existence intersect.

82. Macquarrie's "linguistical-existential" venture, as I have called it, is "on the way towards ἀλήθεια," just as Heidegger's understanding of language is on the way towards "Being." In this respect, I think that Macquarrie's "Heideggerian pathmark" is the same path that Heidegger takes in *On the Way to Language*, through proposing that "language is the house of Being." See note 103.

83. Though partly influenced by Bultmann, Macquarrie's "existential-ontological" framework and approach to existentialism is Heideggerian. As Long suggests, in light of Macquarrie's Heideggerian influences—what I have endeavored to call a "Heideggerian lens"—Macquarrie's comes to the question of human existence by way of "theological inquiry." Long, Existence, *Being, and God: An Introduction to the Philosophical Theology of John Macquarrie*, ix.

existentialism is making a powerful contribution towards renewing some basic Christian words.[84]

As "a powerful contribution" to the hermeneutics of scripture, Macquarrie views existentialism as a style of philosophizing.[85] The existentialism, as Macquarrie appropriates it in his existential theology, does, in fact, attempt to renew "some basic Christian words." This sort of renewal is steered towards those "basic Christian words" that are deemed existential to scripture and must "remain meaningful." Macquarrie's *linguistical-existential* pathmark is predicated on the belief that scripture "stands in continual need of being reinterpreted" is a decidedly existential belief grounded on an ontical understanding of scripture. This is part and parcel of Macquarrie's *Heideggerian lens* and his notion of the *linguistical-existential*. That is to say, the ontics of scripture must be continually reinterpreted, so that the λόγος within it can "remain meaningful"—meaning is made when λόγος in scripture, λόγος in its primordiality, can be *unconcealed* in ἀλήθεια.

At the ontic level, when λόγος is *concealed*, this extent of ληθε makes *what we talk about* in scripture lose its fundamental meaning. In effect, *what we talk about*—especially once it is concretized in the written form—limits *what language is*. Such a limiting concretization and *concealment* turns λόγος into "what language does," or the grammatical/technical. When this occurs, the ontics of scripture reduces the hermeneutic possibilities of λόγος, and *what we talk about*, then, becomes a technical embodiment of the relationship between words and their usage. As a result, the existential meaning of *what we talk about* and λόγος contains a low hermeneutic and *linguistical-existential*.[86] Macquarrie certainly agrees with this assessment, suggesting that, when confronting the words that make up the ontics of scripture:

> [. . .]we may say that they have been made into technical terms, and that they now constitute a kind of esoteric vocabulary which

84. Macquarrie, *Studies in Christian Existentialism*, 136.

85. Macquarrie suggests that existentialism's "style of philosophizing"—to be sure, his style of philosophizing—as a "first and obvious" characteristic ". . .begins from man rather than from nature." Macquarrie, *Existentialism*, 14.

86. What I mean by "low hermeneutic" is that what we talk about is only the ontics of scripture. In other words, "what we talk about" and the ontics of scripture is merely a low, or superficial interpretation of λόγος. I consider this a "low hermeneutic" of λόγος, in contrast to assessing the primordiality of λόγος, which would be, in turn, a "high hermeneutic."

is still in regular use only within the Christian community and which even there is imperfectly understood.[87]

Essentially, when the ontics of scripture as *what we talk about* "constitute a kind of esoteric vocabulary," the meaning made from λόγος is, in fact, reduced to the meaning-making of a specific group or community. But, as Macquarrie rightly points out, when λόγος consists of "technical terms," the meaning made out of those words are not existential, but are meanings restricted to the esoteric opinions and beliefs of a specific group or community. This kind of esoteric vocabulary correlates to an esoteric meaning—this kind of meaning, again, is not existential, but is a *concealment* (ληθε) of λόγος in scripture, which makes it difficult for λόγος to "remain meaningful."

In light of Macquarrie's desire for scripture to "remain meaningful," that focus on the necessity of meaning—that is, venturing beyond esoteric meaning—is rooted in Macquarrie's appropriation of Heidegger's view of ἀλήθεια. That appropriation is steered towards λόγος in scripture, or λόγος in its primordiality—or what I would refer to as λόγος as exoteric meaning.[88] It is only at such a primordial level that the scripture can be truly evaluated in terms of its *primordial being,* or as *what language is.* Eugene Long suggests this too. With respect to what I have called Macquarrie's existential theology of scripture, λόγος in scripture, and λόγος in its primordiality as an articulation of ἀλήθεια, Long proposes that:

> Macquarrie is appealing. . . to Heidegger's view that truth consists in making unconcealed what is being discoursed about, suggesting that religious statements are intended to disclose the being of human existence and its relation to Being itself. . .[89]

As Long points out, Macquarrie's view of ἀλήθεια, like Heidegger's, is based on *unconcealing* "what is being discoursed about," or what I have called *what we talk about.* What that means, then, is that *what we talk about* should be oriented towards ἀλήθεια. To this end, "religious statements," as the ontics of scripture, should "disclose the being or human existence

---

87. Macquarrie, *Studies in Christian Existentialism,* 127.

88. In contrast to what Macquarrie proposes to be "esoteric meaning," I am using the term "exoteric meaning" to propose the opposite: meaning that has existential influence outside of a specific community in a narrow sense, so that that meaning has general, existential value.

89. Long, *Existence, Being, and God: An Introduction to the Philosophical Theology of John Macquarrie,* 9.

and its relation to Being itself." This is the task of Macquarrie's *linguistical-existential* pathmark—a pathmark that must understand the existential difference between the ontics of scripture, the primordiality of λόγος, and what ἀλήθεια is.

The ontics of scripture is *what we talk about* in the general sense. In other words, *what we talk about* is always encased in Christian vocabulary and theological language about God—in this general sense, God is *what we talk about*. Though scripture is the ontics of *what we talk about* when referring to God, it is only language in the general sense—it is the everydayness of λόγος. What this means, then, is that *what we talk about*—even in the general sense, as the ontics of scripture, as the everydayness of λόγος—must be a kind of discourse that is meaningful. As such, meaningfulness leads the way to the primordiality of λόγος, and what ἀλήθεια is. That is to say, meaningfulness in the everydayness of λόγος is Macquarrie's *linguistical-existential* pathmark—that venture is predicated on the *linguistical-existential* necessity of the meaning-making of λόγος. To this end, Macquarrie's venture follows the *Heideggerian pathmark* where:

> [. . .]discourse is meaningful if it brings what is talked about into
> the light, that is, if it *says* something, in what we took to be the
> original significance of 'saying.' Perhaps the notion of meaning has
> to do also with 'placing' the language in some frame of reference
> that we already have, and indeed this seemed to be implied in what
> was said about communication. In any case, what we understand
> here by 'meaning' is closely related with the notion of truth as 'un-
> hiddenness.' We could say that truth is the ideal or limiting case,
> in which that which is talked about has been fully manifested for
> what it is.[90]

The meaningfulness of discourse—making meaning out of the ontics of scripture, or *what we talk about*—is only meaningful if, as Macquarrie argues, "it says something." Essentially, when the ontics of scripture "says something," the meaning that is made "plac[es] language in some frame of reference that we already have"—the *linguistical-existential* meaningfulness of λόγος is the *unconcealment*, or disclosing of λόγος.

The *linguistical-existential* pathmark Macquarrie employs is focused on disclosing λόγος in a narrow sense: the *unconcealment* of *what language is*. Macquarrie's *Heideggerian pathmark* utilizes the *Dasein*-like analytic

---

90. Macquarrie, *God-talk: An Examination of the Language and Logic of Theology*, 75.

possibilities of the *linguistical-existential* to locate the primordiality of λόγος—that is, what is primordial to the everydayness of λόγος—in order to unmask ἀληθεια. To this end, the *unconcealment* of λόγος is the task of Macquarrie's existential theology of scripture—that *unconcealment* is devoted to a *lingustical-existential* pathmark.

CHAPTER 2

"Being" in Tradition and Bultmann's "κηρυγμα"

Rudolf Bultmann's existential theology concerns itself with *primordial being* in tradition. This kind of *being* is exemplified as "kerygma," or "proclamation," in κηρυγμα.[1] For Bultmann, κηρυγμα holds the whole of Christian tradition together as a foundational concept—it is through this κηρυγμα that the history of Christianity develops from the ministry of Jesus and sustains itself theologically. But, Bultmann asserts that κηρυγμα has been suppressed by the superstructures of history, until κηρυγμα becomes buried in what Bultmann denotes as mythology. To this end, though Bultmann views mythology as something that prevents κηρυγμα from unfolding itself to us in modernity, he, nevertheless, believes that "myth" is a very important aspect of the history of Christianity, the historical Jesus, and the development of Christology.

Conceptually, *myth* has its purpose, not just historically, but anthropologically and theologically.[2] Bultmann openly acknowledges this, particularly when *myth* works in tandem with κηρυγμα within Bultmann's existential theology. Yet, *myth* creates a large hermeneutical rift between the New Testament world and our present day—this rift makes the message of Jesus all the more difficult to grasp with the modern mind, and the κηρυγμα itself ungraspable. This rift opens historical distance between then and now—between κηρυγμα and today—until *myth* encases the original

1. Balz and Schneider, eds., *Exegetical Dictionary of the New Testament: Volume 2,* 288.

2. Bultmann, "New Testament and Mythology," In *Kerygma and Myth: A Theological Debate,* 10.

gospel in layer upon layer of hermeneutical excesses. Excesses of this sort must be stripped away, if the κηρυγμα of the original gospel is ever to be accessible and the truth can ever be confronted directly.

Through what Bultmann calls "demythologization"—that is, stripping *myth* away from "the message of Jesus," but not doing away with the essentials of myth entirely[3]—Bultmann uses a *Heideggerian lens* to see through the excesses of mythology. To be clear, the term *demythologization* is an unfortunate and problematic misnomer. What it suggests, as a process, is that *myth* is being taken away, delimited, or negated, to the point that no *myth* remains. This is certainly not true. For Bultmann, *demythologization*, just as Paul Ricoeur rightly surmises, is not a "purely a negative enterprise."[4] *Demythologization* is not so much about completely taking away *myth* through negation, but, instead, is more about reducing—not exactly "stripping away" in the strictest sense of the term—*myth* so that the κηρυγμα of the original gospel conveys a more graspable truth, or ἀληθεια. This means that the act of demythologizing "strips away" only what is necessary, while leaving behind what is essential in *myth*. But, more importantly, to demythologize, as Bultmann argues, means recognizing that the Christian *myth* has *concealed* ('ληθε') the κηρυγμα of the original gospel. To accomplish these ends, Bultmann uses a *Heideggerian lens* that seeks to excavate κηρυγμα from *myth*, in order to uncover ἀληθεια.

3. I must make a note here, for sake of clarify and specificity. My contention that demythologization means to "strip away myth" is in disagreement Morris Ashcraft, who argues the opposite. In light of Bultmann's project, my view is that to "strip away myth" means not stripping away myth entirely, but, instead, leaving behind some essential layers of myth. In other words, I use the term "strip away" to mean that we are not doing away with myth completely, but are recognizing that there are "excesses" to myth that must be stripped away, though not completely eliminating. In Ashcraft's view, ". . .to demythologize the New Testament does not mean that one strips away the myth. Rather, it means that the New Testament must be interpreted existentially." I feel Ashcraft is missing what "strip away" denotes. "Strip away" is similar to deconstruction, which means interpreting existentially—if following Bultmann's argument in "New Testament and Mythology" about what it means to demythologize, it means peeling back the excess layers that surround myth by deconstructing myth, in order to "interpret existentially." Ashcraft, *Rudolf Bultmann*, 14.

4. Ricoeur, "Preface to Bultmann," in *Essays on Biblical Interpretation*, 57.

Bultmann and Heidegger

Bultmann first met Heidegger in 1923 at the University of Marburg. While Heidegger had just begun his professorship there in order to succeed Paul Natorp,[5] Bultmann was already a member of the Marburg theology faculty for two years. Not long after Heidegger's arrival, the two established a collaborative friendship over the next five years, with their relationship continuing long after Heidegger's 1927 departure from Marburg when Heidegger accepted a faculty position at the University of Freiburg in 1928. There, at Freiburg, Heidegger was appointed chair of Professor of Philosophy, ultimately succeeding his mentor Edmund Husserl who had retired. Just as he begins to settle in at Freiburg—the university at which Heidegger would remain for the rest of his academic career, including the brief period when he was elected rector on April 22, 1933[6] and the period when he was banned from teaching from 1945 to 1951—Heidegger publishes *Sein und Zeit* in 1927.

The publication date of *Sein und Zeit* affects any discussion of the relationship between Bultmann and Heidegger, since we can view the relationship in two phases: the period before *Sein und Zeit* and the period afterwards. First, *Sein und Zeit*, as Heidegger's first academic book, was written and published with the intent of qualifying Heidegger for Husserl's vacated chair at Freiburg.[7] In fact, though the book's publication was rushed, the fundamental ideas Heidegger argues in what became an unfinished draft of *Sein und Zeit* are introduced and honed in Heidegger's Marburg courses, most notably courses such as *Platon: Sophistes* (translated as *Plato's Sophist*) of Winter 1924/1925 (GA 19), *Prolegomena zur Geschichte des Zeitbegriffs* (translated as *History of the Concept of Time: Prolegomena*) of Summer 1925 (GA 20), *Logik: Die Frage nach der Wahrheit* (translated as *Logic: The Question of Truth*) of Winter 1925–1926 (GA 21), *Die Grundprobleme der Phänomenologie* (translated as *The Basic Problems of Phenomenology*) of Sumner 1927 (GA 24), and *Phänomenologische Interpretation der Kants Kritik der reinen Vernunft* (translated as *Phenomenological Interpretation of Kant's Critique of Pure Reason*) of Winter 1927/1928 (GA 25). Each of these courses contributed to early drafts of *Sein und Zeit*, and can also be exca-

---

5. William D. Dennison, *The Young Bultmann: Context for His Understanding of God, 1884–1925* (New York, NY: Peter Lang, 2008), 132.

6. Guignon, ed., *The Cambridge Companion to Heidegger*, xx.

7. Ibid.

vated for evidence as to where Heidegger intended to go in the unfinished territory of the book's Division II. In some instances, certain courses can be viewed as, more specifically, early drafts of *Sein und Zeit*—Thomas Sheehan sees *Logik: Die Frage nach der Wahrheit* as an early draft, while Theodore Kisiel considers *Prolegomena zur Geschichte des Zeitbegriffs* as such.[8] What must be maintained is that it is difficult to say if any one course served as an "early draft" of *Sein und Zeit*—we can say, however, that, in all these courses during a very short period in time, Heidegger purposely worked and re-worked through material that eventually found its way into sections in *Sein und Zeit*. In doing so, Bultmann participated in this working and re-working not just during early drafts of what would become *Sein und Zeit*, but during the courses of the period in which Heidegger offered confrontation s with Husserl and his phenomenology, Plato, and Kant.

When I use the term "participated," I am aware that there are immediate questions raised, since Bultmann and Heidegger did not work in the same fields. That is to say, while Bultmann worked in Marburg's theology department, Heidegger, as it has been noted, entered Marburg's philosophy department, which must not be minimized due to Heidegger's previous work with Husserl at Freiburg when Husserl directed Heidegger's dissertation. Having worked in different departments, we might ask what sort of contribution did Bultmann offer to Heidegger during the writing of *Sein und Zeit* and, in another sense, in what way did Bultmann "participate" in the courses in which Heidegger asserted claims that found their way into the book?

To answer his, we must recognize that there exists overwhelming evidence that there was an active and open dialogue between Bultmann and Heidegger, such that Bultmann's theological roots lean towards Heidegger and Heidegger's philosophical roots lean towards Bultmann. In fact, it has been noted very briefly by William Dennison in the recently published *The Young Bultmann*, that Bultmann and Heidegger "met once a week to discuss theological and philosophical issues," as a means for Bultmann to determine how philosophy could speak to theological concerns, as well as for Heidegger to ascertain the same of theology for philosophical concerns.[9] Yet, even when cited, the sort of comradery between them would

8. Kisiel offers this claim in the epilogue to his 1985 translation of *Prolegomena zur Geschichte des Zeitbegriffs as History of the Concept of Time*. Martin Heidegger, *History of the Concept of Time: Prolegomena*, 321. In the meanwhile, Sheehan suggests the same of *Logik: Die Grage nach der Wahrheit*.

9. Dennison, *The Young Bultmann: Context for His Understanding of God, 1884–1925*,

seem fairly unlikely, if our focus is strictly on their very separate bodies of work—if our intent is to say that philosophy cannot speak to theology any more than theology can to philosophy. Clearly, Bultmann and Heidegger did not agree with this dividing line—to whatever extent that divide surely existed between the two departments to which the two were appointed. The fact that we know, now, the extent to which Bultmann and Heidegger had an active and open dialogue as Marburg colleagues was certainly common knowledge between 1923 and 1928—this was from the moment Heidegger arrived at Marburg until he left for Freiburg. Still, little has been written about the full extent of the Bultmann-Heidegger relationship, especially the moment Heidegger joined the Marburg philosophy department in 1923.

Though there has been quite a bit of scholarship detailing Heidegger's first professorship at Marburg, the only definitive account of this period from Bultmann's perspective is available in Konrad Hammann's recently translated biography *Rudolf Bultmann*. Much has been said about what courses Heidegger taught during his time at Marburg—and I have previously listed many of them as they appear in Heidegger's *Gesamtausgabe*—but what has been omitted from this period a lecture/seminar Heidegger participated in with Bultmann in Heidegger's first semester in Winter 1923/1924: the ethics of Paul,[10] accompanied by Heidegger's paper on Martin Luther's concept of sin entitled *Das Problem der Sünde bei Luther*.[11] To be sure, during this same semester, Heidegger delivered *Einführung in die phänomenologische Forschung* (translated as *Introduction to Phenomenological Research* as GA 17), which, in its Preliminary Remarks, he asserts that the lecture has a two-fold task of "establishing and opening up the horizon within which specific facts of the matter are to be expected [and] concretely working out the facts of the matter that have, step-by-step, been made more accessible."[12] From there, Heidegger outlines the overarching task of the lecture as focused on the "elucidation of the *expression* 'phenomenology,'" providing a "representation of the *breakthrough* of phenomenological research in Husserl's *Logical Investigations*" and presenting a "representation of the *development* of phenomenology from this point on."[13] These considerations, as Heidegger

132.

10. Hammann, *Rudolf Bultmann: A Biography*, 203.

11. Dennison, *The Young Bultmann: Context for His Understanding of God*, 1884–1925, 132.

12. Heidegger, *Introduction to Phenomenological Research*, 1.

13. Ibid.

calls them, revolve around the terms "expression," "breakthrough," and "development" as the essential guiding features of phenomenological research, especially as they come to bear on the meaning of phenomenology through Husserl and, in turn, the extent to which Descartes becomes foundational to Husserl and how the phenomenological is possible. In this respect, *Einführung in die phänomenologische Forschung* attempts to work through Husserl and ascertain how Husserl worked through Descartes as a forerunner, but also intends to take Husserl beyond his method of phenomenology and into an application of it. What we find in this lecture, even as Heidegger's first at Marburg, is a methodological extension of all seven lectures he previously delivered at Freiburg from 1919–1923. There is no doubt that Heidegger had a deep commitment to phenomenology. However, in his last course at Freiburg before leaving for Marburg, *Ontologie: Hermeneutik der Faktizität* (translated as *Ontology—The Hermeneutics of Facticity* as GA 63) of Summer 1923, Heidegger began to make some advancements in phenomenology, by viewing the field within the hermeneutic tradition of Plato and Aristotle through to Augustine and Schleiermacher and arising as an necessary offshoot of the dialectic of Kierkegaard and Hegel. In doing so, Heidegger's intent is to take phenomenology further than Husserl and ensure that the field could be properly contextualized hermeneutically and historically. Though Heidegger begins the lecture by outlining the traditional concept of hermeneutics as such, he follows shortly thereafter by focusing on the idea of facticity and how this especially comes to bear upon the "concept of 'man' in the biblical tradition."[14] It is clear that Heidegger is making a connection between phenomenology, hermeneutics, the idea of facticity, and the concept of man, in order to propose that, essentially, for the concept of man to be conceptualized as an idea of facticity, it must be assessed and understood phenomenologically and hermeneutically. As a starting point, Heidegger briefly discusses Paul and carries forward the Pauline understanding of the "concept of man" into short discussions of Augustine and Aquinas, and an abbreviated settling of the concept among the Reformation thinkers, Calvin and Zwingli, which ultimately ends with an assessment of Scheler.[15] Heidegger evoking Scheler is relevant for Heidegger's attempt to expand phenomenology, since Scheler is certainly committed to the same, but does so by forging a methodological relationship between phenomenology and anthropology—according to Heidegger, this

14. Heidegger, *Ontology: The Hermeneutics of Facticity*, 17
15. Ibid., 17–20.

sort of method, as it pertains to the concept of man, "so little understands Kant's basic approach to the idea of person. . .insofar as it is more dogmatic and allows the borders between philosophy and theology to become even more blurred, i.e., ruins theology and undermines philosophy and its distinctive possibilities of critical questioning."[16] This would seem like an ironic thing for Heidegger to say, if we know, of course, that the collaboration between Heidegger and Bultmann—which begins in the next year— can be deemed as attempting to allow "the borders between philosophy and theology to become even more blurred." Still, we see, in his critique of Scheler, an argument against this. For Heidegger, the following connections are made, by which Scheler, as a phenomenological figure in the same lineage as Heidegger, is used as a fundamental entry point:

> The extent to which Scheler creates confusion in [Kant's] these basic starting points manifests itself *inter alia* in the fact that his idea of person is, right down to its linguistic formulation, exactly the one which the Reformation helped bring to the fore in opposition to the superficial Aristotelianism of Scholasticism, cf. Zwingli, Calvin. Only that in the process what gets overlooked again is that here, i.e., in theology, man's various states, modes of being, must in principle be distinguished (*status integritatis, status corruptionis, status gratiae, status gloriae*) [state of purity, state of corruption, state of grace, state of glory] and that one cannot arbitrarily exchange one for the other.[17]

Immediately following this, Heidegger argues that Scheler "confuses" Luther with Isaiah, with respect to the flesh—as one of "man's various states" or "modes of being"—being in a *status corruptionis*. What makes this assessment of what Scheler gets incorrect about Luther interesting is that, on one hand, it shows that Heidegger is assuredly basing his understanding of the flesh on an understanding of sin allowing it to fundamentally exist in a *status corruptionis*, but, on the other hand, by simply referencing Luther this way, it demonstrates that Heidegger has been reflecting on Luther's understanding of sin, in particular. We can see, too, that this direct reference to Luther and the notion of how sin affects the status of the flesh is linked to how Heidegger understands the "concept of man," the idea of facticity therein, and what phenomenology can accordingly tell us—that is to say, when situating the *Ontologie: Hermeneutik der Faktizität* lecture.

16. Ibid., 22.
17. Ibid.

Rather than speak more about his, if we are more concerned with what this has to do with Bultmann, we find that this reflection on Luther—though occurring very briefly in *Ontologie: Hermeneutik der Faktizität*—is expanded upon after the Summer 1923 lecture into a paper presented in the Winter 1923/1924, in Heidegger's first semester at Marburg. To be sure, we could certainly speculate over the timing, in light of all the previous Husserl-influenced work Heidegger had done at Freiburg. I do not think timing is at play here. In other words, it is likely that the development of Heidegger's paper on Luther's understanding of sin simply arose out of a "preoccupation" Heidegger already had with Luther, which only followed him to Marburg.[18] We can note, of course, that, it is often asserted that there is a "Catholic Freiburg" and a "Protestant Marburg"—and, from this, we can surely surmise that Heidegger's move from the former institution to the latter allowed him to express his work on and position himself as influenced by Luther in a way that he would not have been able to do while at Freiburg. Simply put, the move from Freiburg to Marburg may have placed Heidegger professionally in a position to more explicitly express Luther's influence upon him, but it is more evident that Heidegger, even while at Freiburg, had Lutheran roots long before writing *Das Problem der Sünde bei Luther* (translated as "The Problem of Sin in Luther").

Though Hammann asserts that Heidegger, "presented papers on February 14th and 21st, 1923, addressing Luther's understanding of sin" to Bultmann's seminar on the ethics of Paul, Hamman's dating is shockingly incorrect for Heidegger's *Das Problem der Sünde bei Luther*. Dating the text to 1923 does not align with Heidegger's arrival at Marburg in the Fall of 1924, especially if it is widely known that *Das Problem der Sünde bei Luther* was presented after Heidegger left Freiburg, and that, by the Winter 1923/1924 semester, Heidegger was already appointed to the position of associate professor or "*Extraordinarius*," before being deemed an "extraordinary member" of Bultmann's seminar on the ethics of Paul.[19] What is accurate, however, from Hammann's account is that Heidegger participated in two sessions of Bultmann's seminar and, in doing so, "lectured on the problem of sin in Luther" that expanded on the ethics of Paul, in much the same manner as Heidegger had tied Paul to Luther (and the Reformers) in *Ontologie: Hermeneutik der Faktizität*. Tying the two together would

---

18. Van Buren, *The Young Heidegger: Rumor of the Hidden King*, 150.

19. Congdon, *The Mission of Demythologizing: Rudolf Bultmann's Dialectical Theology*, 597.

have been appealing to Bultmann as a Lutheran, even if his lecture was devoted to Paul. Though, in *Ontologie: Hermeneutik der Faktizität*, Heidegger is approaching the problem of flesh for Luther as something that is oriented towards the ethics of Paul, he is simply rearticulating a kind of phenomenology to religion itself, from which Luther and Paul are both negotiating and questioning: Paul's questioning is in confrontation with the teachings of Jesus, and Luther's questioning is in confrontation with Catholicism—for Heidegger, phenomenology added an ethics to the problems of sin and the flesh as "[humankind's] various states, modes of being," to the extent that reading Paul and Luther phenomenologically gave rise to the richness of their respective critiques. Of course, this argument, as Bultmann could have been aware, was not a new one. Three years earlier, while at Freiburg, Heidegger delivered a seminar in Winter 1920/1921 on Paul and the phenomenology of religion in the lecture entitled, "Introduction to the Phenomenology of Religion," included as the first part of *Phänomenologie des religiösen Lebens* (translated as *The Phenomenology of Religious Life* as GA 60). It is in that earlier Freiburg seminar, as it has been noted by David Congdon, that Heidegger "cites Bultmann's 1914 review article in *Theologische Rundschau*."[20] What Congdon is referring to is an appendix section to *Phänomenologie des religiösen Lebens* entitled, in translation, "Methodological Considerations regarding Paul," in which Heidegger discusses Paul's proclamation "in terms of content, relational, enactmental."[21] From there, after considering the "when," the "how," the "what," and the "who" of a proclamation, Heidegger proceeds to determine how these components of a proclamation are grounded in style.[22] It is here, in referencing Bultmann in comparison to three other takes on Paul's "style," that Heidegger parenthetically argues that "'form'—'style' are not aesthetically typologizing; rather the How of explication, concern, appropriation of the enactmental understanding—decision!"[23] Moreover, Congdon asserts that, in light of this evidence, it is clear that "Heidegger was citing Bultmann well before Bultmann was citing Heidegger."[24] Still, there is something else immensely interesting about Heidegger's reference

20. Ibid.

21. Heidegger, *The Phenomenology of Religious Life*, 93.

22. Ibid., 93–94.

23. Ibid., 94–95.

24. Congdon, *The Mission of Demythologizing: Rudolf Bultmann's Dialectical Theology*, 597.

to Bultmann in the Winter 1920/1921 seminar. I would venture to add to Congdon by suggesting that, aside from Bultmann's 1914 review article, Heidegger was likely also aware of Bultmann's 1910 dissertation, *Der Stil der paulinschen Predigt und des kynisch-stoische Diatribe* (translated as *The Style of the Pauline Sermon and the Cynic-Stoic Diatribe*), in which, as described by William Dennison, Bultmann "focused mainly upon the literary-stylistic relationship between Paul's preaching and the Cynic-Stoic diatribe."[25] Though Bultmann's concern is with the concept of preaching itself and how it "was the vehicle to unite pastor and laity, scholar and common people, and God and humanity."[26] With this in mind, Dennison appropriately asks: "why should [Bultmann] not examine the preaching style of the Apostle Paul in order to receive possible insights that would help mend the gap between scholar and layperson in [Bultmann's] own day?"[27] Just as this essential question is grounded in Bultmann's approach to his dissertation, Heidegger is not just similarly tapping into this concern in the "Introduction to the Phenomenology of Religion" seminar, but he is most certainly using phenomenology to assess Paul's preaching style and what becomes the Pauline proclamation in Paul's two letters to the Galatians, Corinthians, and Thessalonians. Through this preaching style and proclamation, Heidegger reads in Paul, according to John van Buren, a criticism of the addressees as "hav[ing] fallen away from the historical situation and from their authentic selves into the present world [to the extent that] their authentic selves within the historical situation have been closed off to them."[28] Heidegger takes the problem of inauthenticity, as argued by Paul, into a reading of Augustine and Neoplatonism in the Summer 1921 lecture (included as the second part of *Phänomenologie des religiösen Lebens*), which follows the Winter 1920/1921 seminar.

By this Summer 1921 seminar, Heidegger reads in Augustine a "problem of historical objectivity"—this allows for a further falling away from the historical situation towards more inauthentic selves compounded by the present world. For Heidegger, Augustine's use of Plato certainly perpetuates this problem, but the problem is especially rooted in the Church's use of Augustine. What results from this is the eventual situation—albeit,

---

25. Dennison, *The Young Bultmann: Context for His Understanding of God, 1884–1925*, 67.

26. Ibid., 66.

27. Ibid.

28. Van Buren, *The Young Heidegger: Rumor of the Hidden King*, 164.

historical—in which Luther enters, when his central question revolves around the meaning of the authentic self and the falling away from the historical situation. We can see, in Heidegger carefully working through Book Ten of Augustine's *Confessions* in the Summer 1921 lecture, the sort of Neoplatonism that influenced Augustine, the influence it exerted upon the Aristotelianism of Scholasticism derived from Aquinas, and the genesis of the Augustinian Order from which Luther's theological roots originate. Nevertheless, Heidegger's focus on Augustine and Neoplatonism in the Summer 1921 lecture does not singularly bring him to Luther's understanding of sin by the time he presents *Das Problem der Sünde bei Luther*—aside from Augustine, it is also Heidegger's frequent phenomenological work on Aristotle not just in every semester from Summer 1921 to Summer 1923 towards the end of his time at Freiburg, but, in his first semester at Marburg, a seminar and an essay both dated to the Winter 1923/1924.

As Heidegger delivered his first major lecture at Marburg—what has been previously noted as *Einführung in die phänomenologische Forschung* (GA 17)—two phenomenology seminars were concurrently given to a smaller number of students: the second of these seminars was on Book II of Aristotle's *Physics* for advanced students entitled "Phämonenologische Übung für Fortgeschrittene: Aristoteles, Physik B." In an essay in the same semester, Heidegger wrote "Wahrsein und Dasein (Aristoteles, Ethica Nicomachea Z)" on Aristotle's *Nicomachean Ethics*.[29] Taken together, the seminar for the advanced students and the essay can be both viewed as phenomenological exercises on Aristotle—though only the seminar makes this explicit—since both are deeply engaged in using Aristotle as a figure of phenomenological research. Yet, aside from two excursions into a seminar on Husserl to beginners[30] and a talk given to the Kant Society in Hamburg on December 7, 1923,[31] Heidegger's phenomenological readings of Aristotle are, in one sense, examples of phenomenological research, but, in another sense, it demonstrates a concerted effort to confront Aristotle. In fact, in my view, this confrontation mirrors Luther's own confrontation with Aristotle—that confrontation is fundamentally grounded in Luther's

29. Both of seminars are currently unpublished. Only the essay has been published in GA 80, but it is currently untranslated.

30. See the "Chronological Overview," in *Supplements: From the Earliest Essays to Being and Time and Beyond*, 31.

31. Ibid.

wholesale rejection of the assimilation of Aristotelian philosophy into Scholasticism.

If we consider Heidegger's essay on Aristotle's ethics, there is a certain congruence between it and Bultmann's Winter 1923/1924 seminar on "The Ethics of Paul." Through Heidegger's phenomenological reading of ethics in the essay—a return to the topic previously explored in Summer 1923 at Marburg—we see Heidegger working through the same problems raised in *Ontologie: Hermeneutik der Faktizität* about "man's various states, modes of being" in theology, which are evident in *status integritatis, status corruptionis, status gratiae, status gloriae*. Heidegger's notion of "being-true" and "being-there of Dasein," as argued in the essay, address a kind of ethics to "man's various states, modes of being." In particular, the relationship that Heidegger establishes between the essay's "being-true"/"being-there of Dasein" and "man's various states, modes of being" in theology construes a phenomenological ethics to Aristotle. It would seem, however, that Heidegger recognizes, even through his use of Aristotle, that there are theological concerns to "being-true" and "being-there of Dasein." We can certainly speculate how these theological concerns come to bear on Heidegger's talk at the Kant Society, in light of Heidegger inaugural lecture at Marburg. Unfortunately, it is impossible to know exactly what this talk entitled "The Tasks and Paths of Phenomenological Research" argued, since it has never been published.[32] We may be able to connect the talk to Heidegger's first Marburg lecture on phenomenological research—if there is a connection between the two, I would argue that it is more likely that the talk extends the lecture, by venturing further into the scholastic ontology that is discussed in one of the three parts of *Einführung in die phänomenologische Forschung*.

It is through the "tasks" and "paths" of phenomenological research that Heidegger arrives at contemplating Luther's understanding of sin. This was preceded by what has been described as a "shorter discussion" on January 10, 1924 on "the topic of living in faith in connection with Romans 6."[33] Not only has this "shorter discussion" remained unpublished—if we can even say that it was transcribed at all, or actually exists as a text—we could conclude from the subject, perhaps, that Heidegger examined "living in faith" in conjunction with phenomenological research. That is to say, through a reading of the meaning of being dead to sin and being alive in

32. Ibid.
33. Ibid.

Christ in Romans 6, Paul's understanding of sin is fairly straightforward. This Letter to Romans would have served as an example of how "living in faith" employs an ethics about "man's various states, modes of being"—we can surmise that Heidegger's use of Romans 6 is with *status integritatis, status corruptionis, status gratiae, status gloriae* always in mind. Exactly how Heidegger may have interpreted this phenomenologically as the "task" and "research" of phenomenological research is largely unclear for the obvious reasons. It is also unclear, in the discussion of January 10, 1924, if Heidegger would have drawn a connection between Aristotle, Paul, and the notions of "being-true" and "being-there of Dasein."

What is clear, nonetheless, is that the topic of the January 10 "shorter discussion" on Romans 6 directly influenced what followed in *Das Problem der Sünde bei Luther* on February 14 and 21. We can see, in this influence, a means of extending a phenomenological reading of Paul to the same for Luther, or even a means to tie the two to Aristotle. It is more to it than that. Heidegger is working theologically from Paul to Luther, and the understanding of sin arising from both becomes the duality of "being" for human through a negotiation of *status integritatis, status corruptionis, status gratiae,* and *status gloriae.* Because Paul and Luther are both appropriating religious reflection, there are also theological reflections at work, since the concept of sin—and any understanding of it—is a theological problem. Whether or not Heidegger directly tied this theological problem for Paul and Luther to a phenomenological problem can only be approximated, if we recognize that the missing "shorter discussion" of January 10, 1924 and the unpublished "talk" to the Kant Society in Hamburg on December 7, 1923 are the key texts necessary for this connection. The only way we can approximate this connection is with Heidegger's *Das Problem der Sünde bei Luther*—yet, like the textual transmission problems of the "shorter discussion" and the "talk" that immediately precede it, it is difficult to know what Heidegger explicitly argues in *Das Problem der Sünde bei Luther,* since, as it has been noted, "[the] manuscript [is] not scheduled for publication and [is] presumably lost."[34] Though this means that there is no first-hand text of *Das Problem der Sünde bei Luther,* there exists only a second-hand text based on a student transcript, and it is this transcript that is included in *Sachgemäße Exegese: Die Protokolle aus Rudolf Bultmanns Neutestamentlichen Seminaren 1921–1951,* published in 1996.[35] As a protocol paper from a

34. Ibid.
35. Ibid.

student that attended Bultmann's seminar "The Ethics of St. Paul," what we have of Heidegger's *Das Problem der Sünde bei Luther*, as it was presented to the seminar, begins by Heidegger asserting that (or what the student transcribing writes "Prof. Heidegger proceeded roughly as follows"):

> The problem of sin will be treated not insofar as it is an object of religious reflection but rather as a theological problem, and it is from the point of view of this question that Luther's theology will then be examined.[36]

Opening the paper this way, it is possible to suggest that the differentiation Heidegger wants to make between "religious reflection" and a "theological problem" is an interesting juxtaposition. It is, in fact, a necessary move, if we can surmise, from this juxtaposition, that Heidegger is less concerned with "religious reflection" than he is with the existence of a "theological problem," because he sees the latter as aligning more with the "task" and "path" of phenomenological research. If this is his orientation, it is clear, then, that his assertion that "the object of theology is God [and] the theme of theology is man in the how of his being-placed before God"[37] is based on a fundamental understanding of what phenomenology can contribute to both "the object of theology" and "the theme of theology." Such a contribution, though not explicitly stated by Heidegger in light of what has been transcribed, can explain the problem of sin and how that problem specifically impacts the question of the meaning of "being." As the transcript suggests, Heidegger proposes that:

> [. . .] the being of [humankind] is at the same time also a being in the world, and there exists for him also the whole problem of the world. Now, Luther followed a particular direction of theological questioning, one preceding directly from sin. Thus our question reads like this: What does the word "sin" mean when the relation of [hu]man to God is being discussed as a theological problem? This problem is closely connected with the question of [humankind]'s original state (*iustitia originalis* [original righteousness]). What is asked here is the being of [humankind] at the moment he emerged from the hand of God.[38]

36. Heidegger, "The Problem of Sin in Luther," in *Supplements: From the Earliest Essays to Being and Time and Beyond*, 105.

37. Ibid.

38. Ibid.

Here, with the use of inclusive language, because Heidegger's concern is with the "being of [humankind] at the moment he emerged from the hand of God," and the degree to which that concern is underwritten by "the question of [humankind]'s original state," he sees, in Luther's approach to the problem of sin, the problem of how the "being of [humankind]" is able to reconcile "the question of [hu]man's original state." If we can say, then, that the problem of humankind is always-already a problem of sin and that this problem of sin greatly affects, even diminishes the "relation of [hu]man to God," we must conclude, too, what it means to be human is grounded in a state of flux—essentially, our "being" toggles between *status integritatis, status corruptionis, status gratiae,* and *status gloriae* because we are always-already in a *status corruptionis* due to the problem of sin. This was Luther's argument—the corruptibility of sin leads to a *status corruptionis* that the meaning of "being" is always wrestling with, especially in the relation of "being" to God. With this in view, Heidegger considers Luther's articulation of the problem of sin as more than just an important theological problem— for Heidegger, as theologically-contingent as Luther's argument is, there are phenomenological undertones to what Luther is proposing about the problem of sin. Heidegger does not proceed in that direction, but, rather, remains within a theological context. This is why Heidegger, as transcribed, finds that "the fundamental tendency in Luther is found in this manner: the *corruptio* [corruption] of the being of [humankind] can never be grasped radically enough."[39] Even though this is a "fundamental tendency" in Luther, it is apparent, too, that it is also a "fundamental tendency" in Paul. This sort of approach to "the *corruptio* [corruption] of the being of [humankind]" and the sense that "[it] can never be grasped radically enough," as Heidegger suggests, judging from the transcripts, can certainly be seen as fundamental to Bultmann's seminar on the ethics of Paul.

If Paul's ethics can be described as anything—that is to say, when we view an ethical framework to how Paul motivates the early First Century Christian communities of Thessalonians, Romans, and Colossians—it is attempting to confront "the *corruptio* [corruption] of the being of [humankind]." To be sure, Luther's notion of "the *corruptio* [corruption] of the being of [humankind]" is quite different from Paul's. Both Heidegger and Bultmann would have been aware of this. Yet, for Bultmann to have had Heidegger present his *Das Problem der Sünde bei Luther* to Bultmann's seminar on the ethics of Paul suggests that Bultmann considered a point

39. Ibid., 106.

of convergence between Paul and Luther, particularly on their respective understandings of sin and, in turn, how sin itself figures into "the *corruptio* [corruption] of the being of [humankind]." What is also apparent in Bultmann's inclusion of Heidegger's *Das Problem der Sünde bei Luther* in the seminar on Paul is that Bultmann surely viewed something important in Heidegger's phenomenological leanings and interpretations of religion. We can certainly speculate that Bultmann had followed or was aware of Heidegger's phenomenological work at Marburg, and probably, in particular, was familiar with Heidegger's "Einleitung in die Phänomenologie der Religion" in 1920/1921. To this end, it is difficult to know if Bultmann was aware, for instance, as it has already been noted, that Heidegger cites Bultmann's 1914 review article in *Theologische Rundschau* in the "Einleitung in die Phänomenologie der Religion" lecture. Whatever the reason, Bultmann recognizes that Heidegger can effectively contribute to Bultmann's seminar on the ethics of Paul, not only by synthesizing Luther's thoughts on sin with Paul's, but by directly addressing Luther's concerns with the problems of Scholasticism for the Protestant movement against Catholicism. Both of these would have interested Bultmann, especially if we view *Das Problem der Sünde bei Luther* as a follow-up to the "shorter discussion" on Romans 6. To this end, because the former and the latter, for Heidegger, are synthesized in connection with the relationship between the problem of sin and "living in faith," Heidegger's ideas on both Paul and Luther certainly left an "indelible imprint"[40] on Bultmann's theology moving forward from that Winter 1923/1924 lecture on the ethics of Paul.

By the following July 25, 1924, when Heidegger gives a talk to Marburg's Department of Theology entitled "Der Begriff der Zeit" (translated as *The Concept of Time* as GA 64), Bultmann was in attendance, and Hammann notes that Bultmann invited Heidegger to the talk.[41] This invitation arose, according to Hammann, due to Bultmann's "numerous efforts in 1924 and 1925 to involve Heidegger in what then was still a frank discussion with dialectical theology," despite the objections of Karl Barth (1886–1968).[42] Though Barth thought that philosophy, in general, "had nothing to say to theology and in theology," Bultmann disagreed, and considered that Barth's position was "unhelpful to the cause of theology."[43] The Bultmann-Barth

---

40. Ashcraft, *Rudolf Bultmann*, 22.

41. Hammann, *Rudolf Bultmann: A Biography*, 205.

42. Ibid.

43. Ibid.

disagreement was not a new one—that is to say, it was not created from Bultmann's relationship with Heidegger—rather, "the disagreement between the two theologians that has remained latent since 1922, almost inevitably became stronger in the face of [the] grave difference of opinion" about what philosophy had to offer to theology.[44] In other words, Bultmann's move away from the rigid theological views of Barth towards Heidegger "inevitably became stronger," not so much due to Heidegger personally, but because Bultmann was already leaning philosophically before he came in contact in Heidegger. Yet, Bultmann found in Heidegger, as Hammann asserts, a "scholarly comradeship. . . [that] mutated into a comradeship in arms when guests from elsewhere gave lectures in Marburg."[45] Hammann goes on to describe this relationship as a "sense of mission" between Bultmann and Heidegger, systematically revolving around an "interdisciplinary conversation and thereby provid[ing] critical grounding for theology."[46] This, of course, is from Bultmann's point of view as relayed by Hammann, since I would contend that Heidegger's approach to such an "interdisciplinary conversation" would have been used to "provide [a] critical grounding" for philosophy.

In spite of that—whatever biases either Bultmann or Heidegger held within their parts of the relationship—following Heidegger's participation in Bultmann's seminar on the ethics of Paul in Winter 1923/1924 and Heidegger's talk to the Marburg Theology Department on July 25, 1924 at Bultmann's invitation, Hammann notes that "Bultmann and Heidegger soon intensified their contacts with each other."[47] We can take this to mean, then, that, though Heidegger and Bultmann forged a professional relationship that revolved around Heidegger's participation in Bultmann's seminars, that relationship extended itself beyond that into Bultmann's own personal preoccupations. For example, Hammann points out that "after October of 1924, [Bultmann and Heidegger] met each Saturday afternoon to read the Gospel of John together,"[48] which, undoubtedly, directly influenced Bultmann's exegesis of the Gospel of John in his *Das Evangelium des Johannes* eventually published in 1941. Just how Heidegger played an influence on *Das Evangelium des Johannes* cannot be narrowed strictly to

44. Ibid.
45. Ibid., 204.
46. Ibid.
47. Ibid., 205.
48. Ibid.

Bultmann's Saturday afternoon readings with Heidegger, or even the period that followed up to its appearance in seven installments between August 31, 1937 and March 27, 1941.[49] This is only part of a much larger picture, which is certainly worth the time discussing more in-depth—in light of Heidegger's influence upon Bultmann, the development of Bultmann's *Das Evangelium des Johannes* becomes an important example, after Heidegger's participation in Bultmann's seminar of the ethics of Paul and during their Saturday afternoon meetings, of Heidegger's philosophical thinking infiltrating Bultmann's theological work.

Bultmann's work on *Das Evangelium des Johannes* actually predates not just the Saturday afternoon readings, but also Bultmann earliest collaborations with Heidegger. Hammann is careful to note that *Das Evangelium des Johannes* was originally contracted between Bultmann and his publisher on March 17, 1918 with a completion date set for the fall of 1920, "but this deadline could not be met, as Bultmann explained to the publisher numerous times during the 1920s, owing to the still-fluid state of the research."[50] If we take Bultmann at his word, it is true that his research was in a "still-fluid state," not just with whatever manuscript Bultmann was pruning, but with respect to whatever ideas about The Gospel of John circulated in his lecture courses at the time, especially his Winter 1922/1923 lecture, in which, according to Hammann, "he was determined from then on to bid farewell to the idealistic interpretation of the Gospel of John that had dominated the nineteenth century from Ferdinand Christian Baur to Albert Schweitzer."[51] If Bultmann was already moving away from an "idealistic interpretation" of the Gospel of John, his gravitation towards Heidegger is certainly explainable and reasonable, when considering that Bultmann was searching for a way to interpret the Gospel of John that was increasingly philosophical. Bultmann's previously held "idealistic interpretation" had been grounded in "how the history of religions frames questions" into the meaning of the Gospel—for Bultmann to reconsider this, it means that such a framing of questioning did not go far enough.[52] We can certainly view this reconsideration as being influenced by Heidegger, and the framing of questioning Heidegger frequently employed in his Marburg lecture courses on religion, as far back as the Winter 1920/1921 and even

49. Hammann, *Rudolf Bultmann: A Biography*, 311.

50. Ibid.

51. Ibid., 312.

52. Ibid.

the smaller seminar, "Kolloquium über die theologischen Grundlagen von Kant, *Religion innerhalb der Grenzen der bloßen Vernunft*" of Summer 1923 given to advanced students and focused on Kant's *Religion within the Limits of Reason Alone*.[53] Once at Freiburg, Heidegger's lecture on phenomenological research in Winter 1923/1924 surely provided Bultmann with firsthand experience of what the framing of questioning generally looks like, including the "phenomenological exercises" of the smaller seminars of the same semester. This very kind of questioning, theologically speaking, certainly followed Heidegger into his participation in Bultmann's seminar on the ethics of Paul, and into both Heidegger's shorter discussion on Romans 6 and his *Das Problem der Sünde bei Luther*—perhaps we can conclude, too, that Heidegger's direct involvement in Bultmann's seminar on the ethics of Paul allowed Bultmann to employ an existentio-phenomenological framing of questioning about Pauline theology.[54] Whether this framing of questioning towards Paul were similarly deployed during the Bultnann-Heidegger Saturday afternoon readings of the Gospel of John is difficult to say—in my view, these Saturday afternoon readings were undoubtedly influenced by the previously given seminar on the ethics of Paul. Consider, too, that, while involved in the Saturday readings, Bultmann attended two of Heidegger lecture courses (if I may reiterate this): *Prolegomena zur Geschichte des Zeitbegriffs* (GA 20) given in Summer 1925 and *Logik: Die Frage nach der Wahrheit* (GA 21) given in Winter 1925/1926. From this attendance, we can only presume that the manner in which Heidegger frames questions—though, at this point, oriented towards the question of the meaning of being—would have demonstrated to Bultmann how the Gospel of John could be approached.

Nevertheless, according to Hammann, "up to 1926, Bultmann's primary interest" was in framing his questioning with a history of religions context, by 1927, "he developed in a research report the first signs of the existentialist interpretation that he sought to employ in a 'history of mythology' interpretation of the Gospel of John."[55] Though these "first signs" do not appear until 1927, we can still surmise that these signs have their real roots in the years before—that is, if we can say that Bultmann's purpose-

53. See the "Chronological Overview," in *Supplements: From the Earliest Essays to Being and Time and Beyond*, 30.

54. What I mean by "existentio-phenomenological" is the coming together of existential and phenomenological concerns for the sake of questioning the meaning of being in Pauline theology.

55. Hammann, *Rudolf Bultmann: A Biography*, 312.

ful alignment with Heidegger is evidence of this earlier leaning towards existentialist interpretations. They can be traced not just to Bultmann abandoning the "idealistic interpretation" of the Gospel of John in his Winter 1922/1923 lecture course, but also, again, to his including Heidegger in the "The Ethics of Paul" seminar just a year later in Winter 1923/1924. The fact that Bultmann, then, returned to the Gospel of John in another lecture course in Winter 1924/1925—a lecture that, as Hammann describes, "dealt anew with the Gospel"[56] and with the Johannine letters in a concurrently delivered seminar—suggests that Bultmann's relationship with Heidegger obviously awakened in Bultmann a new understanding of the Gospel of John that ventured necessarily from the idealistic interpretation that he had "bid farewell to" in the Winter 1922/1923 lecture. What Bultmann parted ways with was not just the history of religions' framing of questions, but with how such a framing poses only superficial questions that never get to the meaning of being in a text such as the Gospel of John. That, of course, is Bultmann's main concern—it is certainly Heidegger's concern more generally with the phenomenology of religion: allowing a more concrete frame of questioning to reveal a philosophical meaning beneath what religion is and what theology can be.

The shared concern for Heidegger and Bultmann remains how philosophy and theology can speak to one another. By 1927—the year of publication Heidegger's *Sein und Zeit*—their collaboration up to this point transitioned into a planned project to which they would be co-authors and serve "as a way of documenting the time they shared at Marburg."[57] Heidegger, at the time, was already making plans to move on to Freiburg. Nevertheless, during a two significant semester breaks—one between the major lectures, *Geschichte der Philosophie von Thomas v. Aquin bis Kant* of Winter 1926–1927 (GA 23) and *Die Grundprobleme der Phänomenologie* of Summer 1927 (GA 24), and another between the major lectures *Phänomenologische Interpretation der Kants Kritik der reinen Vernunft* of Winter 1927/1928 (GA 25) and *Metaphysiche Anfangsgründe der Logik im Ausgang von Leibniz* of Summer 1928 (translated as *The Metaphysical Foundations of Logic* as GA 26)—Heidegger delivers the lecture "*Phänomenologie und Theologie*" in Tübingen on March 9, 1927 and Marburg on February 14, 1928. In it, as noted by Hammann, Heidegger "addressed the relation between philosophy and theology, and the character of theology

56. Ibid.

57. Ibid., 212

as a form of critical study."[58] But, there another purpose served with the lecture as well. Hammann notes, too, that Heidegger's lecture was based on a "partial verbal agreement with the manuscript of Bultmann's lectures on theological encyclopedia."[59] Bultmann's lecture was entitled "*Der Begriff der Offenbarung im Neuen Testament.*"[60] Moreover, when considering "the various versions" of Bultmann's lecture that were delivered both before and after Heidegger's "*Phänomenologie und Theologie,*" Hammann asserts that, though based on a reference to Ernst Jüngel, it is "scarcely possible today to know which thoughts which of the two thinkers thought first."[61] However untraceable their respective thoughts may be between Heidegger's "*Phänomenologie und Theologie*" and Bultmann's "*Der Begriff der Offenbarung im Neuen Testament,*" and how this may have been part and parcel of the overall planned project between them, the joint-publication of the two texts did not happen. Hammann suggests that this was because of Heidegger's reservations with the scope of the planned project, which are expressed in a letter dated to August 8, 1928. In this letter, as cited by Hammann, "[Heidegger] feared that the publication of the essay might give the fatal impression that he was offering an apologia for Christian theology."[62] This, of course, may not be the whole story. We can certainly place this rejection of the project in context with Heidegger having already received a call to Freiburg on February 25, 1928, his intent on leaving Marburg, and the need to not be tied too closely to the ideology of Protestant Marburg. Whatever the reason, Heidegger's inability to follow through with the project as planned was seen as, for Bultmann, a "withdrawal from the conversation between theology and philosophy"—it was also the parting of ways not just of a professional relationship, but a personal relationship too. Still, we find that Bultmann did not necessarily withdrawal from the theology-philosophy conversation, opting to maintain it within his approach to theology—the spirit of Heidegger's philosophical thought would remain Bultmann's chief interlocutor, in this regard, to the extent that Bultmann's theological thought was forever changed by his contact with Heidegger at Marburg.

Bultmann's contact with Heideggerian thought is clear, specifically when recognizing that his experience is rooted in the "genesis" of *Sein*

58. Ibid., 208.
59. Ibid., 209.
60. Ibid., 212.
61. Ibid., 209.
62. Ibid., 212.

und Zeit.[63] That kind of "indebtedness," as it has been pointed out, helps Bultmann develop a specialized theological concept of *being* utilizing Heidegger's categories.[64] The concept of *being*, as Bultmann suggests, "must be the methodical starting-point of theology [which] grow[s] out of my dependence on Heidegger's existential analysis of an in my effort to explicate existence in faith in a theological or conceptual way."[65] Bultmann makes this assessment quite unapologetically to critics of his Heideggerian influences in the following from "New Testament and Mythology" in *Kerygma and Myth*:

> Some critics have objected that I am borrowing Heidegger's categories and forcing them upon the New Testament. I am afraid this only shows that they are blinding their eyes to the real problem. I mean, one should rather be startled that philosophy is saying the same thing as the New Testament and saying it quite independently.[66]

For Bultmann, the "critics [who] have objected" to his borrowing of "Heidegger's categories and forcing them upon the New Testament" are precisely the kind of "critics" to which Bultmann intends to defend his "Heideggerian" approach. By addressing these "critics," Bultmann's "apologia" here, or so to speak, is focused on what he believes the "real problem" is. That "real problem" must be confronted not just theologically but philosophically, since, as Bultmann argues, "philosophy is saying the same thing as the New Testament and saying it quite independently." This means, then, that, though philosophy and theology are different voices expressing different concerns—and they are, as Bultmann explains, doing this "quite

---

63. Theodore Kisiel suggests in *The Genesis of Heidegger's Being and Time*, from which I have rather deliberately taken the term "genesis," that the two early drafts of *Being and Time* were written in 1924 and 1925. These two drafts were composed while Heidegger was still at Marburg, both of which would have been presented as "talks" to Marburg theologians such as Bultmann. Kisiel, *The Genesis of Heidegger's Being and Time*, 9.

64. Ashcraft, *Rudolf Bultmann*, 22.

65. Bultmann actually uses the term "concept of existence." I have substituted this with "concept of being," which is relatively analogous, since I would argue that "existence" and "being" are one in the same thing. They are both linked to issues of ontology and metaphysics, especially in the manner that Bultmann functions through Heideggerian existentialism. Bultmann, "The Historicity of Man and Faith," In *Existence and Faith: Shorter Writings of Rudolf Bultmann*, 92.

66. Bultmann, "New Testament and Mythology," In *Kerygma and Myth: A Theological Debate*, 25.

independently"—they are ultimately oriented towards the "real problem." So, speaking philosophically, albeit through "Heidegger's categories," should be a part of speaking theologically, as with the New Testament. Not only is Bultmann defending the appropriateness and meaningfulness of his "borrowing [of] Heidegger's categories," but he is explicitly denying that he is "forcing them upon the New Testament." Instead, Bultmann believes that "Heidegger's categories," more than any other method of categorization, makes it possible to truly analyze what the "real problem" is in the New Testament. That problem, in Bultmann's summoning of Heidegger, is the problem of *being*. More precisely, as it pertains to Bultmann's *Heideggerian lens*, the problem is with *primordial being* as it is represented as κηρυγμα—consequently, κηρυγμα is the focus of what I intend to refer to as Bultmann's existential theology of tradition.

Bultmann's Existential Theology of Tradition

When considering Bultmann's existential theology of tradition, we must first define what is meant by "existential theology" for Bultmann and the meaning of "tradition" in Bultmann's thought. Allow me to take up the former, as a way of leading into the concerns and parameters of the latter—we will see that, for us to even call Bultmann's way of theologizing an "existential theology," we do so by taking into account Heidegger's influence upon him, and the extent to which Bultmann remains grounded in a theological view. How Bultmann holds onto his theological concerns, and the m eans by which Heidegger provides a set of tools that Bultmann can use to carry out his concern and proceed forth with a theologically-minded task become essential to what we must define about his existential theology in general, before we specify an existential theology of tradition from it.

There is only one book that explicitly ties Bultmann to existential theology: Norman Young's *History and Existential Theology: The Role of History in the Thought of Rudolf Bultmann* published n 1969. What is especially of interest, here, is the book's publication date, which suggests that it was influenced, at least in part, by the growing influence of Sartre's existentialism in Europe and the fact that much of (if not all) of Sartre's project owes its very existence to Heidegger—to that end, the rehabilitation of Heidegger's reputation allowed for other Heidegger-influenced thinkers to be re-examined, namely Bultmann. It is by this premise that Young's book can be contextualized, since it is clear that, though he is keenly aware of Bultmann's unique relationship with Heidegger, his intent, more largely speaking, is to bring Bultmann under the purview of existentialism. In the "Introduction" to *History and Existential Theology*, subtitled as "An Existentialist Approach," Young begins with the following:

> It seems almost inevitable that any attempt to describe Bultmann's approach to history will make use of the label "existentialist." This is unfortunate in a way, because while there is some truth in saying that Bultmann takes an existentialist view of history, this really tells us very little.[67]

Here, Young is aware of the overwhelming desire to tie Bultmann to existentialism, in light of "any attempt to describe Bultmann's approach to history," simply by way of necessity. But, though Young does not make this plainer, when we speak of existentialism and we call any one thinker an "existentialist," we do so at our own peril. Existentialism, as a school of thought, is a big tint and, even if we can say for sure that what a thinker is doing philosophically (or theologically) has an existential approach, we can over-simplify the scope of their task, by deeply limiting that scope to existentialism. To be sure, existentialism can have many definitions and any definition we apply will be fraught with problems because we must ask, rather inevitably," what makes this or that existentialism" and "whose existentialism are we referring to?" These, of course, are tricky questions that do not yield straightforward answers. Young agrees with this, when recognizing that labeling Bultmann an "existentialist," it is "unfortunate in a way" since "there is some truth in saying [it]."[68] Yet, even when denoting that Bultmann employs an "existentialist view of history, this really tells us very little." That is to say, when we apply existentialism to what Bultmann is doing theologically, and find that the stance he assumes is an "existentialist view," and, in turn, consider that this view sees history differently, what we are saying is not bolstered or concretized, but becomes all the more obscure.

By 1969, at the time of Young's publication of *History and Existential Theology*, this was certainly the case when deeming any thinker as having an "existentialist" or suggesting that they have "an existentialist view" of something. Young notes this, conceding that "the label is used with such

---

67. Young, *History and Existential Theology: The Role of History in the Thought of Rudolf Bultmann*, 13.

68. Ibid.

abandon these days that it is difficult to know in any given case what it is supposed to mean."[69] This is certainly true. Still, we see that Young's willingness to contextualize Bultmann this way demonstrates that he is intent on threading the needle. Clearly, any work with Bultmann requires negotiating his philosophical tendencies with his theological concerns. The issue, here, is how do we speak about the kind of theologizing that Bultmann is doing without using existentialism? We cannot, to be frank. If our interest is in in understanding Bultmann's concept of history, as Young does, we need to read it within an existentialist view, since this is the only view that gives us the best chance of approaching Bultmann's "existential theology," as such.

Young is right to point to "history" as what Bultmann's "existential theology" is directed towards. However, using the term "history" significantly limits what we want to do with Bultmann, because his concern is not just with history, so to speak, but more with tradition itself. Since "history" denotes the object of a historian's reflection, and contains within it certain historiographical presuppositions, these are not Bultmann's concerns with "history" at all. History is not as theological in its comportment as "tradition" is—and, for that matter, when we address "history," we are speaking of the past, and "tradition," though it too speaks of the past, also speaks in a forward-moving fashion about what the past influences and directs. In short, we can do "history" without necessarily thinking about "tradition," but we cannot understand "tradition" without coming to terms with the role that history plays in its development.

For there to be a "role of history" in Bultmann's thought, it means that its structure is systematized around the creation of "tradition." Because of this, Bultmann considers the "role of history" as a proliferation of historical messages that shape the meaning of tradition. In other words, "history" has an effect on "tradition" by speaking to it—what this means, then, is that the role that "history" takes is that of a messenger, with a message that is always-already primordial to what happens in tradition. In this sense, Bultmann's existential theology of tradition is focused on how this message is concealed in and by tradition—what we see in Bultmann's existential theology is working through tradition towards αλεθεια as a means of unconcealing κηρυγμα (the message).

Since Bultmann's existential theology decidedly uses a *Heideggerian lens*, κηρυγμα is the object of that lens. Κηρυγμα is *being* at is most

69. Ibid.

primordial. Through Bultmann, a Heideggerian existential analysis is the only method that can completely evaluate κηρυγμα and explicate it theologically from tradition. In this regard, Bultmann states:

> [. . .]the method is determined by its object; and therefore when I take over the concepts of Heidegger's existential analysis, I also in fact take over the object of his analysis. Thus the object of my theological research is in truth not *existence in faith*, but rather *the natural man.*[70]

If, as Bultmann suggests, "the method is determined by its object," then existential theology is that "method," a "method" that is determined by what is "existential." Tradition is the object that requires an "existential analysis." What Bultmann offers is a kind of "theological research" that is not geared towards "existence in faith," but towards, as he argues, "the natural man." That means, I would suggest, that his understanding of the problem of being as κηρυγμα is not founded on "existence in faith"—that is, looking for κηρυγμα in faith—but is situated in "the natural man" or, as I have denoted, *primordial being.* This, then, is Bultmann's *Heideggerian lens.* Accordingly, Bultmann recognizes that κηρυγμα is in the *primordial being* of human existence, and extends the following:

> Heidegger's existentialist analysis of the ontological structure of being would seem to be no more than a secularized, philosophical version of the New Testament view of human [existence]. For him the chief characteristic of man[kind]'s Being in history is anxiety. Man[kind] exists in a permanent tension between the past and the future. At every moment he is confronted with an alternative. Either he must immerse himself in the concrete world of nature, and thus inevitably lose his individuality, or he must abandon all security and commit himself unreservedly to the future, and thus alone achieve his authentic Being. Is not that exactly the New Testament understanding of human [existence]?[71]

Bultmann's answer to this question is yes. Clearly, the New Testament understanding of human existence is grounded on "authentic Being." Note

70. Bultmann, "The Historicity of Man and Faith," In *Existence and Faith: Shorter Writings of Rudolf Bultmann,* 92.

71. Here, it must be noted that I have substituted Bultmann's term "human life" with "human existence." I do so, because I feel that "human existence" is a more philosophical term than "human life" and, if we are to sustain the philosophical language of Bultmann's *Heideggerian lens,* "human existence" would be a more preferable term. Bultmann, "New Testament and Mythology," In *Kerygma and Myth: A Theological Debate,* 24–25.

that "authentic Being" is about *Being*, which is oriented toward "the existential." I want to make this distinction clear. Human existence, especially in a New Testament framework, is not so much focused on the here and now, but on something beyond the temporal, something that is fundamentally atemporal. "Authentic Being" is that atemporal object, which existentially connects human existence to the past and the future. "Authentic Being," as described, allows human existence to make meaning within itself and further meaning beyond itself. Human existence, as Bultmann argues, is predicated on "a permanent tension between the past and the future." This tension is precisely the problem of *being* for the New Testament view of human existence—it is a tension that is laden with anxiety.[72] The permanence of this tension, with the presence of that associated Kierkegaardian two-fold concept of anxiety, wedges mankind between inauthentic and "authentic Being."[73] Despite the proliferation of the former in what Bultmann calls "the concrete world of nature," it is the latter that must be truly "achieved." The latter, as Bultmann contends, is more important, especially, when following Bultmann's thinking, if κηρυγμα is to lead to *primordial being* as "authentic Being."

Bultmann's understanding of "Heidegger's existential analysis of the ontical structure of being" underscores Bultmann's philosophical preoccupations with the New Testament view of human existence. This is how he intends to theologize through a *Heideggerian lens*. But, what must be drawn out of this *Heideggerian lens* is the extent to which Bultmann's exposure to Heidegger influenced Bultmann's understanding of the philosophical question of *what being is*. Also, to a greater extent, that philosophical exposure leads Bultmann to wrestle with the theological question of *what being is*

---

72. Another way to consider "anxiety" is as "angst." In either case, Heidegger provides an interpretation of anxiety, from which Bultmann is certainly drawing his "anxiety." Heidegger sees "anxiety" as a "basic state-of-mind" of *Dasein*, especially if Bultmann's notion of "tension" is steeped in *Dasein* working itself out through the problem of *being*. Heidegger analyzes "anxiety" along three lines of fear: (1) that in the face of which we fear, (2) fearing itself, and (3) that about which we fear. Bultmann's "anxiety" about the "tension between the past and the future" is a culmination of these. Heidegger, *Being and Time*, 179.

73. For Kierkegaard, the concept of anxiety is two-fold: subjective anxiety and objective anxiety. While Kierkegaard describes "subjective anxiety" as one that is directed inwards (humankind's historical relation to the Fall and Original Sin), "objective anxiety" is directed outwards (in relation to perceived threats from the world). Kierkegaard. *The Concept of Anxiety: A Simple Psychologically Orienting Deliberating on the Dogmatic Issue of Heredity Sin*, 56–62.

in an assessment of κηρυγμα. More importantly, in order to theologically assess *what being is*, what remains integral to Bultmann's *Heideggerian lens* is how κηρυγμα is essential to his conceptualization of two theological concepts: the New Testament view of human existence and the definition of history.

Bultmann's New Testament view of human existence is the starting point of his theology.[74] There, Bultmann employs an "existentialist understanding of man [that] deals with the structure of man's existence," in order to theologically assess *what being is*.[75] That assessment is based on "a basic understanding of human existence" and the acknowledgment that "the New Testament includes the mythologies of Jewish apocalyptic and Gnostic redemption religions."[76] The latter adds hermeneutical layers to the former, until any conceptualization of New Testament human existence is shrouded in a mythical world picture.[77]

So, to move beyond this and actually determine *what being is*, it becomes necessary to devise an existentialist interpretation of the New Testament view of human existence, in order to say, with any shred of certainty, that the New Testament embodies a truth which is all-together independent of its mythical setting.[78] That truth is in *what being is*, and where κηρυγμα resides. But, also, in order to disclose κηρυγμα from the mythical setting that encases it, Bultmann concludes that "theology must undertake the task of stripping the Kerygma from its mythical framework, of 'demythologizing' it."[79] As a result, through his demythologizing, "Bultmann's theological aim is nothing less than the rescuing of the kerygma from the consequences of historical criticism."[80] But, an important part of the task of "stripping the Kerygma from its mythical framework" is through engaging in a very different kind of historical exegesis. That historical exegesis, as Bultmann asserts, ". . .asks about meaning, but in such a way that all history

---

74. Ashcraft, *Rudolf Bultmann*, 23.

75. Ibid.

76. Ibid., 54.

77. Kaufmann, *Critique of Religion and Philosophy*, 212.

78. Bultmann poses this as a question near the beginning of his "New Testament and Mythology" essay. Bultmann, "New Testament and Mythology," In *Kerygma and Myth: A Theological Debate*, 3.

79. Ibid.

80. Künneth, "Bultmann's Philosophy and the Reality of Salvation," In *Kerygma and History: A Symposium on the Theology of Rudolf Bultmann*, 89.

is sketched on one plane, one map."[81] Such a sketch is brought together by two questions: (1) when historical exegesis asks about what is said, and (2) when we ask about what is meant.[82] But, what arises from these questions, and any subsequent answers, is an exegesis that ventures too far afield from historical exegesis. To this end, Bultmann makes the following assessment of the inadequacy of historical exegesis and calls for another kind of exegesis all-together in "The Problem of a Theological Exegesis of the New Testament" (1925):

> The presupposition of every exegesis should be recognition of the uncertainty of our existence, the knowledge that our existence is occasioned in our free act of decision; add to that an attitude toward history which acknowledges it as authoritative and thus sees it not with the detachment of the spectator but in the light of present decision.[83]

Here, Bultmann envisions a kind of exegesis that does not interact with history "with the detachment of the spectator," but with a kind of reciprocal interaction, always referencing the "present decision" of human existence and, by extension, the necessity of *what being is*. To determine *what being is*, *being* itself must be teased out with an exegesis focused exclusively on the primordiality of *being*—that is, the only way to compartmentalize *what being is* from all that surrounds, submerges, and encases it is by engaging in a new kind of exegesis. That kind of exegesis has the exegetical task of uncovering *what being is*.

Though Bultmann first attempts to articulate what this new kind of New Testament exegesis would look like in *History of the Synoptic Tradition* (1921) through form-criticism, he concedes the following near the end of the book's introductory section:

> The aim of form-criticism is to determine the original form of a piece of narrative, a dominical saying or parable. In the process we learn to distinguish secondary additions and forms, and these in turn lead to important results for the history of the tradition.[84]

The "original form of a piece of narrative," as Bultmann defines, is about reaching for *what being is* in a narrative, since "the original form" is *what*

---

81. Bultmann, "The Problem of a Theological Exegesis of the New Testament," 133.
82. Ibid.
83. Ibid., 134.
84. Bultmann, *The History of the Synoptic Tradition*, 6.

being is. This means, just as Bultmann explains, "distinguish[ing] secondary additions and forms" from what he calls "the original form." The only way to accomplish this is by recognizing that the exegetical task is to filter out "secondary additions and forms," in order to isolate "the original form" as something of primordiality—that is, something of primordial, existential resonance. This part of the exegetical task is mainly practical, since it results from beginning with a theoretical understanding about the difference between "the original form of a piece of narrative" and the "secondary additions and forms." For Bultmann, uncovering "the original form of a piece of narrative" means assuming a theoretical understanding about what is "history" and what is "tradition."

Bultmann's theoretical understanding—a Heideggerian understanding, to be certain—is based first on a reconceptualization of *history.* What that means is re-conceptualizing *history* through Heideggerian categories. To this end, Bultmann's definition of *history* is contingent on Bultmann's unique theological stance about *tradition,* especially as "the permanent tension between the past and the future."[85] Bultmann's view of *tradition* is not strictly as a historian, or even in terms of historiography. Instead, Bultmann's view of tradition is a philosophical-historical view. *Tradition,* for Bultmann, is a specialized term that contains existential meaning in it—its meaning arises from not only recognizing the "tension" inherent in the term itself, but through the differentiation between what is "original" and what is "secondary."[86] The meaning inherent in *tradition* is linked to κηρυγμα and, then, κηρυγμα connects to *primordial being*—the means by which Bultmann aligns *tradition* with κηρυγμα and κηρυγμα with *primordial being* is, then, the means by which Bultmann does his existential theology.

Bultmann's existential theology of tradition is chiefly situated in how he conceptualizes the message of Jesus. This *message of Jesus* is the ontical κηρυγμα—it is the "proclamation" from which Christian tradition proceeds and is ultimately sustained. Not only does the whole of Christian tradition spring forth from *the message of Jesus,* but, for Bultmann, a specific focus

---

85. Bultmann, "New Testament and Mythology," In *Kerygma and Myth: A Theological Debate,* 24–25.

86. The term "tradition" contains "tension" mostly because it solicits questions whenever it is used. The first question is: Whose tradition? That is, I am asking about to whom does that tradition belong? Next, there is the following question: What kind of tradition? By that, I mean, how is that tradition being described and defined, and to what ends does that description and definition serve?

on the κηρυγμα primordially inherent in *the message of Jesus* undergirds his notion of the primordality of *being*, especially as a way to do theology of the New Testament. The manner in which Bultmann conceptualizes *kerygma* and the primordiality of *being* become essential to a brand of New Testament theology that is not necessarily systematic in nature.[87]

For example, in the first volume of his *Theology of the New Testament*, Bultmann opens with the following about his understanding of *the message of Jesus* and *kerygma*:

> *The message of Jesus* is a presupposition for the theology of the New Testament rather than a part of that theology itself. For New Testament theology consists in the unfolding of those ideas by means of which Christian faith makes sure of its own object, basis, and consequences. But Christian faith did not exist until there was a Christian kerygma; i.e. a kerygma proclaiming Jesus Christ—specifically Jesus Christ the Crucified and Risen One—to be God's eschatological act of salvation. He was first so proclaimed in the kerygma of the earliest church, not in the message of the historical Jesus, even though that Church frequently introduced into its account of Jesus' message, motifs of its own proclamation. Thus, theological thinking—the theology of the New Testament— begins with the *kerygma* of the earliest church and not before.[88]

For Bultmann, there is a difference between *the message of Jesus* and κηρυγμα. That difference hinges on what he calls "a presupposition," or the notion that something is already implicit in a supposition, such as *the message of Jesus* (*'die Verkündigung Jesu'*).[89] Christian faith is this "presupposition" (*'Voraussetzungen'*)[90]—that is, that faith is a presupposed entity with an existence that is dependent solely on itself. However, as Bultmann points out, ". . .Christian faith did not exist until there was a Christian kerygma," which means, then, that he is aware of the primordiality of κηρυγμα. That primordiality is not just about describing what is primordial about κηρυγμα, but also about denoting what is primordial to *the message of Jesus*. In other words, *the message of Jesus* is simply an ontical ends to a primordial means: the *kerygma* at its most primordial.

---

87. That is to say, Bultmann's *Theology of the New Testament* is not a systematic theology, but, rather, a work of New Testament exegesis. For that matter, Bultmann is not a systematic theologian in the strict sense, but is a New Testament exegete.

88. Bultmann, *Theology of the New Testament Volume 1*, 3.

89. Bultmann, *Theologie des Neuen Testaments*, 1.

90. Ibid.

If, as Bultmann proposes, "theological thinking—the theology of the New Testament—begins with the *kerygma* of the earliest church and not before," then *kerygma* is the most primordial aspect of the "earliest church," as the most primordial representation of what tradition is.[91] So, when considering this at *prima facie*, in order to truly understand what *the message of Jesus* is, it is important to first unfold, as Bultmann argues, "[the] ideas by means of which Christian faith means sure its own object, basis, and consequences." The only way to "unfold those ideas" is by hermeneutically-reducing "Christian faith" to κηρυγμα. Such a reduction is phenomenological in the Husserlian sense.[92] Moreover, any such reduction, if focusing exclusively on Bultmann's κηρυγμα, is at the heart of the existential task of interpreting the ontics of tradition.

Κηρυγμα in Tradition and the "Historical-Existential" Pathmark

Bultmann's pathmark in existential theology is focused on κηρυγμα in tradition. The demythologization program that Bultmann undertakes is a venture that pursues a *Heideggerian pathmark* of κηρυγμα as an object of primordiality. In this regard, Bultmann's demythologizing task—what
have referred to as an existential theology of tradition—is concerned w
isolating κηρυγμα by utilizing the "historical-existential." To do this,
mann's program deconstructs what tradition does, or how traditio
ates, at the ontic level, in order to disclose what tradition is as
Demythologization as deconstruction is about unmasking the
ity of tradition. To demythologize means to deconstruct trad
to unmask the primordiality of κηρυγμα, since traditior
κηρυγμα in ληθε. The underlying intent, then, is to conc
ing is in *unconcealment*, or as ἀληθεια—that is, concept
tradition as the primordiality of tradition.

91. I am thinking about "what tradition is" as Bu
church," particularly from the standpoint of Bultmar
"primitive Christianity" in an eschatological comr
Jesus's disciples. Bultmann, *Primitive Christianity*

92. This reduction, as Edmund Husserl c
which is an intentional act of limiting the un
thing" can be better comprehended with s
Phenomenology and to a Phenomenologic

For Bultmann, there arises an existential need to venture beyond the ontics of tradition towards the primordiality of tradition. Bultmann first conceives of this need in *History of the Synoptic Tradition* and reiterates this concern in *Theology of the New Testament*. Though Bultmann's approach to the ontics of tradition is by way of a New Testament scholar, perhaps working from the perspective of a pseudo-historian. To be more exact, Bultmann's sense of history—and tradition, for that matter—is based on Heidegger's notion of the historical.[93] This influence is behind Bultmann's Heideggerian understanding of what history is and what tradition is.[94] Even though the former is important, the latter is a more critical, existential concept to Bultmann's demythologizing program—in Bultmann's view, tradition has become so mythologized that it requires deconstructing—demythologizing, as he calls it—if there is ever to be any hope of grasping ἀλήθεια (*unconcealment*). Essentially, Bultmann's goal is to grasp tradition's *Heideggerian being* "in the sense of the true"[95] through *unconcealment*. In this sense, the only way to truly make *unconcealed* meaning out of tradition is by not focusing on what it looks like at the ontic level (the message of Jesus), but the *primordial being* (the κηρυγμα of the earliest church) within it. Bultmann's *historical-existential* venture, as such, seeks to translate the ontics of tradition into what tradition is at its most primordial—it is the determination of the earliest church as an *unconcealment* of the primordial mode of *being* for κηρυγμα.

As a *Dasein*-like entity with analytic possibilities, the *historical-existential* is the focal point for what Bultmann calls "theological thinking— theology of the New Testament."[96] This kind of "theological thinking" is akin to Heideggerian thinking, which is situated in the kind of thinking necessary to pose the question of the meaning of *Being*. Similarly, Bultmann's "theological thinking" about "what tradition is" and the New Testament poses the question of the meaning of κηρυγμα. Heidegger's *Being* embodied in Bultmann's notion of the primordiality of tradition, as the primordiality of κηρυγμα in tradition. Moreover, just as Heidegger conceives of *Being* as one of two analytic possibilities of *Dasein*, κηρυγμα, as the

Heidegger, *Being and Time*, 30.

Ibid.

Like Heidegger, Bultmann's notion of being "in the sense of the true" is derived [from Brent]ano's idea of "truth in the proper sense." Brentano, *The Origin of the Knowledge of Right and Wrong*, 69–70.

[No]te 46.

primordiality of tradition, is an analytic possibility of the entity that I have called *historical-existential*.

By utilizing the *historical-existential*, Bultmann makes a careful, existential distinction between two elements in tradition: the existentiality of the message of Jesus and the existentiality of the κηρυγμα of the earliest church. In this sense, Bultmann's distinction—a distinction between existentialities—is based on the everydayness of the former and the primordiality of the latter. That is to say, this distinction is respectively made between the ontics of tradition and the primordiality of tradition. Only by tracing *primordial being* through the primordiality of tradition is it possible to *unconceal*, disclose, or reveal κηρυγμα as *what being is*—what this means, then, is that only the primordiality of tradition is on the way to ἀληθεια. The purpose of Bultmann's demythologizing program is to provide a "clearing"[97] for ἀληθεια—Bultmann's act of stripping away the layers of myth means to *unconceal* the primordiality of tradition as κηρυγμα.

97. See note 72.

CHAPTER 3

"Being" in Reason and Tillich's "καιρος"

Paul Tillich's existential theology is oriented towards *primordial being* in reason—that is to say, Tillich uses a Heideggerian understanding of reason to explore the primordiality of *being*. The concept of reason, as such, is an ontical construction that conceals *what being is* at a primordial level. In this way, reason is only superficial, and is only concerned with being-in-the-world: *being* in an ontical state, not *what being is*. Tillich's *Heideggerian lens* places emphasis on καιρος, or "event,"[1] as a critical element of addressing *what being is*, so that all ontical facts, as they are revealed to human existence, are oriented towards ἀλήθεια.

When conceptualizing *what being is*, then, Tillich's notion of καιρος becomes inextricably linked to the phenomenon of "thrownness"—as an "event," "being-thrown" is the Heideggerian facticity of "being-thrown-into-the-world," so to speak, and recognizing that *being*, in itself, is ultimately contingent on a world initially shrouded in existential mystery.[2] "Thrownness" is not just a particular event in the life of human existence, it is an existential event that defines *what being is*. Accordingly, human existence must make meaning out of "thrownness," in an effort to unconceal καιρος.

In effect, Tillich's "thrownness" is the first facticity in a series of facticities that human being must existentially work out, when making meaning

1. In a more complete sense, "kairos" refers to "eschatological filled time, time for decision." Balz and Schneider, eds., *Exegetical Dictionary of the New Testament: Volume 2*, 232.

2. "Thrownness" is a Heideggerian term adopted by and appropriated into Tillich's existential theology. The term, as Tillich endeavors to use it, is about being "thrown into existence" in such a way that an entity exists as it has to be and as it can be. Heidegger, *Being and Time*, 321.

from the human situation, as a whole.[3] This kind of situation is not only existential, but it is epistemological, since it is grounded on a subjective rationalism that leads towards άληθεια. It is only through καιρος—a stand-in for *what being is* when *being* undergoes *unconcealment*—that άληθεια is even possible. In other words, the event of human existence itself is purely ontical, because that event merely refers to what being has become—therefore, "what being has become" is not *what being is*.[4] Again, *what being is* must be *unconealed* in its most primordial state. "What being has become" is an ontic state that layers καιρος in *concealment* ('ληθε'), through the imminence of the event of "being-thrown" into human existence.[5]

Even though καιρος is an imminent event, Tillich situates that imminence within an existential stream of historicity and temporality—in that historical-temporal stream, καιρος refers to the past and the future from the positionality of the present.[6] What this means is that, when καιρος is *unconcealed* as άληθεια, that *unconcealment* reveals so much more than just the present existential situation of *what being is*. To this end, Tillich's ultimate concern is about how "what being has become" ontically can be reasoned into *what being is* primordially. This approach to the concept of reason undergirds Tillich's Heideggerian approach to "the event" as καιρος—Tillich's *Heideggerian lens* reasons through the ontics of "being-thrown" into human existence, in order to rationalize the καιρος within and further expose άληθεια.[7]

---

3. "Thrownness" as what I call "the first facticity" can be derived from Heidegger's following statement: "The expression 'thrownness' is meant to suggest the facticity of its being delivered over." What makes "thrownness" a facticity is, as Heidegger suggests, the extent to which it is "that it is." Heidegger, *Being and Time*, 174.

4. As a note, I am drawing a distinction here between "what being has become" and "what being is." That distinction aligns respectively with "the ontical" and "the primordial."

5. Here, when I say "ontic state," I am rearticulating Heidegger's term "ontical." In *Being and Time*, Heidegger explains that an ontical "is made to underlie the ontological." Heidegger, *Being and Time*, 127.

6. Since καιρος is about the immediate present, it is situated between concepts of the past and future.

7. "Being-thrown" is based on ontics, since it is the groundwork of what is ontical.

Tillich and Heidegger

Tillich was a professor of systematic theology at the University of Marburg very briefly from 1924 to 1925, having arrived at a time when Bultmann and Heidegger were already there—with Bultmann having joined the theology faculty in 1921 and Heidegger the philosophy faculty in 1923. It is apparent that Tillich was meant to replace Rudolf Otto, but Otto did not leave upon Tillich's appointment—in fact, Otto would remain at Marburg until 1929. Perhaps, this was at the heart of Tillich's short tenure at Marburg—if Otto's staying directly influenced or was the deciding factor for Tillich's leaving, it is not possible to say here. What has been asserted, however, is that Tillich, upon arriving at Marburg, faced the considerable opposing influence of Barthian supernaturalism underwritten with an anti-humanistic attitude, which Tillich ultimately disagreed with. This seems unlikely, since Bultmann, while also at Marburg, and outlasting Tillich, would have experienced the same Barthianism. Also, too, Tillich found ideological, albeit philosophical, comradery in Bultmann and Heidegger, which would have bolstered and emboldened his own theology against the proponents of Barthian theology. Yet, as Tillich briefly explains in *My Search for Absolutes*:

> [. . .] my friendly adviser the minister of education, Karl Becker, forced me against my desire into a theological professorship in Marburg. During the three semesters of my teaching there[,] I encountered the first radical effects of neo-orthodox theology on theological students: Cultural problems were excluded from theological thought; theologians like Schleiermacher, Harnack, Troeltsch, Otto were contemptuously rejected; social and political ideas were banned from theological discussions.[8]

Here, if we take Tillich at his word, we will find more questions than answers. It would seem that, given Tillich's Lutheran background, he would have found the theological atmosphere at Marburg welcoming, or at least conducive to differing opinions of theologians under the tent of dialectical theology. Something must be said, however, about Tillich's contention that "Karl Becker, forced me against my desire" to join the faculty at Marburg. Such a statement remains unclear, and it is only asserted in this one instance in any of Tillich's accounts of the period. From it, we can assume that, in one sense, that Tillich did not want to go to Marburg, and, on another sense, only took the professorship out of some degree of

8. Tillich, *My Search for Absolutes*, 42.

unarticulated obligation to Karl Becker. If that is so, it may be possible to suggest that Tillich, at the time of joining the Marburg Theology Department, did not intend to stay at Marburg for very long, having only appeased Becker over Tillich's previously held sensibilities and presuppositions about either Marburg or the Theology Department itself. For that to be Tillich's starting point, clearly he was looking for a reason to further support his leaving Marburg. As clear as he may be about how he experienced "the first radical effects of neo-orthodox theology," it seems that such an experience does not mesh with Bultmann's—if we can similarly align them philosophically and theologically, and orient them individually with Heidegger. I do not wish to presume that Tillich did not "encounter" what he says he "encountered." For Marburg to be described as "Protestant Marburg," I question the extent to which neo-orthodoxy curtailed the theological thought of Marburg students. This neo-orthodoxy confronted Bultmann within the Theology Department, and countered Heidegger coming from the Philosophy Department, and yet, neither of them experienced an antagonism to their syntheses of philosophy and theology that forced either of them to leave Marburg altogether. Consider Tillich's claim another way. We do know that the Marburg Theology Department routinely held talks between theologians—both those within the department itself and other visiting from outside—but also, in particular, between Heidegger and the Theology Department itself. When considering the latter alone, it becomes all the more puzzling to fully take Tillich's claim. To whatever extent the "radical effects of neo-orthodoxy," as Tillich calls it, influenced, oppressed, or prevented Marburg theological students from fully engaging with "cultural problems," it is impossible to view this outside the context of Tillich's own lectures, since his interests were in the relationship between culture and theology. He could very well mean it this way, if suggesting, too, that "social and political ideas were banned from theological discussions," and his lectures can be contextualized through these kinds of discussions. Additionally, we see Tillich pointing out that the theological thinking of Friedrich Schleiermacher (1768–1834), Adolf von Harnack (1851–1930), Ernst Troeltsch (1865–1923), and Rudolf Otto (1869–1937) "were contemptuously rejected." There is an underlying significance, for Tillich's own theology, in invoking each of these theologians—all four figures, in one way or another, attempted to engage, through their respective theological thought, a dialogue between "religion" and the social, the political, and the cultural. It is this term "religion," as it is espoused in the works of Schleiermacher,

Harnack, Troelsch, and Otto, in which Tillich is most interested. Though he never explicitly mentions the term in his reflections in *My Search for Absolutes*, his preferring "religion" over theology may have been "contemptuously rejected" and "banned" from the theological discussions of the day, due to Barthian forces. Tillich would later write in his *A History of Christian Thought*:

> [. . .] the impact of Barth on Germany was so great that when I returned to Germany in 1948, I was immediately criticized by my friends for still using the word "religion." It had been, so to speak, eradicated from the theological discussion in Germany.[9]

In this, though Tillich is speaking more generally about Germany, it seems like that his thoughts were not far from his experience at Marburg. We can see in this statement, too, references to the teaching positions he held after Marburg up to 1933: Dresden Institute of Technology, the University of Leipzig, and the University of Frankfurt. By 1933, Tillich would leave Germany for the United States, having accepted and joining the faculty at Union Theological Seminary in New York. To have returned to Germany in 1948, as he explains, to say that he was "immediately criticized by [his] friends for still using the word 'religion" points not just to his frequent use of the term in his "Philosophy of Religion" courses at Union, but points directly to his formative years at Marburg. Since Marburg was Tillich's first true professorship following his five-year stint as a *Privatdozent*[10] at the University of Berlin, Marburg holds an important place in the development of Tillich's early thought. Still, if it was while at Marburg that Tillich experienced resistance to his theological discussions, the three semesters of lectures delivered there demonstrate his attempts—however brief—at countering what was deemed as the status quo of neo-orthodoxy.

The problem that remains is if Tillich's Marburg experiences alone dictated his leaving Marburg for Dresden, or if, when viewed another way, the resistance he encountered at Marburg was simply a validation of his initial reservations about joining the Marburg faculty in the first place—in other words, it was not really about the resistance, but about requiring a reason to leave Marburg. An argument can be made to either end. For whatever the reason—a reason that to the best of my knowledge, is only

9. Tillich, *A History of Christian Thought: From Its Judaic and Hellenistic Origins and Existentialism*, 404.

10. "Privatdozent" is the German word for "lecturer." Tillich, *My Search for Absolutes*, 41.

articulated by Tillich in *My Search for Absolutes*, and largely omitted from any biographical discussions devoted to the period—Tillich left Marburg and gladly accepted an offer from Dresden as Professor of Religious Studies in 1925, even though, at the time, Dresden did not have a theology department. Even then, in a matter of eight years, Tillich would leave Dresden, join Leipzig, leave Leipzig, join Frankfurt, and leave Frankfurt—such constant professional turnover suggests, to which Tillich certainly generally implies, that he experienced similar resistance to his theological thought and teaching at these other institutions, and Marburg was only the first of these occurrences. However, because Marburg is so formative for Tillich's early professional career, and because it is only at Marburg that Tillich comes in contact with Bultmann and Heidegger, the latter of which Tillich owes a specific indebtedness to his theological development.

In that very short time at Marburg, Tillich taught only three semesters: Summer 1924, Winter 1924/25, and Summer 1925, which have been collected and published in 1986 as *Dogmatik: Marburger Vorlseung von 1925*. This currently untranslated collection presents all of Tillich's Marburg lectures, as the preliminary sketches of an approach to systematic theology that Tillich would eventually expound upon in the three volumes of his *Systematic Theology*, published in 1951, 1957, and 1963. The first volume, in particular, contains many of the ideas that Tillich worked through during his time at Marburg, especially in the lecture Tillich delivered in his final Marburg semester entitled *Dogmatik*, and subtitled with the epigraph *"Theologie muss Angriff sein."*

Though, once leaving Marburg, Tillich would go on to deliver, also in 1925, another *Dogmatik* lecture at Dresden, the genesis of Tillich's work on what became *Systematic Theology* is understandably rooted in his time at Marburg. Tillich's Marburg period is, without question, a very formative period in his development as a theologian and a philosopher. Still, because his time at Marburg was so brief, and his contacts with the likes of Rudolf Bultmann and Martin Heidegger were temporary, it is difficult to not say that both Bultmann and especially Heidegger had a significant influence on how Tillich came to understand the relationship between theology and philosophy. It remains largely unclear how much participation Tillich had in the Bultmann-Heidegger relationship, or more specifically with either man individually. For example, it is still relatively difficult to know if Tillich attended the July 25, 1924 talk Heidegger gave to Marburg's Department of Theology—this, of course, was Heidegger's *"Der Begriff der Zeit"* and Bultmann was in attendance. It may be safe to assume that Tillich was there, but a lack of evidence validating this makes such an assumption only an assumption. The same can be said about Tillich's possible attendance in Heidegger's lectures—as Bultmann is said to have attended them over a series of three semesters—during the time both were at Marburg. We can certainly recognize that Heidegger delivered, in Tillich's first semester of Summer 1924, a major lecture on Aristotle entitled "*Grundbegriff der aristotelischen Philosophie*" (translated as *Basic Concepts of Aristotelian Philosophy* as GA 18)[11] and a small seminar for advanced students entitled "*Die Hochscholastik und Aristoteles.*"[12] These lectures, as they came to bear on Heidegger's approach to Aristotle most notably, would have been of particular interest for Tillich at the time. The following semester of Winter 1924/1925, too, would have been of interest for Tillich, when Heidegger delivered a major lecture on Plato entitled "*Interpretation Platonischer Dialoge* (Σοφιστής, Φίληβος)" (appearing in *Plato's Sophist* in GA19)[13] and the seminar "Übungen zur Ontologie des Mittelaters (*Thomas, de ente et essentia, summa contra gentiles*)."[14] As both of them are concerned with Heidegger's analysis of the question of the meaning of being through interpretations of Plato and Aquinas, Tillich would have found both interpretations—though assuredly phenomenological in nature—quite informative for Tillich's understanding of "the science of being" with respect to Part Two of his previously published *Das System der Wissenschaften nach Gegenständen und Methoden* from 1923. Towards the end of this same Part Two, Tillich provides a brief discussion of history, which would have provided an interesting standpoint he could have possibly brought into an attendance in Heidegger's *Geschichte des Zeitbegriffs* lecture (GA 20) of Summer 1925— one of the lectures that Bultmann is said to have attended, though I must be clear that it is uncertain if Tillich attended it too.

Up to this point, we have mainly speculated about Tillich's contact with either Bultmann or Heidegger during his time at Marburg, for the chief purposes of ascertaining Tillich and Heidegger's relationship. What that relationship was, it surely cannot be compared to the Heidegger-Bultmann relationship, since, as a point of comparison, we can safely conclude

---

11. See the "Chronological Overview," in *Supplements: From the Earliest Essays to Being and Time and Beyond*, 31.

12. Ibid.

13. Ibid.

14. Ibid., 31–32.

that Tillich did not allow Heidegger to present at Tillich's lectures and, furthermore, that Tillich did not make any professional alignment with Heidegger. It may be possible, however, judging from a passing statement from Konrad Hammann's biography on Bultmann, that Tillich and Heidegger knew one another while they were both at Marburg. In another way, there is a high probability that Tillich and Heidegger participated in symposiums or colloquiums that involved "out-of-town speakers" invited to Marburg by the Department of Theology to present lectures.[15] As they both provided "critical opinions"[16] of visiting speakers, we can assume—or be reasonably led to assume—that Tillich and Heidegger served on panels or committees together. Because this remains just speculation, what kind of relationship Tillich had with Heidegger while at Marburg—either professional or personal—can move no further than conjecture, particularly since Tillich himself does not sufficiently shed very much light on this.

Part of the problem, if all-together setting aside any relations with Bultmann within the Marburg Theology Department, with understanding and explaining the relationship between Tillich and Heidegger while the two were at Marburg is that Tillich, for the most part, minimizes it. To be sure, Tillich references Heidegger in passing in *My Search for Absolutes*, another interesting reference—though still fleeting—points to Tillich's Marburg period with Heidegger in, oddly enough, *A History of Christian Thought*, at the end of a chapter entitled "The Enlightenment and Its Problems." In it, at one point, Tillich Tillich draws a connection between pietism and existentialism, particularly proposing that they "have much to do with each other."[17] Immediately thereafter, Tillich writes, "I am reminded of the atheistic sermon which Heidegger once gave us in his pietistic categories."[18] What Tillich asserts, here, requires unpacking. First, if we address Tillich's labeling of Heidegger's "atheistic sermon," we will want to question, on one hand, why Tillich would use the term "atheistic" and, on the other hand, what does Tillich mean by "sermon"? In parsing it this way, the former may be applicable, while the latter is puzzling. For Tillich—and even Bultmann, for that matter, Heidegger's approach to religion would have been relatively "atheistic," in the sense that Heidegger is not concerned with explicit refer-

---

15. Hammann, *Rudolf Bultmann: A Biography*, 146.

16. Ibid., 146.

17. Tillich, *A History of Christian Thought: From Its Judaic and Hellenistic Origins and Existentialism*, 366.

18. Ibid.

ences to God or theism in what Tillich calls existentialism. Rather, Heidegger does take a theistic tone philosophically, which Tillich would have been able to interpret quite effortlessly, especially as it is conceptually tied to the question of the meaning of being. For Tillich to see this otherwise—to see an "atheistic" aspect to Heidegger—suggests to me that Tillich is placing it in the context of Heidegger and existentialism. In other words, Tillich is not viewing this "atheism" with respect to Heidegger's *Einleitung in die Phänomenologie der Religion* lecture of Winter 1920/1921 (appearing in GA 60), or even Heidegger's participation in Bultmann's seminar on the ethics of Paul in Winter 1923/1924—both that occurred before Tillich arrived at Marburg—or even, for that matter, Heidegger's participation in the July 25, 1924 "talk" for Marburg's Department of Theology. Even with the high possibility of Tillich having attended this "talk," it would appear that he did not interpret Heidegger's understanding of time in the context of religion. This is only speculation. What ventures a little further from speculation is the probability that Tillich's labeling of Heidegger "atheistic sermon" refers to *Sein und Zeit*—if we can view the former term as accurate, and the latter as a rather dismissive. That is to say, if we can, with some certainly, assume that Heidegger did not actually deliver an "atheistic sermon"—when imagining Heidegger's participation along with Bultmann and Tillich in various theological discussions within the Department of Theology—it becomes all the more apparent that Tillich is, indeed, referring to *Sein und Zeit* and tying it to existentialism. Granted, in the short time Tillich was at Marburg, Heidegger was writing, as Theodore Kisiel argues, the first draft of *Sein und Zeit*. From this, we can make assumptions about what Tillich knew of these early drafts and speculate that this knowledge, to whatever degree, deeply affected his philosophical approach to theology—if we can say that *Sein und Zeit*, in particular, is pivotal to Tillich's experiences with Heidegger. This, of course, cannot be said enough, even if, at this point, the true nature of Heidegger's influence on Tillich is not as clear and concrete as one would like. To complicate matters, Tillich is not as full-throated about his Marburg period with Heidegger, and seems, instead, to suggest that this period alone will not help us fully understand what influence Heidegger had upon Tillich—we can start here, but we will need to trace Tillich's career before coming to Marburg.

Before Marburg, Tillich carried with him an extensive teaching background, having previously taught philosophy as a *Privatdozent* of Theology at the University of Berlin from 1919–1924. In addition, Tillich's academic background included a Doctor of Philosophy degree from University of Breslau and a Licentiate of Theology from Halle—the latter, at the time, being the highest theological degree that could be earned in Germany.[19] For both degrees, Tillich's dissertations focused on the German philosopher Friedrich W. J. Schelling (1775–1854), who is one of the two key philosophers during the critical German Idealism period post-Kant and pre-Hegel.[20] The first dissertation from 1910 is entitled *Die religionsgeschichtliche Konstrucktion in Schellings positiver Philosophie, ihre Voraussetzungen und Prinzipien* (translated as *The Religious Historical Constitution in Schelling's Positive Philosophy: Its Presuppositions and Principles*), while the second, from 1912, is entitled *Mystik und Schuldbewusstein in Schellings philosophischer Entwicklung* (translated as *Mysticism and Guilty Conscience in Schelling's Philosophical Development*). We see, from these dissertations, that Tillich was appropriating Schelling's philosophy to address Tillich's own theological concerns with the meaning of religion and the extent to which human existence fundamentally exists in relation to that overarching meaning of religion. For Tillich, these early concerns, though expressed through his use of Schelling, revolved more broadly around epistemology and metaphysics. In light of these early concerns, Tillich remarks much later in his career, in *A History of Christian Thought*, that "what I learned from Schelling became determinative of my own philosophical and theological development."[21]

We can certainly ponder a moment over why Tillich viewed Schelling as "determinative of [his] own philosophical and theological development," and not, for example, Georg W. F. Hegel, who was just as concerned with the epistemology as a "science" and a "system," and how this might speak to human existence and the meaning of religion. However, what Tillich saw in Hegel was what he saw in Kant—two ends of a "bridge" beginning with Kant as "the one who began German classical philosophy, and Hegel is the end."[22] Schelling is, of course, a figure that Tillich is right to position on

19. Taylor, ed., *Paul Tillich: Theologian of the Boundaries*, 14.

20. The other philosopher is Johann Fichte. But, perhaps it is worth noting that, in addition to Fichte and Schelling, there is a third philosopher during this generation of thinkers that is often considered as important, even if only tangentially: Karl L. Reinhold. See "Preface" to the collection entitled *Between Kant and Hegel: Texts in the Development of Post-Kantian Idealism*, vii-xi.

21. Tillich, *A History of Christian Thought: From Its Judaic and Hellenistic Origins and Existentialism*, 435.

22. Ibid.

this bridge—along with Johann G. Fichte (1762–1814)—but Tillich is also right to consider Schelling as more than just a bridge between Kant and Hegel, suggesting that Schelling was an "independent" philosopher that "had an influence reaching beyond Hegel up to our time." Through this, Tillich explains that:

> [. . .] Schelling synthesized or combined Kant's critical epistemology and Spinoza's mystical ontology. But Schelling was more than this synthesis. [. . .] Schelling became the philosopher of Romanticism. He represented not only the beginning of romantic thinking in the philosophy of nature. There were elements of this already in Fichte and even in Kant's third *Critique* where he introduced the *Gestalt* theory of biological understanding of life. But Schelling kept pace with the different changing periods of Romanticism, and the decisive turning point was when Romanticism started to become existentialism. In this sense Schelling is far more than a bridge between Kant and Hegel. Long after Hegel's death, he was the greatest critic of Hegel. In Schelling the second phase of Romanticism became existentialist.[23]

And so, for Tillich, Schelling is "prior to Kierkegaard,"[24] as the beginning point of what is known as existentialism and the existentialist movement. This distinction is obviously important for Tillich, especially if we recall the connection he makes between existentialism and Heidegger. It is clear that Tillich recognized in Heidegger's thinking a lineage through existentialism ultimately oriented towards Kierkegaard, and not Schelling. It is safe to say that Heidegger would not have agreed with positioning Schelling "prior to" Kierkegaard, or that the former assumes a trajectory through the latter. As Tillich was aware of what would become the first draft of *Sein und Zeit*, it would have been clear that, though Tillich viewed Heidegger as an existentialist in a line tracing back to Schelling, Heidegger did not view Schelling the same way and, for that matter, did not consider himself as an existentialist—particularly, if we hold to Tillich's reading of Heidegger's existentialism in *Sein und Zeit*. Tillich finds in Schelling the origins of existentialism, and not in Kierkegaard. Tillich's appropriation of Schelling in this manner seems just as creative as Heidegger's own appropriation of Schelling in his lecture of Summer 1936. What Tillich accomplishes—in a manner that contrasts with Heidegger's—is a validation of Schelling's in-

23. Ibid., 438.
24. Ibid., 437.

fluence over Kierkegaard. When Tillich asserts that, "in fact Kierkegaard attended Schelling's Berlin lectures in the middle of the nineteenth century, and used many of Schelling's categories in his fight against Hegel,"[25] this is undoubtedly summoning his two Schelling dissertations and how they each used Schelling's a transition towards a new way of thinking about Schelling's importance beyond Hegel, and beyond German Idealism alltogether. The path Tillich forges in his two dissertations led him directly towards a theological confrontation with dialectical theology—particularly with the likes of Emil Brunner and Karl Barth—by the time he arrived at Marburg. This previous work on the dissertation telegraphed the problems Tillich would eventually have at Marburg, since, from the dissertation work,[26] Tillich developed an understanding and approach to the philosophy of existence from a Christian perspective.[27] As Tillich describes them, the two dissertations "dealt with Schelling's philosophy of religion."[28] Though this is generally true, more specifically, Tillich discovered in Schelling a way to synthesize "philosophical and theological impulses," since both could "enrich one another in Christian thought."[29] Such sentiments would have been problematic, and certainly give some credence to the resistance Tillich faced while at Marburg, if he used Schelling to carry forward the synthesis of his own "philosophical and theological impulses."

In speaking of Tillich's impulses towards philosophy and theology, Mark K. Taylor notes in the "Introduction" to a selected works of Tillich entitled *Paul Tillich: Theologian of the Boundaries* that:

> [The vision of philosophy and theology enriching one another] even permeated his early years of ministry, when, just after ordination in his twenty-sixth year, Tillich sought to communicate the Christian message to the poor of the Moabit workers' district in Berlin. Tillich found the traditional languages of church and theology not sufficient to convey the meaning of Christian terms, even those as familiar as 'faith.'[30]

Clearly, if Tillich found "the traditional languages of church and theology" insufficient, especially if he was concerned with "convey[ing] the meaning

---

25. Ibid.

26. See Kegley, ed., *The Theology of Paul Tillich*, 395.

27. Taylor, ed., *Paul Tillich: Theologian of the Boundaries*, 14.

28. Tillich, "Autobiographical Reflections," *The Theology of Paul Tillich*, 10.

29. Taylor, ed., *Paul Tillich: Theologian of the Boundaries*, 14.

30. Ibid.

of Christian terms," then, as Tillich remembers in his *My Search for Abso-lutes*, "a new way had to be found." Tillich found that "new way" at Marburg, which certainly arose primarily from the resistance he encountered. To be sure, he was keenly influenced by those talks between theology and phi-losophy faculty members about what philosophy could say to theology and vice versa, though it is impossible to measure the actual extent of that influ-ence. Whether or not Tillich thought of that "new way" he hoped to find at Marburg situated in a prior understanding of Heidegger is still unknown. In other words, if Tillich viewed Heidegger's work, both before Marburg and while at Marburg, as essential to what he wished to do with Schelling this "new way" is not articulated anywhere in Tillich scholarship. If an in-terest in working further with Heidegger existed, Tillich never expressed this, even in light of Heidegger's eventual work with Schelling in Summer 1936. To the best of my knowledge, Tillich does not reference Heidegger's "Schelling" in any of his published work, though scholarship into Tillich's many "philosophy of religion" lectures at Union from Fall 1936 to Spring 1945 has yet to fully reveal this.

Though Tillich's time at Marburg lasted only about a year and a half—in terms of the three semesters of teaching—it left "a mark" on Til-lich's thought, since it was during that time, in particular, when Tillich was introduced to existentialism in its twentieth-century form.[31] Heidegger was at the center of that introduction—though Heidegger would disagree with being that "center"—into what was a "new way" of thinking, and how this "new way" was what Tillich had been searching for before coming to Marburg. We can take it, too, that, through his early dissertating work on Schelling, Tillich was in search for this "new way." But, as J. Heywood Thomas aptly points out in *Paul Tillich*:

> In some ways it was not a new way of thinking—at any rate, Tillich regards himself as having been prepared for it by three things—his familiarity with Schelling, his knowledge of Kierkegaard and the contact he had had with 'the philosophy of life.'[32]

In Thomas' suggestion, here, that "it was not a new way of thinking" can be taken at face value. It may mean to be, perhaps, a veiled reference to Heidegger—if we can say that Heidegger had already conceived of this new way of thinking, through his work on phenomenology towards the end of

31. Thomas, *Paul Tillich*, 3.
32. Ibid.

his time at Freiburg, and into his Marburg period when Tillich encountered him. Looking at it in this context, it is possible to agree with Thomas, not necessarily to slight Tillich, but to give credit to Heidegger. Nevertheless, Tillich's "new way of thinking" is developed from Heidegger's "new way of thinking," even if Tillich was "prepared for it." Though Thomas notes that Tillich's preparation for his "new way of thinking," is based on "familiarity with Schelling" that prepares him for constructively working with the issues brought forth by existentialism in its twentieth-century form, and how his "knowledge of Kierkegaard" plays just as prominent a role. To some extent, the "contact [Tillich] had had with the 'philosophy of life'" can be ascertained as questioning the meaning of being, if we view this as a contact between Kierkegaard's early nineteenth-century version, Schelling's "existentialism," as Tillich interpreted it, and what Tillich recognized as "existentialism" in Heidegger. Tillich's encounter with the latter, in particular, proved to be much more impacting upon his thinking and the development of the first volume of his *Systematic Theology*. Though Tillich certainly credits Schelling as significant during the early development of his theological thinking, he recalls the time at Marburg with Heidegger's existentialism— as an influence on his mature thinking—in the following way:

> In Marburg, in 1925, I began work on my *Systematic Theology*, the first volume of which appeared in 1951. At the same time that Heidegger was in Marburg as professor of philosophy, influencing some of the best students, existentialism crossed my path. It took years before I became fully aware of the impact of this encounter on my own thinking. I resisted, I tried to learn, [and] I accepted the new way of thinking more than the answers it gave.[33]

This "new way of thinking" presented Tillich with a new way to ask questions, particularly from a theological standpoint. Using the existential categories of Heidegger's *Dasein*-analytics, Tillich's influence by Heideggerian thought "required that he state the problem of God in a new way."[34] That is, for Tillich to approach the problem of God in a "new way," he had to engage that problem through a "new way" of thinking about God. Though, as Tillich concedes, "I accepted the new way of thinking more than the answers it gave," the means by which he approached the problem of the meaning

---

33. Tillich, *My Search for Absolutes*, 42.

34. Edie, "The Absence of God," in *Christianity and Existentialism*, 136–137.

of God is constructed similarly to Heidegger's "question of the meaning of Being," as expressed in the outset of *Sein und Zeit*.[35]

Tillich's time at Marburg was not only an immensely important time for Tillich, but was also critical in Heidegger's career: Let us place Tillich in Heidegger's context. Tillich's three semesters at Marburg parallels Heidegger's initial drafting and writing of *Being and Time*. In fact, Tillich's short professorship at Marburg coincides with Heidegger's first draft of *Being and Time*—Heidegger scholar Theodore Kisiel names this early draft as "The Dilthey Draft," which he dates between July 1924 and April 1925."[36] In that draft, Heidegger wrestles with the concept of time, in which he investigates the intersectionality of temporality and historicality. This intersection between "the temporal" and "the historical" are critical to Heidegger's "treatment of the question of Being."[37] As Heidegger explains at the end of the "Second Introduction" to *Being and Time*, "the temporal" plays a role in the interpretation of *Dasein*, while "the historical" is among the "basic features of a phenomenological destruction of the history of ontology, with the problematic of Temporality as our clue."[38] Both "the temporal" and "the historical" must be adequately reckoned with when asking "the question of the meaning of Being"—in order to ask such a question, the meaning of *Being* must be situated within the parameters of "the temporal" and "the historical." These parameters of situatedness are precisely what Heidegger is ultimately concerned with, especially on the way towards ἀλήθεια, even at a Husserlian categorical-intuitive level.[39] Tillich takes up this same concern theologically, employing a *Heideggerian lens* focused on uncovering

35. Though Tillich's chief interest is in the problem of God and Heidegger's is with the problem of Being, Heidegger conceptualizes "Being" with the same teleological framework as Tillich's "God." Nevertheless, I do not wish to claim, here, that Heidegger's "Being" is equivalent to Tillich's "God." I do not find that such a connection is prudent, at this time. However, like Heidegger's confrontation with "the question of the meaning of Being," Tillich confronts the problem of God by working out the question of meaning of God "concretely." Heidegger, *Being and Time*, 1.

36. Kisiel suggests that there are 3 early drafts of Being and Time: 1.) "The Dilthey Draft," 2.) "The Ontoeroteric Draft," and 3.) "The Final Draft." Kisiel, *The Genesis of Heidegger's Being and Time*, 311–361.

37. Heidegger, *Being and Time*, 63.

38. Ibid.

39. Theodore Kisiel argues that Heidegger's question of the meaning of *Being* is based on the categorical intuition of Edmund Husserl in *Logical Investigations*. Kisiel, *Heidegger's Way of Thought: Critical and Interpretative Signposts*, 96.

ἀλήθεια—what Tillich utilizes is the notion of καιρος as an "existentiell"[40] in what is expressed as an existential theology of reason.

Tillich's Existential Theology of Reason

Let us parse what is meant by "existential theology of reason" by situating Tillich's "existential theology," as such. The fact that Tillich's work with "being" and "Being" within a theological context makes his "existential theology" quite obvious. Still, such an assertion warrants further explanation, since the relationship between Tillich and "existential theology" can be easily contaminated by the larger issue of existentialism. To be sure, Tillich does get assimilated into the discussions of existentialism—either fairly or unfairly—and this does, at least on a fundamental level, helps us ascertain what Tillich intends to do with the "being" of human existence and the "Being" of God. At this most fundamental level, we find that Tillich is much more than just an existentialist—or just part of a school of thought—which is all the more the reason why Tillich's theology is an "existential theology." Yet, we must be very careful here with what we mean by "existential theology"—over-emphasizing the "existential" aspect to Tillich's existential theology can take us too far afield from what is precisely meant by "existential theology of reason."

To my knowledge, there is no other scholarship that explicitly considers, by name, "Tillich and existential theology," or "Tillich's existential theology." Rather, there are two notable books that seem to point to Tillich's existential theology, though the assertions in both are focused on how Tillich works through a theological understanding of being: Bernard Martin's *The Existentialist Theology of Paul Tillich* published in 1963 and Adrian Thatcher's *The Ontology of Paul Tillich* published in 1978. In both cases, though the authors assess Tillich's approach to "being" and how this approach to influenced by Heidegger, neither actually label Tillich's theological stance through Heidegger as an "existential theology."

Of the two, Martin's *The Existentialist Theology of Paul Tillich* comes the closest to asserting an "existential theology" in Tillich's thought, but, instead, settles for describing Tillich's thought as an "existentialist theology." This is quite different from "existential theology," since, if we take Martin's

---

40. Heidegger describes the "existentiell" as an interpretation that "can demand an existential analytic," which directly leads to what is "possible and necessary" within that which is existential. Heidegger, *Being and Time*, 37.

argument, it is through an "existentialist theology" that Tillich "draws a sharp distinction between philosophy and theology and ascribes a separate function to each, particularly in connection with the doctrine of [human being]."[41] As interesting as this point is, and though it provides a plausible understanding of how Tillich envisions the relationship between philosophy and theology, I would disagree with the notion that Tillich "draws a sharp distinction" between the two. More aptly, Tillich uses philosophy to develop his theological approach, and allows his theology to sustain its inquiry philosophically. If we view it this way, there is no "sharp distinction" between the two, since they are both contingent on the other, particularly with respect to how Tillich outlines the doctrine of human being. Though that doctrine is effectively explained differently in philosophy than it is in theology, the Heideggerian lens that Tillich usesphilosophy to understand "being" in ways that theology cannot, as much as he uses theology to understand "being" in ways that philosophy cannot. How Martin misses this is evident in the sense that Martin labels Tillich's theology as an "existentialist theology"—we can take this to mean, then, that Martin sees Tillich's theology as "existentialist," as exhibiting the scope and limits of a broader existentialism. While that is true, it greatly marginalizes Tillich's "Heidegger"—when we see Tillich's theology through the Heideggerian lens that it deserves, we find that his theology is more accurately an "existential theology," because it decidedly employs Heideggerian language.

Though Thatcher's *The Ontology of Paul Tillich* begins by taking into account how both "ontology" and "the ontological question" in Tillich's theology, Thatcher contends that "the method and content of this kind of ontology is of course strikingly different from the earlier versions of the same subject."[42] What makes it "strikingly different," as Thatcher rightly notes, is that, if we can say that Tillich has an ontology to his theology, it is obviously influenced by Heidegger and Heidegger's wish to destroy fundamental ontology. In light of this, when we discuss Heidegger's question into the meaning of Being, it is an ontological question—this same question, for Thatcher, is fundamental to Tillich's conceptualization of how "being" and "Being" function in his theology. This fundamentality is derived from an "existentialist theology," with its concerns tied to human existence exclusively—rather, Tillich presents an "existential theology," to the extent that it uses a Heideggerian lens to "reason" through not just human existence and

41. Martin, *The Existentialist Theology of Paul Tillich*, 27.
42. Thatcher, *The Ontology of Paul Tillich*, 2.

"being," or even God's existence and "Being," but the existential dependency of both on the other.

Tillich's "existential theology" comes by way of a philosophical-theological explication of ontology and the ontological question, but also a resistance to—albeit, an avoidance of—the "existentialist" tendencies to focus on only how "being" is affected by God's "Being." For Tillich, it is not just about a human-God relationship and the degree to which what it means to have "being" is relative to how "being" encounters "Being." Rather, Tillich conceives of the encounter "Being" has with "being." To do this, Tillich's "existential theology" transitions into an "existential theology of reason," since the situatedness of "being" towards "Being" and vice versa is an ongoing revelation of how "being" rationalizes itself and rationalizes "Being" relation to "being." What that means, then, is that "being" searches for αλεθεια in itself, but also in "Being." Either directedness—whether inwardly projected or outwardly—is grounded in the unconcealment of "being" or "Being" respectively in αλεθεια. This occurs by way of καιρος—it is the "event," through reason, that allows "being" to reflect inward to itself and reflect outward to "Being" in a revelatory manner.

The centerpiece of Tillich's "existential theology of reason" is καιρος, since it grounds Tillich's conceptualizations of "reason" and "revelation" in an inextricable, meaning-making relationship. To this end, I will defer any discussion of καιρος for the moment and discuss, instead, as a very important frame of reference, the dialectical, interdependent connection Tillich makes between "reason" and "revelation"—these two concepts shape Tillich's existential theology of reason.

Though both have individualized existential concerns, the connection between "reason" and "revelation" is one of existential interdependence—for Tillich, "reason" is just as much existentially-oriented towards "revelation" as "revelation" is toward "reason." This interdependence, which is predicated on mutual meaning-making, is, as Alexander McKelway explains, "a relationship in which both sides affect each other, and at the same time remain independent."[43] Moreover, the means by which "both sides affect each other" is through a question-answer relationship. In McKelway's view, Tillich's understanding of "reason" and "revelation" is undergirded by the notion that "the questions affect the answer, and in the light of the answer the questions are asked."[44] In other words, "reason" proposes questions that

---

43. McKelway, *The Systematic Theology of Paul Tillich: A Review and Analysis*, 45.
44. Ibid.

seek answers in "revelation," and "revelation" presents questions that seek answers in "reason"—what arises from this question-answer relationship is a correlation between the two. It is a correlation that can be likened to Aristotle's correspondence theory.[45] McKelway assesses Tillich's correlation as a "method" that:

> [. . .]begins with the human question and proceeds in this way: first the human situation is analyzed in order to determine the existential questions which arise from it. Then the Christian message is presented in a way which demonstrates its answer to those questions. The questions are 'existential,' meaning that they express man's deepest and ultimate concern. The analysis out of which the questions arise is also 'existential.'[46]

Tillich's "method of correlation," as it has been coined, begins with the human existential situation, which "yields questions which theology must answer."[47] That "answer," of course, is in "the Christian message." What makes "the human situation" existential is "the existential questions which arise from it"—those "existential questions" attempt to locate meaning for "the human situation" by locating meaning in the existential answers of "the Christian message." This "correlation," then, as Leonard Wheat explains, "is a process whereby philosophical questions are correlated with theological answers derived from the traditional Christian message."[48]

In order to truly understand Tillich's method of correlation, it is important to consider it as a two-fold correlation: two correlated existential elements correlating to two correlated existential elements. In effect, Tillich's notion of "reason" is tied to "the human situation," while his concept of "revelation" is linked to "the Christian message"—this is part and parcel of Tillich's "method."

From what I have called a "two-fold correlation," McKelway suggests that "existential analysis and the questions which arise from it are one side of the correlation [and] the other side is the theological answer derived from revelation." George F. Thomas agrees with McKelway, describing Tillich's

45. For Aristotle, this "correspondence theory" was about referring to truth, or that which is true. Aristotle explains this "theory of truth" in the following way in Line 1011b from *Metaphysics*: ". . .nothing truly is in [the sense of truth], that anything must be true for something else, and that necessarily all things are relative to each other. . ." Aristotle, *Metaphysics*, 82.

46. McKelway, *The Systematic Theology of Paul Tillich: A Review and Analysis*, 45–46.

47. Ibid., 46.

48. Wheat, *Paul Tillich's Dialectical Humanism: Unmasking the God above God*, 82.

"method of correlation" as a question-answer between "the 'question' of Reason with the 'answer' of Revelation."[49] In other words, questions spring forth from "reason," while "revelation" provides the answers for "reason." There is a "sort of relation" between the questions and answers "reflects a genuinely dialectical process."[50] This question-answer "method," which John Clayton describes as "questioning and being questioned; answering and being answered," is a method that is dialectical at its essence.[51] Tillich's dialectical method—the method of correlation—between questions and answers, indeed, inarguably determines the systematic structure of his whole theological system.[52] Nevertheless, even if Tillich's "method" is obvious, McKelway is careful to note the following:

> The method of correlation is implied in Tillich's definition of theology. When he states that the nature of theology is apologetic, and its function is to answer the questions implied in the human situation, his method can only be to correlate those questions with that answer.[53]

Though Tillich's "method" may be implied, it is an extension of Tillich's explicit apologetics of "the nature of theology." That is because, in the particularities of his "method," Tillich wishes to use "the nature of theology" to supply the theological answers to the philosophical questions inherent in "the human situation." While Tillich situates "the nature of theology" in a theological understanding of revelation and God, "the human situation" is predicated on a philosophical understanding of reason and *being*—it is a theological-philosophical framework with which Tillich begins the first volume of his *Systematic Theology*, subtitled *Reason and Revelation: Being and God*.[54] As such, McKelway explains:

49. Thomas, "The Method and Structure of Tillich's Theology," In *The Theology of Paul Tillich*, 133.

50. Clayton, "Questioning and Answering, and Tillich's Concept of Correlation," in *Kairos and Logos: Studies in the Roots and Implications of Tillich's Theology*, 127.

51. Ibid., 131.

52. Thomas, "The Method and Structure of Tillich's Theology," in *The Theology of Paul Tillich*, 133.

53. McKelway, *The Systematic Theology of Paul Tillich: A Review and Analysis*, 45.

54. When considering the subtitle of Tillich's first volume of *Systematic Theology*, there are two things I wish to suggest for further clarity. The first is this: when I suggest "a theological understanding of revelation and God," this stands to suggest "a theological understanding of revelation *through* God." Secondly, when I suggest "a philosophical understanding of reason and being," this stands to suggest "a philosophical understanding

Paul Tillich's *Systematic Theology* begins with an analysis of reason and the doctrine of revelation. Thus, from the first, he establishes the criteria, basis, and verification of his philosophical and theological assertions, and shows the rationality and intelligibility of revelation.[55]

To this end, Tillich's "analysis of reason" and "the doctrine of revelation" are based respectively on "philosophical and theological assertions." These "assertions," as such, as filtered through Tillich's *Heideggerian lens*—it is by way of this *Heideggerian lens* that Tillich "establishes the criteria, basis, and verification of his philosophical and theological assertions" about *being*.

Like Heidegger's task that is devoted to the question of the meaning of *Being*, Tillich's "method" is devoted to the meaning of "the human situation"—or, as the first volume suggests, it is the situational, meaning-making juncture between the existentialities[56] of *being* and God—but his is a question of the meaning of *being* in "the human situation" and to what extent "revelation" through God holds the answers to what "the human situation" means. As Heidegger's outlines his own question, Tillich's question is, like Heidegger's, rooted in humanity's "situation"—though Heidegger seeks answers in the "revelation" of *Being*,[57] Tillich seeks answers in the "revelation" of God. In other words, Heidegger and Tillich have the same philosophical starting point, as each formulates their questions in search of theological answers.

Though it may seem that Heidegger's task is not analogous to Tillich's "method," both are, in fact, working from the same "philosophical and theological assertions." Of course, if there is a difference, it is in how they individually balance their fundamental "assertions" between "the theological" and "the philosophical." Obviously, Heidegger tilts more to "the philosophical" and Tillich leans more towards "the theological," since they

---

of reason *in* being."

55. McKelway, *The Systematic Theology of Paul Tillich: A Review and Analysis*, 71.

56. I use the plural term "existentialities" in reference to the singular "existentiality," which I have endeavored to call something that has the potentiality of containing meaning. Hence, "existentiality" is a juxtaposition of the terms "existential" and "potentiality."

57. Heidegger does not use the specific term "revelation" in *Being and Time*. Yet, it is clear that "Being," as the capitalization of the word obviously implies, serves a revelatory purpose for Heidegger. This is because "the question of the meaning of Being" involves revealing "what being is." This especially comes to bear on Heidegger's *Dasein* and the use of the term "revealed"—in this regard, Heidegger argues that: "As a resolute, Dasein is revealed to itself in its current factical potentiality-for-Being, and in such a way that Dasein itself is this revealing and Being-revealed." Heidegger, *Being and Time*, 355.

respectively prefer to be called a philosopher and a theologian. That is not to say, then, that neither is fixed in "the philosophical" or "the theological." With this in mind, "the theological" is not totally absent from Heidegger's assertions[58] any more than "the philosophical" is missing in Tillich's assertions. Especially for Tillich, his "method of correlation" is not fixed exclusively in "the theological" or "the philosophical." This is precisely because, like Heidegger's task, there is more to Tillich's "method of correlation" than simply corresponding philosophical questions with theological answers. Wheat agrees with this in the following:

> [. . .]there is more to correlation than Tillich spells out. When we examine his thought carefully it is evident that he is attempting something far more ambitious than correlating philosophical questions with theological answers. Indeed, in their orientation the questions are as much theological as philosophical. And Tillich's answers, once understood, are as much philosophical as theological. In fact, the answers are 100 percent philosophical, only the language belongs to theology.[59]

If Tillich is, indeed, "attempting something far more ambitious than correlating philosophical questions with theological answers," as Wheat suggests, it is something that undoubtedly uses a *Heideggerian lens*. The fact that Tillich's questions and answers are both "as much theological as philosophical" means, then, that his "method" is also "as much theological and philosophical." In fact, Wheat argues that Tillich's "method," as such, "involves the creation of triangular analogies [with] three concepts—theological, philosophical, and humanistic—[that] are joined by a three-way analogy."[60] This means that, along with concerns rooted in both "the theological" and "the philosophical," Tillich's "method" incorporates "humanistic" concerns. The triangularity between Tillich's understandings of "the theological," "the philosophical," and "the humanistic" is rooted in the existential interconnectedness of the three concepts, particularly since Tillich's "method" begins with human life—this is where Tillich's questioning begins.

Tillich's concept of human life is derived from Schelling's positive philosophy.[61] It is based on the notion that, according to Jerome

---

58. See note 59.

59. Wheat, *Paul Tillich's Dialectical Humanism: Unmasking the God above God*, 83.

60. Ibid., 85.

61. This should be relatively apparent, even on a holistic level, since Tillich's

Stone, "human life involves a separation from the divine ground, [and] a resulting polarization within human life. . ."[62] The manner in which Tillich conceptualizes "human life" is through positive philosophy—Schelling's, of course—in order "to think philosophically about the divine activity in myth and revelation."[63] Stone goes so far as to suggest that Schelling's positive philosophy parallels "Tillich's notion of a theonomous philosophy, a philosophy which unites the autonomy of reason with an ultimate concern for the divine ground and activity."[64] Through Schelling's brand of positive philosophy, Tillich's "autonomy of reason" is at the heart of what he calls his "theonomous philosophy," and it is punctuated with working out "theonomous" issues of "ultimate concern" along with "divine ground and activity."

Essentially, "theonomous philosophy" is an existential compromise Tillich's makes between Schelling's positive philosophy and Heideggerian philosophy—it becomes the means by which Tillich's "method" keeps a foothold in both. However, Tillich's self-proclaimed "theonomous philosophy" is his response to and re-appropriation of Heideggerian philosophy— a philosophy that Tillich views as containing "emphatic atheism"[65]—even

---

wrote two dissertations on Schelling, and both involved analyses of Schelling's positive philosophy.

62. To prevent myself from going too far afield into Schelling's philosophy, I have omitted the following from Stone: ". . .between the First and Second, and a movement toward reconciliation of the polar elements with each other and with the divine, resulting in an enrichment of the divine life." Stone, "Tillich and Schelling's Later Philosophy," 20.

63. Ibid., 29

64. Ibid.

65. Bernard Martin quotes Tillich, when Tillich describes his "theonomous philosophy" as a method that "establishes a doctrine of man, though unintentionally, which is both the doctrine of human freedom and human finiteness; and which is so closely related with the Christian interpretation of human existence. . .in spite of Heidegger's emphatic atheism." I do disagree with Tillich here. I do not believe that Heidegger's atheism, if we can call it that, is especially "emphatic." Instead, I believe, as George Hemming argues in *Heidegger's Atheism*, that Heidegger just refuses to use a theological voice in *Being and Time* (as with the rest of his corpus). That refusal, as such, is not really "emphatic" as much as it is about Heidegger needing to be elusive about what he means by *Being*. I believe Heidegger's elusiveness is connected to his unwillingness to be penned down theologically, in an effort to work from a strictly philosophical standpoint. Mostly this is due to Heidegger's belief that, like the history of western philosophy, Christian theology is bogged down with Platonism. To this end, I do not believe Heidegger truly has an "emphatic atheism." Though in all likelihood, Tillich's assertion of Heidegger's "emphatic atheism" may be rooted in Tillich's belief that Heidegger does not go far enough in *Being and Time*, especially with Heidegger's explication of the meaning of *Being*, and the degree to which it is possible to argue that *Being* is, in fact, a stand-in for God. Martin, *The*

though Tillich's brand of "theonomous philosophy" is filtered through Schelling's positive philosophy and ultimately assumes a stance with a *Heideggerian lens*. Tillich's task of "theonomous philosophy" is to establish a relationship between his distinct brands of theonomy and autonomy,[66] which becomes foundational to Tillich's *Heideggerian lens* and accompanying "method." In light of what Tillich's "method" proposes through "theonomous philosophy," Bernard Martin describes Tillich's "theonomous philosophy" as a kind of philosophy that "turns towards the unconditional for its own sake, using the conditioned forms to grasp the unconditional through them."[67] For Tillich, the unconditional and the conditional are respectively issues of *Being* and *being*—like Heidegger, Tillich's sense of *Being* is "unconditional" and, therefore, *being* is "conditional" upon *Being*.[68] What this stands to suggest, then, is that Tillich's "method," while dialectical, is also "theonomous," since it existentializes reason's "autonomy" at the level of *being* in relation to revelation's "theonomy" at the level of *Being*. In other words, *being* is "conditional"[69] since its autonomy of reason must existentialize "unconditional" *Being* through a theonomy of revelation.

While *Being* is Heidegger's notion of "the theological" and *being* is Tillich's notion of "the philosophical," Tillich's *Heideggerian lens* assumes both his own notion of "the philosophical"—as a "theonomous philosophy"—and Heidegger's notion of "the theological." Not only does Tillich use *being* to formulate philosophical questions about the "autonomous" meaning of "the human situation," but he uses *Being* to conceptualize Heideggerian theological answers[70] about the "theonomous" meaning of "revelation."

Existentialist Theology of Paul Tillich, 18.

66. Tillich, *The System of the Sciences: According to Objects and Methods*, 205.

67. Martin, *The Existentialist Theology of Paul Tillich*, 31.

68. If following Martin's assessment of Tillich's "theonomous philosophy," it seems quite apparent that Martin is making the same connection as I am. For Tillich's "theonomous philosophy" to, as Martin explains, "turn towards the unconditional for its own sake," Tillich's approach to philosophy is turning towards something that is beyond the here and now. In light of his assessment, Martin certainly believes that Tillich is "turn[ing] toward" *Being*. I certainly agree with that, as well as the fact that "conditional forms" refer to *being*.

69. As I have discussed in my Introduction, Robert Gall seems to suggest this, proposing that there is a "conditionedness of beings as a whole." Gall, *Beyond Theism and Atheism: Heidegger's Significance for Religious Thinking*, 25.

70. When I say "Heideggerian theological answers," I am referring to where the argument in *Being and Time* does not go—that is, the incomplete Part II which, as I have aforementioned in my Introduction, is meant to be Heidegger's most theological part of

What results from this is a dialectical existentiality between them at the critical point of Tillich's conceptualization of καιρος—this is Tillich's existential theology of reason.[71]

Καιρος in Reason and the "Rational-Existential" Pathmark

Tillich's pathmark in existential theology is devoted to καιρος in reason—this venture pursues a *Heideggerian pathmark* of "kairos" as an object of primordiality. As the primordiality of *being*, καιρος discloses *what being is* on the way to ἀλήθεια. That is to say, καιρος is what *being* looks like when it is in a state of primordiality and, then, opens the possibility for *unconcealment*, or ἀλήθεια—in effect, primordial *being*, once disclosed, makes it possible for *being* to be *unconcealed* as what it already is.[72] By way of Tillich's *Heideggerian pathmark*, the "rational-existential" venture he takes attempts to translate "what being has become," or *being* in its ontic state into *what being is*, or the primordiality of *being* on the way to ἀλήθεια.

In Tillich's existential theology of reason, the *rational-existential* is a *Dasein*-like entity with two analytical possibilities: the ontics of reason and the primordiality of reason. The former is "what being has become," and the latter is *what being is*—these two modes of *being*, then, must be existentially-distinguished from one another, in order to point towards ἀλήθεια, as the *unconcealment* of *being*. This latter mode is the focus of Tillich's *Heideggerian lens* and his use of the *rational-existential*—that "lens" is devoted to *unconcealing*, disclosing and revealing *primordial being* that has become hidden beneath the ontics of reason.

Reason, at the ontic level, is not *what being is* any more than it is ἀλήθεια—instead, it is, as I have endeavored to call it, "what being has become." When encountering reason at the ontic level, what is encountered, then, is simply "being-in-the-world"—that is to say, reason, in a form of ontical *being*, must adjudicate the ontical state of existence. For Tillich, then, the ontics of reason is predicated on "thrownness," the Heideggerian term for "being-thrown" into existence—another way to consider "thrownness"

Being and Time. It is the territory that Heidegger does not venture far enough into, as Tillich argues.

71. I use the term "dialectical existentiality" to refer more explicitly to two things that share a dialectical relationship so that, from that relationship, mutual meaning is exchanged.

72. See note 40.

is as being-thrown-into-the-world, or as Tillich terms "estrangement."[73] To this end, Tillich finds in "estrangement" a separation of freedom from destiny.[74] Like Heidegger's term "thrownness," Tillich's "estrangement" refers to a series of facticities: the fact of "being-thrown," the fact of recognizing that *being* is inextricably tied to "worldliness" or bonded to "worldhood," and the fact that, when *being* is "thrown," *being* that must be "in the world."[75] All of these facts—though ontical—make up the facticity of estrangement as "thrownness" within Wittgenstein's case.[76] Moreover, Tillich's theological sense of "thrownness," through "estrangement" as a facticity of what it means to be human in relation to the Fall and the concept of sin, is about "being-thrown" into the human situation as an "event"—Tillich proposes that "the state of existence is the state of estrangement."[77] In such a situation of "estrangement," humanity (existence) must account for the ontics of their *being* by orienting the meaning of *being* towards a primordial meaning made in *primordial being*. In this regard, the "event" is all about orienting *being* toward primordiality. This means, then, that humanity's "event" cannot consider ontical *being* as a point of existentiality, but, instead, must seek existentiality in the primordiality of *being*—the existentiality of the latter is rationalized through the *rational-existential* on the way to ἀλήθεια.

The existentiality of *primordial being* is made possible with καιρος, or "the event." As such, when speaking about "the event"—especially if defining it in a prefatory fashion as an "immanent event"[78]—Tillich has a particular, specialized definition of καιρος as "a historical moment."[79] For Tillich, καιρος has a "unique and universal sense" for Christian faith, which is "the appearing of Jesus as the Christ."[80] To this end, καιρος has a special significance that is "decisive for our present situation."[81] As such, in Tillich's view, καιρος has an "ethics" to it that is understood in terms of "ethics in a

73. Tillich, *Systematic Theology Volume 2: Existence and the Christ*, 72–73.

74. Ibid., 62.

75. Ibid.

76. I am considering the term "facticity" in terms of the logical atomism of Wittgenstein. As Wittgenstein suggests in the first few propositional statement from *Tractatus Logico-Philosophicus*, the world is made up of facts and those facts, when collected, make up "the case." Wittgenstein, *Tractatus Logico-Philosophicus*, 1.

77. Tillich, *Systematic Theology Volume 2: Existence and the Christ*, 44.

78. See Deleuze, *Pure Immanence: Essays on a Life*.

79. Tillich, *Mortality and Beyond*, 89.

80. Tillich, *The Protestant Era*, 46.

81. Ibid., 47.

changing world."[82] In order to understand "the ethics of καιρος," it is prudent to begin first with defining Tillich's καιρος in the general sense, before going any further with my narrower definition of καιρος as an analytic possibility of the *rational-existential*—in this regard, I will momentarily table the latter to discuss the former.

In *Gilkey on Tillich*, Langdon Gilkey, who was a student of Tillich's at Union Theological Seminary, describes καιρος in the following manner: "*Kairos* represents the unity in a specific time of the eternal and the unconditioned with the historical, the finite, the particular, the concrete, and so the relative."[83] What Gilkey describes is the extent to which Tillich's καιρος is an "event," since it "represents the unity in a specific time"—as an "event," Tillich's καιρος is the embodiment of "a specific time of the eternal and the unconditional." Moreover, Gilkey seems to suggest that Tillich's καιρος unifies "the eternal and the unconditional," "the historical, the finite, the particular, the concrete," and "the relative" into a singular moment of what I would call "existentiality." Existentiality is about the unification of various temporal elements into a Deleuzean event of immanence. In effect, Tillich's καιρος unifies the ontics of reason with the primordiality of reason—it is a point of existentiality that unifies all concepts of time into an "event" capable of translating the ontics of reason into the primordiality of reason, on the way to ἀλήθεια. In other words, the situatedness of Tillich's καιρος as a unifying "event" leads directly to the *unconcealment* of *primordial being*. On a more fundamental level, though I am going a bit further than Gilkey, he seems to agree with this, offering the following assessment about Tillich's καιρος:

> [. . .]*Kairos* unites, first of all, past and future, old and radically new, origin and demand, being and the fulfillment of being. It also unites in temporal fashion the universal and the particular, the absolute and the relative; its coming represents the appearance of the Eternal Now in our particular historical moment, a coming that manifests the new possibilities of creation (origin) in that time. . . a new appearance leading toward fulfillment.[84]

As both "being and the fulfillment of being," which is predicated on "a new appearance leading toward fulfillment," καιρος leads the way to ἀλήθεια—this is "a new appearance" and the "fulfillment." What Gilkey is describing,

82. Tillich, *Mortality and Beyond*, 89.
83. Gilkey, *Gilkey on Tillich*, 11.
84. Ibid.

then, is the existentiality that is made possible through καιρος. Because καιρος is both "being and the fulfillment of being," it is respectively the existentialities of *being* at the ontic and primordial levels—καιρος makes meaning out of not just ontical *being*, but also *primordial being*.

To be clear, καιρος is not ontical—καιρος is always concerned with the primordial. In other words, καιρος operates strictly in primordiality, and not in the ontical. However, for καιρος to be "being and the fulfillment of being," as Gilkey proposes, it is important to not confuse Gilkey's description with suggesting that καιρος contains ontical *being*. Instead, καιρος has what I would call "transitional being," or a mode of *being* that is in transition between ontic and primordial levels. This is because καιρος itself is transitional, since its own existentiality is chiefly concerned with providing "a new appearance leading toward [the] fulfillment" of ἀληθεια, *unconcealment*, and the "fulfillment of being." To this end, "a new appearance leading toward fulfillment" is not just the "fulfillment" of *primordial being*, but, more importantly, the "new appearance" of *being* in *unconcealment*. That is to say, καιρος leads the way to ἀληθεια. What this means, then, is that, by focusing on the unification of the "past and future, old and radically new, origin and demand," καιρος is devoted to the analytical possibility of not what *being* looks like "in the world," but *what being is*. Essentially, since καιρος leads away from "being-in-the-world," its focus on the primordiality of *being* is meant to move beyond "the ontical" restrictions of "worldhood." In this sense, James Adams suggests the following:

> Only in the *Kairos* may one escape the toils of spatialization, for the *Kairos* demands time-thinking rather than space-thinking. This insight becomes decisive not only for Tillich's philosophy of history but also for his theory of truth.[85]

Adams recognizes that "the toils of spatialization" is "worldhood"—these "toils," as such, are in what Tillich calls "the ethics of a changing world." But, the fact that καιρος "demands time-thinking rather than space-thinking" means that it grounds its "ethics" more in the temporal than the spatial. The "demands" of the former over the latter is Tillich's Kantian "moral imperative," which is "the demand to become actually what one is essentially and therefore potentially."[86] Like Kant, Tillich adjudicates his "moral imperative" through his concept of reason. In this respect, Tillich ". . .deals with

---

85. Adams, *Paul Tillich's Philosophy of Culture, Science, and Religion*, 55.
86. Tillich, *Mortality and Beyond*, 20.

the concept of reason and the categories belonging to it and leads to the existential problem implied in reason, to which the answer is: revelation."[87] Just as Adams suggests, the "demands" of καιρος through the concept of reason leads to Tillich's "theory of truth," as ἀληθεια, *unconcealment*, and the "fulfillment of being"—to be precise, Tillich's "ethics" of καιρος and the "ethics" inherent in his concept of reason is a critical point of existentiality, adjudication, *unconcealment*, and the "fulfillment" of *primordial being*. Gilkey notes this by arguing that:

> [. . .]Tillich introduces his understanding of reason, of creative thinking and doing, and the essential relation of these to their divine depths, in presenting his understanding of theology and its method in part one of his *Systematic Theology*. . . Reason to Tillich is the creative, culture producing power of human being (and so of being).[88]

Tillich's approach to and understanding of reason, as Gilkey argues, is, in fact, "the creative, culture producing power of human being." Though Tillich describes this power as historical,[89] any historicity to Tillich's understanding of reason is linked to the historicality of καιρος. What I mean, then, is the historical positionality[90] of the "event" of "estrangement" or "thrownness"—what I shall coin in short as simply "historicality," as an amalgamation of the terms "historical" and "positionality"—is existentialized by empowering the everydayness of *being* as *primordial being*. This empowerment is accomplished, as Richard Grigg proposes in *Symbol and Empowerment*, through the extent to which "being itself can be symbolized"[91] as the *unconcealed* answer to the question of being as ἀληθεια. In other words, Tillich asserts that:

> The question of being is not the question of any special being, its existence and nature, but it is the question of what it means to

87. Tillich, *The Protestant Era*, 92.

88. Gilkey, *Gilkey on Tillich*, 35.

89. Tillich, *Theology of Culture*, 30.

90. When I speak of "historical positionality," I am speaking not about Bultmann's sense of "the historical," but a different sense of "historical" in Tillich, one that is related more to Tillich's καιρος than any understanding Tillich may have that aligns with Bultmann's κηρυγμα. Put more simply, Tillich is more concerned with "the event" of human existence, as it relates to revelation, rather than "the message of Jesus" as it relates to revelation.

91. Grigg, *Symbol and Empowerment: Paul Tillich's Post-Theistic System*, 53.

be. It is the simplest, most profound, and absolutely inexhaustible question of what it means to say something *is.*[92]

To this end, "what it means to say something *is*" is the goal of Tillich's *rational-existential* pathmark into the concept of reason, using καιρος to point to *primordial being* and ἀλήθεια.

92. Tillich, *Biblical Religion and the Search for Ultimate Reality*, 6.

CHAPTER 4

"Being" in Experience and Rahner's "χάρις"

Karl Rahner's existential theology investigates *primordial being* in experience. With a transcendental slant utilizing a *Heideggerian lens*, Rahner envisions experience as contingent on χάρις, or "grace,"[1] as a representation of ἀλήθεια. In this way, experience is only an ontical representation—it is the means by which χάρις constitutes its "being-in-the-world." But, when considering χάρις in its most primordial as *what being is*, Rahner's concept of experience is rooted on *concealment* ('ληθε') and "being-there." That is, experience, at its ontical level, is simply "what is there"—this "there-ness" conceals *what being is*, or the "is-ness" of χάρις.

To be clear, Rahner's conceptualization of χάρις is a conceptual understanding about the difference between *what experience is*, and what experience does. Of course, what experience does—as in denoting that something experienced has an experiential quality to it—is the everydayness of experience.[2] Experience, as it has happened, is referred to as *what is experienced*. Yet, as Rahner seems to suggest, *what is experienced* is the ontical aftermath of "what experience is." In other words, *what is experienced* is the "there-ness" of experience, even if it may appear to be *what experience is*. As such, *what is experienced*, then, is not *what being is*. Moreover, *what is experienced* is only a second-hand awareness of *what experience is*, since *what experience is* an articulation of χάρις and, in turn, *what being is*. Again, *what is experienced* is not ἀλήθεια, and Rahner's existential theological task

---

1. Balz and Schneider, eds., *Exegetical Dictionary of the New Testament: Volume 3*, 457.

2. See note 30.

is to disclose *what experience is* and the ἀλήθεια of experience in its most primordial form.

Through a *Heideggerian lens*, Rahner apperceives a primordiality to experience, something primordial enough to perceive *what is experienced* as a *concealment* ('λῆθε') of *what experience is*. Rahner's *Heideggerian lens* engages in this kind of thinking about the concept of experience—it is based on the extent to which *what is experienced* is something that is not immediately knowable in itself, in a Kantian manner.[3] This cannot happen until there is an active engagement in thinking a kind of thought[4] about *what experience is*, particularly if *what experience is*, as χάρις, is unmasked as the existentiality of *primordial being*.

Rahner and Heidegger

Having already been ordained as a Jesuit priest in 1932 and entered his final year of "tertainship" in the Society of Jesus, Rahner became a doctoral student at the University of Freiburg from 1934 to 1936, primarily as a condition for eventually teaching philosophy at Pullach. His intent, in arriving at Freiburg, was to pursue a doctorate in philosophy, particularly by focusing his research on the philosophy of Immanuel Kant and Joseph Maréchal, a Belgian Jesuit. These two figures, along with Pierre Rousselot, a French Jesuit, were pivotal in Rahner's reading of Thomas Aquinas' metaphysics before arriving at Freiburg. Rahner's interest in metaphysics, especially of Aquinas and what became derived as Thomist metaphysics, led

---

3. As a note, I think it is important to explain what I mean by "immediately knowable itself." I am adopting Kantian language about things-in-themselves to describe what I mean by the term "what experience is." As Kant argues in *Critique of Pure Reason*, though objects of understanding, such as what I have called Rahner's concept of experience, are not immediately knowable, "we must yet be in position at least to think them as things in themselves." Kant makes this claim in the Preface to the Second Edition of *Critique of Pure Reason* of 1787. What Kant means here is that we cannot allow the unknowable aspects of things to adjudicate our ability to reference the "thinghood" of something. That "thinghood," or something that as a "thing-in-itself," is its "is-ness." This kind of Kantian thinking is in the background of Heideggerian thinking and, in turn, a foundational component of Rahner's *Heideggerian lens*. But more importantly, Kantian language about "things-in-themselves" is implied in Rahner's *Geist in Welt*, especially as a means of understanding transcendental knowledge: "what experience is," as such, is about experience itself and, subsequently, it is a presupposition of transcendental knowledge. Kant, *Critique of Pure Reason*, 27.

4. See note 23.

him to find a common strain of thought between Kant and Maréchal, insofar as it provided a conceptual bridge between Kantian metaphysics and Thomist metaphysics. The latter, in particular, was essential for Rahner's early theological studies, when considering that his studies, in this regard, were chiefly influenced by Maréchal as "the first Catholic philosopher to enter seriously and sympathetically into Kant's work in order to rescore Aquinas' theory of knowledge in a transcendental key."[5] For Rahner this research interest in Maréchal and, in turn, Kant, became a deciding factor for his gravitation towards Heidegger—it was with *Sein und Zeit* published in 1927 arguing for a destruction of the history of ontology, his 1929 lecture on Kant, and his overall use of Husserl's phenomenology that allowed Heidegger to become another influence for Rahner's pre-Freiburg studies.

Even though he viewed, with "real enthusiasm," Heidegger as "the *enfant terrible* of the new existential phenomenology," once at Freiburg, Rahner, along with Johannes Lotz, fell under the orbit of the Martin Honecker, a neo-Thomist.[6] Though it has been argued that both Rahner and Lotz intended to "take their doctorate [at Freiburg] under Heidegger," which has even been noted by Hugo Ott, Ott disagrees, suggesting, instead, that this "is entirely without foundation, since at that time [Heidegger] would never have accepted a Jesuit as a doctoral candidate."[7] This, of course, is certainly likely, given Heidegger's political involvement with National Socialism and, more generally, Freiburg's political climate and the demise of "ideologically affiliated chairs of philosophy" that brought tension between Heidegger and Honecker.[8] If following this, it would seem more plausible that Honecker would take on Rahner and Lotz as doctorate students, for no other reason than professional preservation at Freiburg and, perhaps, as a means to endure Heidegger's position as a "powerful and domineering thinker and teacher."[9] Whatever the reason—that is, whether it is possible to say that Honecker's interest in Rahner and Lotz was not strictly a result of Jesuit comradery—Honecker jointly mentored Rahner and Lotz, and it was from Honecker that Rahner attended courses in Greek philosophy,

---

5. Sheehan, *Karl Rahner: The Philosophical Foundations*, 4.
6. Ott, *Martin Heidegger: A Political Life*, 274.
7. Ibid.
8. Ibid., 275.
9. Ibid.

two courses in ethics, and a course on Franz Brentano,[10] which were interspersed with Heidegger courses.

To be sure, by the time Rahner arrived at Freiburg, Heidegger had been there for six years, after having left Marburg in 1928 to occupy Freiburg's Professor of Philosophy chair vacated by the retired Edmund Husserl. In fact, by 1934, Heidegger had just completed a disastrous year as Freiburg's Rector, ultimately ending in his resigning from the position the same year.[11] This experience with the Rectorship had a profound influence on two lectures given towards the end of 1933, subsequently collected in GA 36/37 of the *Gesamtausgabe* as *Sein und Wahrheit* (translated as *Being and Truth*): *Die Grundfrage der Philosophie* of Summer 1933 and *Vom Wesen der Wahrheit* of Winter 1933/1934. These lectures, along with *Logik als die Frage nach dem Wesen der Sprache* (translated as *Logic as the Question Concerning the Essence of Language* as GA 38) in the Summer of 1934, form a composite of Heidegger's examination of the relationship between truth and logic, particularly in light of the deeply politicized and polarized climate of 1933–1934 that directly led to Heidegger's failed Rectorship. In my view, these lectures, though not attended by Rahner, provide an important context for the lectures that Rahner eventually attended in 1934–1936. Across these lectures, with *Die Grundfrage der Philosophie* serving as an essential starting point, Heidegger proposes a groundwork for philosophy (*"grundlage der philosophie"*) that hinges on the extent to which "truth" (*"Wahrheit"*)[12] can be approached at its very "essence" (*"Wesen"*) and to what degree "logic" (*"Logik"*) stands in as a "question" (*"Frage"*) into the meaning of the "essence of language" (*"Wesen der Sprache"*). The close proximity of these lectures suggest, too, that Heidegger conceives of an intersectionality between "being," *Wahrheit*, "logic," and "language"—and it is possible to ponder, as well, that this intersectionality arose from a collision between politics and philosophy.

When viewed together, Heidegger's investigations into *Wahrheit* and "logic" certainly prove to be influential to Heidegger's approach to figures

---

10. Sheehan, *Karl Rahner: The Philosophical Foundations*, 5.

11. Guignon, ed., *The Cambridge Companion to Heidegger*, xx.

12. It must be noted that *Wahrheit* is rather erroneously translated as "truth," especially by the translators of *Sein und Wahrheit*. "Truth" does not accurately express what Heidegger means by *Wahrheit*. At this point, in order to maintain the potency of the word's meaning for Heidegger, I will retain *Wahrheit*. However, *Wahrheit* will be eventually replaced by the more appropriate translation for ἀλήθεια, which is the chief focus of this thesis.

such as Hölderlin and Schelling in his major lectures of Winter 1934/1935 and Summer 1936, respectively. What Rahner thought of these investigations is largely unclear, though we do see these concerns manifest themselves in the eventual development of Rahner's *Heideggerian lens*—*Wahrheit* and "logic," as overarching themes, can definitely be read into Rahner's theology, even if it is difficult to ascertain to what extent Rahner was aware of the specifics of the lectures prior to his entry into Freiburg at the end of 1934. If the two lectures collected into GA 36/37 as *Sein und Wahrheit* were ever indirectly experienced by Rahner is unknown as well—that is to say, we can only speculate whether Rahner read the lectures in transcript. Though this is purely speculation as a way towards understanding Rahner's *Heideggerian lens*, the *Sein und Wahrheit* lectures surely informally shaped Rahner's general theological perspectives of *Wahrheit* and "being" as separate preoccupations about God. More narrowly, however, the intersectionality of *Wahrheit* and "being" helps to frame Rahner's Catholicism through his respective confrontations with Kant, Maréchal, and Thomist metaphysics. These are confrontations with *Wahrheit*. In *Vom Wesen der Wahrheit*, Heidegger presents an analysis of "the essence of *Wahrheit*." This "essence" is the very essence of *being* itself—that is, there is an existential intersectionality between essences of *Wahrheit* and *being*. What this means, then, is that where there is "the essence of *Wahrheit*," there resides *what being is*, and where the essence of *what being is* there resides *Wahrheit*.[13] To be sure, the "essence of *Wahrheit*" is *primordial being*, where Heidegger's intent is to establish a "*Grundfrage*" for a philosophy of *Wahrheit*, through a narrow conceptualization of authentic *being*. In other words, authentic *being* is *what being is* at its most primordial. This issue of primordiality is particularly important to Rahner's early theology, because it marks a transitional period—perhaps even a kind of *die kehre* for him, in a way—that shifts his theological studies into philosophical-theological studies, which don a decidedly *Heideggerian lens*.

Consider the climate in which Rahner devoted himself to his theological-philosophical studies. Rahner arrived at Freiburg during what was undoubtedly the height of National Socialist influence in Germany, not just as it infiltrated the German political structure, but as it came to bear on the administrative infrastructure of Freiburg itself. Nowhere is this more evident than with Heidegger's rise and fall from Freiburg Rector—a rise and

---

13. In other words, "the essence of *Wahrheit*" is "what being is." It is at this juncture where it is possible to find ἀλήθεια and, then, being at its most primordial.

fall that can be credited to the incompatibility of politics and philosophy for Heidegger. Still, it is clear that, even after resigning from the Rectorship, Heidegger was wary of the implications of politics on philosophy, as much as he was of philosophy upon politics. There were dangers fundamentally inherent in both, especially when politics and philosophy utilize the intersectionality between being, truth, logic, and language for very different purposes. In being aware of this, the *Sein und Wehrheit* lectures of 1933–1934 inform the lectures that followed in the semesters of 1934–1936. But more importantly, in addition to the *Sein und Wahrheit* lectures, there are other texts parallel to the period that position Heidegger's politics over and against his philosophy—these texts can be categorized as overtly political texts. The first of these is Heidegger's inaugural address as Freiburg Rector entitled "The Self-Assertion of the German University" given on May 27, 1933. In it, as with the two *Sein und Wahrheit* lectures, there exists an intersectionality between *Warhreit* and logic grounded in Heidegger's collective charge for Freiburg teachers and students to "fully understand the glory and greatness of this new beginning [in order to] carry within ourselves that deep and broad thoughtfulness upon which the ancient wisdom of the Greeks drew."[14] To do so, Heidegger's charge, as Rector, was focused on "leading this university spiritually and intellectually," by what could be called as spiritual and cultural reawakening, through a reconsideration of the meaning of self.[15] This same sentiment is echoed in *Die Grundfrage der Philosophie* (translated as *The Fundamental Question of Philosophy*), the first of the *Sein und Wahrheit* lectures from the Summer of 1933. Here, as with the rector address, Heidegger begins by calling for "spiritual-political mission" as a means of approaching not just what it is "the fundamental question of philosophy" but how that question comes to bear on "the fundamental happening of our history." Between the texts, we can notice Heidegger drawing upon like-minded terminology and phrases such as "the German people" as *Volk*, "endurance," "constancy," and "fate." These overt commonalities between the Summer 1933 and the Rector Address should not be surprising, since the aforementioned lectures are the first lectures Heidegger delivers after assuming the Rectorship. Rather, what may be surprising, however, is that, since Heidegger resigned from Rector in April 1934, they become the only lectures Heidegger delivered while

---

14. Heidegger, "The Self-Assertion of the German University," in *The Heidegger Controversy: A Critical Reader*, 38.

15. Ibid.

working in the dual role as professor and rector—if we take into account that the second lecture, *Vom Wesen der Wahrheit* (translated as *On the Essence of Truth*), complied in *Sein und Wahrheit* was delivered in the Winter of 1933/1934 and the next lecture not delivered until the Summer of 1934. Over the course of delivering these two lectures, there are concurrently dated texts that trace Heidegger's administrative involvement at Freiburg, such as short articles he had published in the Freiburg Student Association newsletter known as the *Freiburger Studentenzeitung*.[16] These texts are overtly political in nature, following directly from issues and promises raised in the Rector Address. Though, in another sense, though the *Sein und Wahrheit* lectures seem superficially overtly philosophical—if we are to see them as a counter to the politicization of the concurrently produced texts—both lectures, instead, are covertly politically in nature, to the extent that *Die Grundfrage der Philosophie* and *Vom Wesen der Wahrheit* can be more accurately viewed, just as the translators of *Being and Truth* would agree, as espousing politically-charged language and becoming an example of what, for Heidegger, National Socialist philosophy looks like.

The relationship between Heidegger's active political involvement with National Socialism, his elevation to Freiburg Rector with the administrative duties therein, and the *Sein und Wahrheit* lectures as ground-zero of a political philosophy all make the period of 1933–1934 a critical period, not just professionally for Heidegger, but for Rahner as a student entering into his doctoral studies at Freiburg, hoping to work with Heidegger. It is safe to say that Rahner entered this atmosphere with a certain about a naivety. I do not mean this in the general sense, since Rahner would have surely been aware of National Socialism's distortion of Christianity and Heidegger's espousal of this—probably as much from the Rector Address as from the *Sein and Wahrheit* lectures—but more narrowly with respect to Rahner's understanding of how this fit into the Nazis' long-term goals. More specifically, what Rahner knew about the reasons behind Heidegger's resignation from Freiburg Rector and his party-going but complicated participation in the Nazi party is, for the most part, unknown—especially since much of the political and professional intrigue revolving around Heidegger would have been more clandestine by Rahner's arrival in the Fall of 1934. In my view, if Rahner had been more aware of Heidegger's true relationship with National Socialism, even after his stepping down from the Rectorship

---

16. See "Political Texts, 1933–1934" in *The Heidegger Controversy: A Critical Reader*, 40–60.

but still espousing the Nazi ideology, Rahner would not have not been so eager to work with Heidegger. We can only speculate what Rahner knew. It has been noted, however, that, according to Peter Fritz, upon attending his first lecture course from Heidegger in the Winter 1934/1935, Rahner "would not have known as he listened to Heidegger's Hölderlin lectures the unspeakable things that the Nazis were planning and would do over the next decade."[17] As true as this may be, there remains no way to know what Rahner could have teased from any of Heidegger's lectures from 1934–1936, for that matter—the fact that Rahner took four semesters of coursework under Heidegger, and affectionately referred to him as his teacher, seems to suggest that Rahner was largely unaware. Given his Jesuit background, we can assume that, if he had been aware, Rahner would have avoided Heidegger's lectures all together.

As an influence upon him that was more important than the handful of Honecker lectures he attended, Heidegger's lectures provided Rahner with a more effective means of critiquing Aquinas, Kant, and Maréchal, yes, but also demonstrated a more proficient manner of confronting Catholic theology, similarly to how Heidegger's *Sein und Zeit* confronted Western philosophy. The difference is with their respective seminal figure of focus. While Heidegger sought to confront Plato as the seminal figure from which the whole of Western philosophy became eventually misdirected, Rahner viewed Aquinas similarly as an essential figure in the development of Thomism and how it adversely influenced the role of scholastic philosophy on the Catholic Church. This seems to be the goal of Rahner's work with Aquinas before arriving at Freiburg and, to be sure, it followed him into the work he wished to do with Heidegger, by attending Heidegger's lectures.

At the time of Rahner's admittance to Freiburg, any student wishing to work with Heidegger did not automatically guarantee acceptance into Heidegger's lectures. For Rahner, especially, as a Jesuit and as a student in the orbit of Honecker, it would have been much more unlikely that he would have been able to attend Heidegger's lectures at all—this sort of restriction would have been placed more so by Heidegger himself than by Freiburg's philosophy department. Yet, as it has been noted by Geffery Kelly, "Rahner was fortunate in being allowed to enroll in the highly restricted seminars of Heidegger."[18] Not only did this fortunate enrollment in Heidegger's

17. Fritz, *Karl Rahner's Theological Aesthetics*, 88.

18. Kelly, "Introduction," In *Karl Rahner: Theologian of the Graced Search for Meaning*, 6.

lectures place Rahner in unique group of Heidegger-interested Jesuit students—along with Johannes Lotz and Fernando Huidobro Polanco, all of which Heidegger acknowledges as being frequent visitors to his house[19]— but Rahner's professional theological career, thereafter, was undeniably stamped with Heideggerian influence. Often, Rahner resisted having his career tied so heavily to Heidegger, arguing, instead, that Maréchal exercised much more of an influence over him. Though Maréchal was important to Rahner's theological thought, it was Heidegger that provided a philosophical framework by which Rahner could better assess Maréchal. This is especially so, when considering that Rahner eventual dissertation would be a synthesis of Maréchal and Heidegger, and not Maréchal and some other figure. The reasons for highlighting Maréchal over Heidegger seems steeped more out of convenience than fact, if we can tie this preference to Heidegger's relationship with National Socialism and how tainted Heidegger's reputation became, particularly in the years after World War II. Nevertheless, more privately, Rahner held significant affection for Heidegger, despite the fallout over the more full-throated revelations of Heidegger's Nazi ties and his subsequent lack of contrition. In fact, as noted in Thomas Sheehan's *Karl Rahner: The Philosophical Foundations*, "Rahner preserved until his death a list of the lecture courses and seminars he took from [Heidegger] who forty years later [Rahner] would call his one and only teacher."[20]

To my knowledge, Sheehan provides the only detailed list of the lectures and seminars Rahner attended under Heidegger, which represents all four semesters at Freiburg from 1934 to 1936: Winter 1934/1935, Summer 1935, Winter 1935–1936, and Summer 1936. Thanks to Sheehan, these four semesters can be examined more thoroughly by separating the lectures from the seminars—while the lectures had a larger number of students in attendance, the seminars, being more "advanced" in nature, had fewer students and tended to function as an *Arbeitskreis*.[21] In order to highlight this difference between the two in relation to the contents of the lectures versus the seminars, allow me to consider the lectures first.

Rahner attended the following Heidegger lectures: *Hölderlins Hymnen "Germanien" und "Der Rhine"* (translated as *Hölderlin's Hymns*

---

19. Ott, *Martin Heidegger: A Political Life*, 275.

20. Sheehan, *Karl Rahner: The Philosophical Foundations*, 5.

21. This is a term that can be applied to some of Heidegger's seminars devoted to smaller numbers of students. Roughly translated, it can mean "working group."

"*Germania*" *and* "*The Rhine*") in Winter 1934–1935 (GA 39), *Einführung in die Metaphysik* (translated as *Introduction to Metaphysics*) in Summer 1935 (GA 40), *Die Frage nach dem Ding: Zu Kants Lehre von den transzendentalen Grundsätzen* (translated as *What is a Thing*, with a new translation in preparation as *The Question Concerning the Thing: On Kant's Doctrine of the Transcendental Principles*) in Winter 1935/1936 (GA 41), *Schelling: Über das Wesen der menschlichen* (translated as *Schelling's Treatise on the Essence of Freedom*) in the Summer 1936 (GA 42).[22] All of these lectures can be considered as Heidegger's major lectures, if we tend to Heidegger's categorization of these to Division I of the *Gesamtausgabe*. To this end, the lectures are consecutively listed as GA 39, GA 40, GA 41, and GA 42, and we can notice that these lectures lead Heidegger towards his first two Nietzsche lectures (in GA 43 and GA 44)—and they mark, not just the beginning of an important period in Heidegger's thought, but reflect a rather turbulent period that propels Heidegger towards Nietzsche.

Though we can surely ponder over Rahner never attending the Nietzsche lectures, knowing that they commenced just as he concluded his Freiburg years, and we can speculate what affect Heidegger's reading of Nietzsche would have had on Rahner, Heidegger's reading of Hölderlin, for Rahner, is certainly a worthy beginning point for Rahner's work with Heidegger. There, in *Hölderlins Hymnen "Germanien" und "Der Rhine"* in Winter 1934–1935, Heidegger considers how reading Hölderlin's poetry presents an avenue towards thinking about philosophy, without necessarily reducing Hölderlin's work to a kind of philosophy itself. In other words, Heidegger uses Hölderlin's poetry to speak to how we can think and philosophize, but, in doing so, striking a careful balance between the ideals of poetry and the aims of philosophy—the intent is to not reduce Hölderlin to a philosopher, but, rather, allow his poetry to ground what it means philosophize. Reading Hölderlin's "Germania" and "The Rhine," then, becomes an exercise in philosophizing through the act of poetizing—and poetizing embodies philosophizing. Still, through this approach to Hölderlin, Heidegger practices a Nazi ideology through this poetizing and philosophizing about the two poems, though at no point in time in the lecture does Heidegger explicitly use the term Nazism or National Socialism—instead, on occasion, as a stand-in, Heidegger refers to Germany and the fate of the

---

22. The German titles and dates of these seminars are accordance with the chronology in Heidegger's *Gesamtausgabe*.

German people as that which is tied to a destiny of what must be philosophized and poetized.

The destiny that underwrites the philosophizing and poeticizing of Heidegger's reading of Hölderlin's is similarly underwritten in the philosophizing and politicizing of Heidegger's reading Hegel and Schelling in *Seminare: Hegel—Schelling* (GA 86), most notably in the seminars that appear in the collection from the 1930s and 1940s. Among these, one has been translated into English in 2014 as *On Hegel's Philosophy of Right*. As with Heidegger's use of Hölderlin's poetry, he made similar use of Hegel's *Philosophy of Right*, interpreting from Hegel's concept of right an ethics to which he could develop a political thought about National Socialism and Nazism. Unlike the Hölderlin lecture, if judging from the *Gesamtausgabe* categorization of *Seminare: Hegel—Schelling*, it would appear that the translated *On Hegel's Philosophy of Right* was not just a "seminar," but, more accurately, it was given as an advanced seminar attended by a smaller number of students, particularly if noting the fragmentary nature of the text.

Given Sheehan's list of the courses and seminars Rahner attended under Heidegger, the only Hegel seminar included in *Seminare: Hegel—Schelling* given in Winter 1934/1935 is not the same as "seminar, upper level: Hegel, *Phänomenologie des Geistes*."[23] This lone seminar entitled *Hegel, Rechtsphilosophie* is the text that has been translated into *On Hegel's Philosophy of Right*. With that in mind, it would appear that Rahner did not attend this specific seminar, even though it was, in fact, very likely a "seminar, upper level." We can conclude this, not simply from the incompatibility of the subject—*Hegel, Rechtsphilosophie* from the *Seminare: Hegel—Schelling* collection versus the "Hegel, *Phänomenologie des Geistes*" from Rahner's list—but because, as pointed out by the 2014 translators, *Hegel, Rechtsphilosophie* was given only in the Winter 1934/1935 and not across both that semester and the Summer 1935, as was the "seminar, upper level: Hegel, *Phänomenologie des Geistes*," according to Rahner's list. Accordingly, this leads us to the question: what Hegel seminar did Rahner attend that lasted across two sequential semesters?[24] For Rahner to have attended such a seminar at the time, if it was not what has been translated as *On Hegel's Philosophy of Right*, it is immensely difficult to know precisely what Hegel seminar Rahner attended in the Winter 1934/1935 and again in Summer 1935. The problem that arises here is not just with narrowing down

23. Sheehan, *Karl Rahner: The Philosophical Foundations*, 5.
24. Ibid.

the two semesters that Rahner is said to have attended Heidegger's Hegel seminar, which will prove relatively elusive. Once setting aside the *Hegel, Rechtsphilosophie* seminar, our focus will be on adhering to the content of the seminar Rahner had from Heidegger: *Phänomenologie des Geistes*.

What this means, then, is that, for Rahner to have had a seminar on Hegel's *Phänomenologie des Geistes* during Winter 1934/1935 and Summer 1935, we will need to further speculate what that seminar was, since, as it currently exists, the *Gesamtausgabe* does not corroborate Rahner's list, as it has been presented by Thomas Sheehan. To start, it must be noted that Heidegger's first lecture on *Phänomenologie des Geistes* was given in the Winter 1930/1931, his fifth major lecture at Freiburg. Afterwards, it has been argued by Joseph Arel and Niels Feuerhahn, the 2015 translators of *Hegel* (GA 68), that Heidegger delivered three seminars on *Phänomenologie des Geistes*, all of which are gathered in GA 86's *Seminare: Hegel—Schelling.*[25] If following Arel and Feuerhahn, the first of these is not until Summer 1942 entitled *Hegel, Phänomenologie des Geistes*, the second in 1942, simply entitled *Hegel*, and a third dated to Winter 1956/1957 entitled *Gespräch von der Sache des Denkens mit Hegel*. In between the second and the third, Heidegger's two other Hegel lectures pertinent to the subject are found in the second part of GA 68 in *Erläuterung der "Einleitung" zu Hegels "Phänomenologie des Geistes"* and *Hegels Begriff der Erfahrung* dated to 1942–1943, which, itself, appears twice: first in shorter form in the *Holzwege* collection in 1950, then in a longer form in 1970. From all of these Hegel seminars devoted to *Phänomenologie des Geistes*, we can possibly ascertain that the content across these lectures are similar and comprised of fairly recycled material, especially with the seminars around 1942, if, in extending Arel and Feuerhahn's assessment of the second part of GA 68, Heidegger largely focuses his exegetical attention on Hegel's introductory section of *Phänomenologie des Geistes*. We might ask, then, a question about the manner that this focus in 1942 relates to the fact that, as Arel and Feuerhahn argue, the Winter 1930/1931 lecture "omits discussion of both the 'Preface' and the 'Introduction' and instead devotes [it]self to the explication of Sections A and B of [*Phänomenologie des Geistes*]."[26] Though we can easily speculate as to why this is the case, our concern with tracing what Hegel lecture Rahner had limits us from doing so. What remains at hand, however, is how does this devotion fairly-concentrated in 1942 across three separate

25. Heidegger, *Hegel*, xiv.
26. Ibid.

lectures come to bear on the two semesters of the "seminar, upper level: Hegel, *Phänomenologie des Geistes*" Rahner attended in Winter 1934/1935 and Summer 1935?

If we keep in mind that Hegel's introductory section to *Phänomenologie des Geistes*, in brief, asserts that there is a fundamental contradiction between what we can know of the world in relation to how we can know the Absolute, when our knowledge of the Absolute greatly influences what we can know of the world—the consciousness bridges this divide. For Heidegger, working through *Phänomenologie des Geistes* would have revealed that there was something essential in knowing the Absolute, as a contingency for knowing the world, as well as the ability to harness the consciousness as a means of knowing the world and, in turn, tapping into the Absolute. What Heidegger would do with this, not so much in the first 1930/1931 lecture, but certainly by the time Rahner attended the "seminar, upper level: Hegel, *Phänomenologie des Geistes*" in the consecutive semesters of Winter 1934/1935 and Summer 1935 is appropriate Hegel, the concepts of knowledge and the consciousness, the notion of the Absolute, and the role of *Geistes* for the purposes of outlining how the fate of the German people could be awakened to unfold their collective destiny. This sentiment would have been carried forward into the three separate Hegel courses given in 1942, which finds its way into the second part of *Hegel* in *Erläuterung der "Einleitung" zu Hegels "Phänomenologie des Geistes"* as the following claim: "For the Germans the historical moment way come in which they would have to become attentive to that which awaits them as their own. That which is their own can only be appropriated in their essential confrontation that lets the essential become question-worthy."[27] Here, Heidegger views the "essential confrontation" as "the German relation to the metaphysics of German Idealism," and the underlining question-worthiness of "what remains entangled in an either-or." For Heidegger, as he comes to the close of this 1942 lecture, trying Germans to metaphysics means confronting the metaphysics of Schelling and Hegel "as the return to Leibniz" and the conceptualization of an "absolute metaphysics."[28] What makes this absolute metaphysics "absolute" is that it is a "modern metaphysics"[29]—it is the metaphysics of National Socialism and, when implied this way in 1942, we can only speculate if a similar articulation was previously delivered to

27. Ibid., 108
28. Ibid., 110–111.
29. Ibid., 111.

Rahner in the two "upper-level" Hegel seminars of Winter 1934/1935 and Summer 1935, and, therefore, we can only theorize how such an articulation influenced Rahner's understanding of Hegel and metaphysics.

What need not be speculated is that Heidegger found a connection between Hegel's *Geistes* and metaphysics proper, as a way to rationalize the fate and destiny of the German people led by National Socialism. Here, while delivering the second of the two Hegel lectures Rahner attended, this connection is the impetus for the "fundamental question of metaphysics" at the outset of *Einführung in die Metaphysik* in Summer 1935. The next, *Die Frage nach dem Ding: Zu Kants Lehre von den transzendentalen Grundsätzen* of Winter 1935/1936, more specifically concerns itself with exploring how Kantian metaphysics "shaped and essentially clarified" Leibniz's metaphysics and becomes a bridge, through Kant's transcendental philosophy, to the metaphysics of Schelling and Hegel.[30]

Taken together as major lectures, from *Einführung in die Metaphysik* and *Die Frage nach dem Ding: Zu Kants Lehre von den transzendentalen Grundsätzen*, Rahner, broadly speaking, was presented with Heidegger's take on the fundamental problem of metaphysics as it pertains to the meaning of the question of metaphysics itself, as Heidegger's first return to the subject matter, since the Summer 1931 when he gave the *Aristoteles: Metaphysik IX* lecture. Prior to that, and all while at Freiburg since 1928, Heidegger's most recent, focused treatment of the subject had been in the book, *Kant und das Problem der Metaphysik* published in 1929 and, quickly thereafter, the 1929/1930 lecture, *Die grundbegriffe der Metaphysik: Welt, Endlichkeit, Einsamkeit*. By the time Heidegger returned to metaphysics for a lecture course in Summer 1935, Rahner and others in attendance would have been presented not just with re-articulations of Heidegger's previous work on subject, or even what could be described as more mature ventures into the field, but, instead, would have encountered an approach to metaphysics— that is, the fundamental problem of it, the question of what it means to do it at all, and the extent to which exegesis of seminal figures such as Aristotle and Kant remain pertinent—that attempted to use metaphysics in much the same manner as Heidegger used Hölderlin (and Hegel): to justify the ideology of National Socialism. Here, Heidegger's reading of metaphysics, in terms of how it espouses the fate and destiny of the German people, views it as a foundation running beneath all else, so that it is the framework upon which philosophizing, poeticizing, and politicizing are constructed.

30. Ibid., 110.

As with Rahner's previous major lecture on Hölderlin, the two metaphysics lectures undoubtedly shape Rahner's eventual *Heideggerian lens,* through Rahner's confrontation with Heidegger's views on the fundamental destruction of the conventional—albeit, historical, or traditional—examination of metaphysics. This destruction is predicated on how Heidegger conceives of the constructive apparatus that is called the history of metaphysics. That is, the history of the understanding of being must be destructed, if it is to be interpreted as a constructive framework. Constructively, then, "for Heidegger the whole history of human thought and existence has been dominated and characterized by [humankind]'s understanding of being."[31] Just as Heidegger previously argues in *Sein und Zeit,* "the whole history of human thought," beginning from Plato and carrying forward through the Western philosophical tradition, has incorrectly approached the question of *being.* Not only is this case similarly made in the *Einführung in die Metaphysik* lecture, but the case is also asserted with respect to Kant's "transcendental" in *Die Frage nach dem Ding: Zu Kants Lehre von den transzendentalen Grundsätzen.* In this latter seminar—which Rahner lists as *Grundfragen der Metaphysik*—in particular, Heidegger examines Kant's metaphysics, specifically with respect to Kant's *"Lehre"* of transcendental principles—these "transcendental" principles become, for Heidegger, a way to understand Kant's system of reason, which Kant delineates in the three *Critiques.*[32] With Kant already an interest of Rahner's, Heidegger's take on metaphysics by 1935 affected not just how Rahner viewed Kantian metaphysics, but would have, by extension, deeply influenced how he had come to understand Aquinas' own metaphysics. Much of this was due to Heidegger's own approach to Kant and metaphysics, which had largely matured from the 1929 *Kant* book and the extent to which that early reading of Kant was decidedly phenomenological—it does not veer too far afield from his earlier Marburg course, *Phänomenologische Interpretation von Kants Kritik der reinen Vernunft* of Winter 1927/1928. However, what we find in the two metaphysics lectures that Rahner attended is a focus on critiquing the transcendental as somewhat of a stand-in for Heidegger's earlier overlay of the phenomenological. In addressing the transcendental in the latter lecture after providing a foundational understanding of what

31. In the 1959 English translation of *Einführung in die Metaphysik,* the translator makes this excellent summative assessment at the outset of the "Translator's Note." Heidegger, *An Introduction to Metaphysics,* vii.

32. Immanuel Kant's three Critiques: *Critique of Pure Reason, Critique of Practical Reason,* and the *Critique of Judgment.*

makes the transcendental possible through the question of metaphysics in the former lecture, it is interesting that the only evidence of Rahner's critique of these two lectures appears as critical notes for the former lecture *Einführung in die Metaphysik*, which appear in Rahner's papers. Though these notes challenge much of Heidegger's reading of metaphysics in the Summer 1935 lecture, I argue that it is possible, too, to believe that Rahner was just as critical of Heidegger's handling of the transcendental, if there is a plausible conflict for Rahner between the "Heideggerian Kant" and the "Rahnerian Thomas," which is seemingly implied by Peter Fritz.[33] What Fritz suggests is that "Rahner learns from Heidegger's Kant book how to avoid speaking epistemologically, and how to recast human subjectivity into a metaphysics of knowledge based on the imagination."[34] I feel this is certainly true, but only to an extent. It is not the Kant book that Rahner encounters in the two metaphysics lectures of Summer 1935 and Winter 1935/1936. Though we can split hairs here, what Rahner learns from Heidegger by the mid-1930s is far removed from the Kant book, if we consider that the National Socialist agenda of the lectures does not yet rear itself in the Kant book and, more importantly, the Kant book is closer to Husserl's phenomenology—the two metaphysics lectures totally avoid this, opting to speak, instead, by the second of the two, transcendentally. To this end, Sheehan suggests that "Rahner's formulation of the transcendental approach is markedly Kantian and, to that degree, not well suited to Heidegger."[35] Fritz cites this from Sheehan, challenging it as marginalizing Rahner, at best, into "a deviant Heideggerian who strays towards Kant, and at worst, a careless, superficial exegete of Heidegger who gets his teacher wrong despite serious effort to understand him."[36] I do not read Sheehan's assertion this way. In my view, Sheehan would likely agree with Fritz. The case that Sheehan makes is with regards to how Rahner eventually develops an understanding of the transcendental more aligned with Kant's and not a "Heideggerian Kant"—or, to be sure, an understanding that is articulated through a "Rahnerian Thomas"—which is "not well suited" to Heidegger's phenomenological approach to Kant. Clearly, since Sheehan is focused on an "early Rahner," the point that he makes is completely valid and grounded in recognizing that Rahner diverges, at the end of his Freiburg studies, from

---

33. Fritz, *Karl Rahner's Theological Aesthetics*, 47.

34. Ibid.

35. Sheehan, *Karl Rahner: The Philosophical Foundations*, 116.

36. Fritz, *Karl Rahner's Theological Aesthetics*, 47.

Heidegger's bias towards his own early phenomenological reading of Kant. The term "bias" is still a bit strong, since, in the decade after composing *Sein und Zeit*, Heidegger was surely attempting to reconcile his early phenomenological work with National Socialism—as Rahner would witness, the latter undoubtedly win out for the sake of expediency. Nevertheless, what Sheehan does not address, any more than Fritz does, is how what Rahner learned in the two metaphysics lectures of the mid-1930s positioned an "early Rahner" into a confrontation between his own "Rahnerian Thomas" version of Aquinas and the "Heideggerian Kant" version of Kant of *Die Frage nach dem Ding: Zu Kants Lehre von den transzendentalen Grundsätzen* in Winter 1935/1936.

Also, during the Winter 1935/1936, according to Rahner's list as it has been reproduced by Sheehan, Rahner attended a "seminar, middle level: Leibnizens *Weltbegriff und der Deutsche Idealismus*."[37] This seminar is included in the currently untranslated Ga 84 entitled *Seminare: Leibniz—Kant—Schiller* (2013), with four other seminars: one dated to Summer 1931, two to Winter 1931/1932, and one to Summer 1934. As the latest of these, "Leibnizens *Weltbegriff und der Deutsche Idealismus*" is the only seminar dedicated to Leibniz, while the others are focused on either Kant or the Kantian dialectic. It is, in fact, the only lecture on Leibniz that Heidegger gave at Freiburg, with the only other occasion he focused on Leibniz occurred in his final lecture at Marburg, *Metaphysische Anfangsgründe der Logik im Ausgang von Leibniz* in Summer 1928. In particular, the Leibniz seminar of Winter 1935/1936 presents Leibniz's "world-concept" or concept of the world through monadology and how this view, published by Leibniz in 1720, acts as a precursor to German Idealism in the late 18th and early 19th centuries, or what becomes known as Post-Kantianism. In this way, we can see Heidegger's reason for grouping this Leibniz seminar with the Kant-focused seminars, as a means of situating Leibniz within a trajectory of thought that gave birth to Kant's thought and, eventually, the reactions to Kant—particularly to his *Kritik der reinen Vernunft* of 1781—by Hegel, Fichte, and Schelling. To be sure, this makes thematic sense, particularly if we can see the grouping of the seminars in GA 84 under the umbrella of German Idealism. Yet, given the time period, Heidegger's reading of Kant's *Kritik der reinen Vernunft* in Summer 1934 and Leibniz in Winter 1935/1936 are most assuredly slanted towards rationalizing National Socialism and Nazi ideology. For his use of Leibniz and monadol-

---

37. Sheehan, *Karl Rahner: The Philosophical Foundations*, 5.

ogy, Heidegger is also tying the monad to Kantian metaphysics. Though the connection is fairly straightforward, we might wonder why Heidegger does not work through Leibniz's early treatise, *Discourse on Metaphysics* as a more direct comparison subject-for-subject to Kantian metaphysics. This is because, in my view, which Heidegger seems to share by even giving "Leibnizens *Weltbegriff und der Deutsche Idealismus*," Leibniz's later work on the monad is more closely related to Kantian metaphysics, especially if we can say that the monad more directly influenced Kant. Leibniz, at his most philosophically mature, outlines the monad as a simple substance that enters into composites, eliciting a pre-established harmony directly challenging Cartesianism. What Rahner would have experienced, then, in this seminar—though it remains unclear if he was ever fully aware of it—is Heidegger's use of Leibniz in much the same manner as Hölderlin, Hegel, and Kant, as another important figure that can be prefigured and fashioned into the National Socialist thinking.

In his final semester at Freiburg in Summer 1936, Rahner attended Heidegger's major lecture course, *Schelling: Vom Wesen der meschlichen Freiheit* (translated as *Schelling's Treatise on the Essence of Human Freedom* in 1985) appearing in GA 42 and what Rahner lists as a "seminar, upper level: Kant, *Kritik der Urteilskraft*," which does not appear at all in the *Gesamtausgabe*. Setting aside the "seminar, upper level" for now, the major lecture of Schelling as a thematic continuation of the Leibniz seminar of the previous semester and, from the two semesters before that, the two Hegel seminars—it is Heidegger's positioning of Schelling as an important figure comported to Hegel and Leibniz. Here, however, we notice that Heidegger delivers *Schelling: Vom Wesen der meschlichen Freiheit* as a lecture, and not a seminar. Since we see his treatment of Hegel and Leibniz directed to the limited attendance of "upper-level" seminars, Heidegger's Schelling lecture delivered to a larger number of students suggests that, by 1936, Heidegger recognized in Schelling—though more obscure in the German Idealist tradition than Hegel and Fichte—certain guiding principles that was meant to form the ethical backbone of National Socialism. In the translation of *Schelling: Vom Wesen der meschlichen Freiheit*, Joan Stambaugh points out that the lecture occurs in a crucial point in Heidegger's development, especially by offering preliminary articulations of *Ereignis* and how that term would be more fully articulated in *Beiträge zur Philosophie (Vom Ereignis)*, which were privately composed 1936 to 1938. Even as it occurs in *Schelling: Vom Wesen der meschlichen Freiheit*, the term *Ereignis* comports Heidegger towards using Schelling to examine the metaphysics of evil. For Heidegger, his discussion of "the metaphysics of evil" begins with first extrapolating, as the task of his interpretation of Schelling's 1809 treatise *Philosophical Inquiries into the Nature of Human Freedom and Matters Connected Therewith*, how the fall of the Holy Roman Empire, as a period known to National Socialism as the First Reich. In doing so, Heidegger's assessment of the question of the essence of freedom and the metaphysics of evil point not just to the conditions of the fall of the First Reich, but the conditions that allow for the birth of the Third Reich. We can see a certain irony in Heidegger's work with the metaphysics of evil, in hindsight all of Nazist atrocities. In 1936, for Heidegger, the metaphysics of evil had more to do with what was done against the German people, rather than what was currently being done to the mere existence of those that threatened National Socialism, and the question of the meaning of being German. Because of this, Heidegger found a necessity in interpreting Schelling, arising from the extent that "[Schelling] did not. . .bring his questioning to that metaphysical place into which Hölderlin had to project himself poetically,"[38] which would have reminded Rahner of his first lecture course from Heidegger. More importantly, Rahner would have recognized that Heidegger was tying together Hölderlin, Hegel, Schelling, Leibniz, and Kant as thinkers always-already philosophizing about National Socialism before Hitler ever came to power in 1933. Not only would Rahner have located this theme by Summer 1936 with *Schelling: Vom Wesen der meschlichen Freiheit*, but he would have certainly witnessed Heidegger's "seminar, upper level: Kant, *Kritik der Urteilskraft*," though we can only speculate, as a systematic companion to the Schelling lecture—the return to Kant, at this point, signals that Heidegger's use of *Kritik der Urteilskraft* was meant to provide an aesthetic framework to the metaphysical foundations explored in Hölderlin, Hegel, Schelling, Leibniz, and Kant.

With Rahner's Freiburg doctoral studies taken as a whole, the four major lectures and the four seminars greatly influenced Rahner's overall approach to philosophy and what can be deemed as his *Heideggerian lens*. More specifically, too, Rahner's Heidegger lectures and seminars influenced his philosophy of *being*, particularly as a distinctly Heideggerian philosophy of the relationship between metaphysics, *Wahrheit*, and the transcendental. Coming from a theological background, and setting aside the undertones of National Socialism, Heidegger's lectures and seminars

---

38. Heidegger, *Schelling's Treatise on the Essence of Human Freedom*, 4.

across four sequential semesters from Winter 1934/1935 to Summer 1936 helped Rahner confront *what being is*, when conceptualizing that *primordial being* is situated in concepts of *Wahrheit*, what metaphysics tells us, and a recognition of the transcendental. These three concepts, especially as Heideggerian elucidations, provide the theoretical framework from which Rahner's theological investigations become philosophical in nature. Not only would this more generally come in conflict with Rahner's dissertation advisor Martin Honecker, but would prove to be a specific problem for the topic to which Rahner had been assigned by Honecker from Thomist philosophy—Rahner was tasked to explore the epistemological problem from the *Summa Theologiae* of Thomas Aquinas. It has been often noted that Honecker rejected Rahner's "draft thesis" and the reason often given is that Honecker believed Rahner's dissertation was "too much influenced by Heidegger."[39] This is not entirely true, even if Honecker had already positioned himself as an ideological opponent of Heidegger at Freiburg and such a reason would reflect bias. What is more likely, however, as rightly noted by Hugo Ott, is that Rahner's dissertation "failed to meet the academic standard demanded by Honecker."[40] There is no way to know what this means specifically. We can conclude that Lotz's dissertation met Honecker's "academic standard," because, unlike Rahner's, Lotz remained true to a prescribed scholastic framework,[41] even though Lotz was certainly influenced by Heidegger too.

To see Heidegger's influence on Rahner's dissertation, let us take a closer look his dissertation entitled *Geist in Welt: Zur Metaphisik der endichen Erkenntnis bei Thomas von Aquin*, which is a culmination of his philosophical study during those Freiburg doctoral years.

Rahner's Existential Theology of Experience

In order to discuss Rahner's "existential theology of experience," our focus will be on determining what Rahner's "existential theology" is. As our starting point, there are certain assumptions that are inevitable and necessary, when considering that the way that Rahner theologizes is from a philosophical perspective and the philosophizing he embarks on is always theological in nature. Of course, in tying Rahner to existential theology, it

39. Ott, *Martin Heidegger: A Political Life*, 276.

40. Ibid.

41. Ibid.

may be difficult to see the relationship between the two, especially since, currently, there is no other scholarship that explicitly thinks of Rahner and existential theology, argues for Rahner's existential theology, nor recognizes that Rahner's theology is an "existential theology." While this may seem problematic, in one sense, and make it seem as if any relationship between Rahner and "existential theology" already run-aground any meaningful discussion, it is unmistakably apparent that there is a certain element of Rahner's theology that is existentially comported to a Rahner's philosophical understanding of existence fundamentally rooted in Heidegger's influence upon him—it is Rahner's frequent use of the concept and notion of "grace."

Much of the available Rahnerian scholarship certainly pinpoints "grace" as an important part of how Rahner theologizes, particularly as an "existential" component of Rahner's overall philosophical conceptualization of existence. Sections from four books can be viewed as outlining Rahner's theology in this manner: the Leo O'Donovan edited *A World of Grace: An Introduction to the Themes and Foundations of Karl Rahner's Theology* published in 1981, *Karl-Heinz Weger's Karl Rahner: An Introduction to His Theology* published in 1980, Donald Gelpi's *Life and Light: A Guide to the Theology of Karl Rahner* published in 1966, and Herbert Vorgrimler's *Understanding Karl Rahner: An Introduction to His Life and Thought* published in 1986. What is obvious in each—though not quite as obvious in Vorgrimler—is that Rahner's theology depends on the notion of grace, perhaps more than any other theological concept. For Rahner, grace brings human existence and God's Being together, at the point of existential importance for both. Nevertheless, when we speak of grace in this manner, we find that it, too, has an existence to it—it has a "being"/"Being"—that places humanity's "being" and God's "Being" in a connectedness and mutual belongingness that is not just theological, but is philosophical-theological. That is to say, "grace" is what turns Rahner's theology into an "existential theology," especially as a means of positioning humanity to God, and God to humanity. In this way, Rahner's "existential theology" becomes an "existential theology of experience," because grace, in itself, is an experience that humanity and God share, though the former receives it and the latter bestows it.

What must be understood, then, is that grace, in itself, as a human experience and a God-experience is a vehicle by which αλεθεια is possible— "grace," as such, opens the possibility for the meaning of human existence to be unconcealed, and the meaning of God's existence to be equally unconcealed. In other words, grace allows for "being" to exist in its most primordialty, as well as "Being" to exist in the same state. Yet, for experience—or an existential theology of experience—to lead to an unconcealment of either "being" or "Being," the focus of Rahner's Heideggerian lens must be ultimately and primordially on χάρις.

Geist in Welt—despite being considered as philosophical/theological juvenilia in comparison to his more mature *Foundations of Christian Faith* and the *Theological Investigations* volumes—is the cornerstone of the *Heideggerian lens* that Rahner applies to his ventures into existential theology of experience. Though not explicitly focused on "grace" as χάρις, *Geist in Welt* still exhibits Rahner's interests in the transcendental, the ontical, and the primordial—these three interests are focused, then, on *what being is*, or the primordiality of *being*. To be clear, what makes *Geist in Welt* important is that it contains "the basic philosophical position developed [in the work] in dialogue with modern philosophy provid[ing] the unifying principle and presupposition of Rahner's whole theology."[42] In this regard, then, *Geist in Welt* represents an important point in Rahner's theology, and a jumping off point from which his existential theology ultimately takes shape.

In the introduction to the 1968 translation of *Geist in Welt* entitled "Karl Rahner and the Kantian Problematic," Francis Fiorenza observes:

> [*Spirit in the World*] represents Rahner's attempt to confront the medieval scholastic philosophy of Thomas Aquinas with the problems and questions of modern philosophy, especially as formulated by Immanuel Kant in his critical and transcendental philosophy.[43]

Rahner's "attempt to confront" the thought of Aquinas with "the problems and questions of modern philosophy" denotes that Rahner is concerned with deconstructing Aquinas in the same manner that Heidegger is with deconstructing the Plato and Platonism. Like Heidegger, Rahner's awareness of "the problems and questions of modern philosophy" is rooted in an understanding that something is out of joint in philosophical modernity—it is the sense modern philosophy's "problems and questions" can be explained, somehow, and even answered through a reassessment of the medieval scholasticism of Aquinas. That much is clear. But, for Rahner, to

---

42. Rahner, *Spirit in the World*, xix.

43. Ibid.

go back to Aquinas—just as Heidegger goes back to the Plato—there are intermediate points along the way that must be reckoned with. These are unavoidable points that must be explained, in themselves, if there is ever to be any substantive reckoning with Aquinas. One of those such points is Kant, and interpreting Kant's critical and transcendental philosophy. However, Rahner's Kantian interpretation is only tangential and implicit, operating mainly in the periphery, since, as Fiorenza suggests:

> [. . .]*Spirit in the World* does not contain an explicit interpreta-
> tion of Kant. It does not indicate to what extent Rahner would
> have avoided the misunderstanding of other students of Marechal
> insofar as he would have followed the more adequate later inter-
> pretation of Heidegger. The influence of Heidegger is nevertheless
> important for Rahner's understanding of the objectivity of human
> knowledge. . .[44]

To say that Rahner "would have followed the more adequate later interpre-
tation of Heidegger" seems to rightly suggest that Rahner mainly based his Kantian interpretation on Heidegger's lecture course on Kant. That course was likely Heidegger's "Die Frage nach dem Ding: Zu Kants Lehre von den transzendentalen Grundsätzen," which, as mentioned in my "Rahner and Heidegger" section, Rahner attended in the winter semester 1935/1936. From that course, Rahner would have developed a Heideggerian "understanding of the objectivity of human knowledge," particularly through Heidegger's own existentialist lens. It is through this lens that Rahner in-
terprets Kant and, then, uses that Heideggerian-influenced lens on reading Question 84 Article 7 from Thomas Aquinas' *Summa Theologiae*.

In Question 84 Article 7, Aquinas posits the following question:

> Whether the intellect can actually understand through the in-
> telligible species which it is possessed, without turning to the
> phantasms?[45]

This question is, on one hand, concerned with metaphysics, but, on the other, questioning metaphysics in terms of epistemology—it is not only an individual question of being, or even an exclusive question of knowing, but it is a critical question of knowing and being. This question, as such, along

---

44. Ibid., xl-xli.

45. Kreeft, ed. *A Summa of the Summa: The Essential Philosophical Passages of St. Thomas Aquinas' Summa Theologica*, 317.

with its objections, its counter-objection, its solution, and its answers to the objections, in their totality, are the focus of Rahner's *Geist in Welt*.[46]

Though the chief task of *Geist in Welt* is to provide an interpretative study of Thomas Aquinas' metaphysics and epistemology, Rahner focuses that analysis, at least in part, through Heideggerian existentialism, rather than Maréchal's Thomism.[47] Just as it has been rightly noted, *Geist in Welt* has major Heideggerian influences, particularly from Heidegger's *Sein und Zeit* and *Kant und das Problem der Metaphysik*.[48] From these two early works of Heidegger, Rahner's *Geist in Welt* attempts to, through an analysis of Aquinas, "ground transcendental epistemology in a new reading of human being influenced by Heidegger."[49] Rahner's "new reading," as it as, ultimately develops from Rahner having located an intersectionality between Heidegger's concept of *Dasein* and Aquinas' concept of the dynamism of the human mind.[50] This connection is especially crucial not just to the way in which Rahner does theology, but critical to his synthesis of philosophy and theology—it is an intersectionality that is as much theological as it is philosophical. What consequently results from this intersectionality is Rahner decidedly venturing into transcendental-existential territory in *Geist in Welt*, with Thomistic metaphysics of knowledge seated in his philosophical notions of "the transcendental" and "the existential."[51]

Published as *Spirit in the World* in the 1968 English translation, Johannes Metz describes Rahner's "transcendental and existential philosophy" in the following from the "Forward" to the 1994 edition of *Geist in Welt*:

46. It must be noted that Rahner translates Aquinas' Latin *"Utrum intellectus possit actu intelligere per species intelligibiles quas penes se habet, non convertendo se ad phantasmata"* slightly differently than Kreeft does, which has been cited in note 191. Rahner, *Spirit in the World*, 3–11.

47. Other than Heideggerian existentialism, Rahner's dissertation is influenced by two Jesuit philosophers: Pierre Rousselot (1878–1915) and Joseph Maréchal (1878–1944).

48. Thomas Sheehan, a major Heidegger scholar, makes this argument. He explains that Rahner "attempts a reinterpretation of certain possibilities implicit in Aquinas' theory of knowledge and being." Sheehan goes on to argue that Rahner is attempting to "retrieve" from Aquinas "a theory of being founded in the structure of human being which expresses itself in acts of predicative knowledge." Sheehan, "Metaphysics and Bivalence: On Karl Rahner's *Geist in Welt*," 21–22.

49. Ibid.

50. Kelly, "Introduction," In *Karl Rahner: Theologian of the Graced Search for Meaning*, 7.

51. Rahner, *Spirit in the World*, xvi.

> *Spirit in the World* uses a Thomistic metaphysics of knowledge
> explained in terms of transcendental and existential philosophy
> to define [humankind] as that essence of absolute transcendence
> towards God insofar as [humankind] in [its] understanding and
> interpretation of the world respectfully 'pre-apprehends' ('*vorg-
> reift*') towards God.[52]

As Metz points out, the "Thomistic metaphysics of knowledge" that Rahner
explains in *Spirit in the World* is linked to a conceptualization of understanding. Rahner is not just concerned with humankind's interpretative understanding of itself, but humankind's "understanding and interpretation
of the world." In this latter sense, Rahner contends that that "understanding" and that "interpretation of the world" is an act teleologically-oriented
towards the "essence of absolute transcendence towards God," as such.[53]

Clearly, in *Spirit in the World*, Rahner recognizes that human knowledge is limited whenever that knowledge is encased in human being,
or compartmentalized in human existence—human knowledge, when
anchored to human being's worldliness, cannot fully comprehend the
God's "absolute transcendence," as such. In other words, humankind may
comprehend God and, perhaps, apprehend God, using all the tools of
humankind's existential situation—that is, with the use of what I will call
situational ontology.[54] If human being can comprehend/apprehend anything of existential value from what amounts to an ontical situation, strictly
speaking then, that meaning does not contain enough transcendental value
to conceive, grasp, and explain God's "absolute transcendence." Rather,
humankind is only able to comprehend/apprehend what I would call an
"ontology of knowledge"—the existential situation of physical humanness
in all its practical, moral and ethical worldliness—instead of a metaphysics
of knowledge: a kind of knowledge which lies beneath human ontology but
is hidden within it.

---

52. Ibid.

53. I use "as such" here to denote that "God's absolute transcendence" is, altogether,
always different from anything conceivable, graspable, or even explainable by humankind. God's embodiment as "absolute transcendence" becomes what Rahner refers to as
a "holy mystery" in his *Foundations of Christian Faith*. Though I wish to make a quick
note of it now, I will discuss this with more detail later.

54. This term represents a combination of human being and the human being's existential situation. Together, humankind is encased in "situational ontology," since it must
make-meaning of itself as a human being, as well as make-meaning from the situation
that human being is confronted with at the very point of recognizing existence.

Rahner's use and interpretation of "Thomistic metaphysics of knowledge" is meant to express a need to transcend any ontology of knowledge. These two kinds of knowing are based on either an ontology of knowledge as apprehension, or a metaphysics of knowledge as the ability to "pre-apprehend." To be sure, Rahner is concerned with the latter, especially as a way for humanity to "know" God. If, as Metz argues, Rahner's *Spirit in the World* is concerned with how humankind "pre-apprehends towards God," then that concern with epistemological metaphysics is also a concern with *what being is*. To "pre-apprehend towards God" means systematically embarking on a kind of metaphysics that "pre-apprehends" *what being is*. That is, of course, any pre-apprehension aligns "what God is" to *what being is*. Not only is it clear that Rahner is making this essentialist connection in *Spirit in the World*, but his entire system of metaphysics[55] is rooted in a Heideggerian-influenced understanding of *what being is* and, then, what ἀλήθεια is. To this end, Rahner's early concern in *Spirit in the World* with the human ability to "pre-apprehend towards God" is a philosophical-theological examination of *what being is* as *primordial being* and ἀλήθεια.

If the possibility of pre-apprehension "towards God" is predicated on the possibility of pre-apprehending *primordial being* and ἀλήθεια, then humanity must apprehend the relationship between nature and grace. That is, this relationship provides the scope and limitations of what it means to be human in relation to the world and to God. This relationship, though not explicit in *Spirit in the World*, is certainly at the heart of Rahner's study of Aquinas' metaphysics and epistemology. While "nature" is an issue of epistemology, metaphysics is oriented toward "grace"—both embody Rahner's understanding of the existential situation humanity finds itself in when searching for *primordial being* and ἀλήθεια. Not only do these terms "nature" and "grace" play important roles in *Spirit in the World*, but they recur as the hallmarks of Rahner's theology thereafter. More specifically, "grace" or χάρις, for Rahner's *Heideggerian lens*, encompasses the means through which humanity's being can pre-apprehend God's Being, through *primordial being* and ἀλήθεια.

---

55. See note 100.

Χάρις in Experience and the "Experiential-Existential" Pathmark

Rahner's pathmark in existential theology searches for χάρις in experience—this venture pursues a *Heideggerian pathmark* of "grace" as a supernatural object of the primordiality of experience.[56] Through Rahner's existential theology of experience, *what is experienced* must be translated from its ontic state into what it already is[57] as *primordial being*—meaning, as the existential embodiment of *what experience is*. What this means is that Rahner's χάρις is related to the "experiential-existential" as one of its *Dasein*-like analytical possibilities.[58] As Rahner argues, χάρις "penetrates our conscious life, not only our essence but our existence too."[59] In this regard, when utilizing a *Heideggerian lens*, χάρις is a particular, conditional, and affective *Dasein*-like entity[60] by which humanity pre-apprehends the ontics of experience (our existence) and unmasks primordial being toward ἀλήθεια (our essence).

The "experiential-existential" pathmark that Rahner takes is devoted to pre-apprehension (*'Vorgriff'*). For Rahner's purposes of philosophizing within theology,[61] pre-apprehension is that which discloses χάρις in its primordial transcendence and, then, reveals ἀλήθεια. To pre-apprehend not only means differentiating *what is experienced* from *what experience is*, but drawing an existential distinction between "there-ness" and "is-ness." When engaged in pre-apprehension, it becomes possible to divide the ontics of experience (*what is experienced*) from experience itself, or experience at its

56. Rahner, *Nature and Grace: And Other Essays*, 4.

57. See note 40.

58. See note 46.

59. Karl Rahner, *Nature and Grace: And Other Essays* (New York, NY: Sheed and Ward, 1963), 26.

60. I use the term "entity," since Rahner proposes that "grace is not a thing, but a particular condition of a spiritual person." What seems to underlie this description of "grace" is its *Dasein*-like analytic possibilities (which I will discuss in more detail). Especially, to the extent that "grace," as Rahner continues to describe, is "the determination of a subject" even though it is "formally distinct from this subject." Accordingly, the same can be said of Heidegger's *Dasein*, and the degree to which *Dasein*'s analytical possibilities—as with "grace" as χάρις—are "affective" and "conditional" upon the ontics of experience, or human existence. Rahner, "Philosophy and Theology," in *Theological Investigations: Volume VI: Concerning the Vatican Council*, 72–73.

61. Rahner, "Philosophy and Philosophising in Theology," in *Theological Investigations: Volume IX: Writings of 1965–1967*, 47.

most primordial (*what experience is*)—to be clear, while the former places *primordial being* in *concealment* with "there-ness," the latter *unconceals* the primordial state of "is-ness" and χάρις. To this end, pre-apprehension is the meaning-making key to Rahner's existential theology of experience—it is part and parcel of his *Heideggerian pathmark* and the *Heideggerian lens* through which he searches for ἀλήθεια.

Pre-apprehension, as Rahner argues, is not self-explanatory.[62] In other words, though pre-apprehension allows for the *experiential-existential* conceptualization of χάρις and ἀλήθεια, it is not self-edifying or even self-revelatory. There may be a supernatural given-ness to the communicative-ness of χάρις,[63] but ἀλήθεια is not a given. That is, since ἀλήθεια prefers to exist in a state of *concealment* or λήθε, pre-apprehension requires working out χάρις as a *Dasein*-like possibility of the *experiential-existential*. For Rahner, pre-apprehension "must be understood as due to the working of that to which man is open, mainly, being in an absolute sense."[64] Furthermore, in his systematic work *Foundation of Christian Faith: An Introduction to the Idea of Christianity*, Rahner explains pre-apprehension as:

> . . .[the] subjective, non-objective luminosity of the subject in its transcendence is always oriented towards the holy mystery, the knowledge of God is always present unthematically and without name, and not just when we begin to speak of it.[65]

By defining pre-apprehension as "subjective, non-objective luminosity of the subject," Rahner is clearly separating his definition from any Husserlian subject-object connotation of the term.[66] Similarly to Heidegger's argument in *Being and Time*, Rahner's *Heideggerian lens* must move beyond such subject-object relations. Yet, situating subjectivity with respect to objectivity becomes Rahner's critical move of foundational, existential necessity—it involves conceptualizing what transcendence is for subjectivity, and how

62. Rahner, *Foundations of Christian Faith: An Introduction to the Idea of Christianity*, 34.

63. Rahner, *Nature and Grace: And Other Essays*, 21; 26; 32.

64. Rahner, *Foundations of Christian Faith: An Introduction to the Idea of Christianity*, 34.

65. Ibid., 21.

66. When I refer to "subject-object relations," I am referencing Husserl's constitutive notion of intersubjectivity, which Husserl explains as "we as human beings, and we as ultimately functioning-accomplishing subjects." Husserl, *The Crisis of European Sciences and Transcendental Phenomenology: An Introduction to Phenomenological Philosophy*, 182–183.

any conceptualization of transcendence is based on some objectified understanding of the primordiality of χάρις on the way toward ἀλήθεια. That is to say, *what is experienced* is subjective and *what experience is*, in the primordiality of experience as χάρις, is meta-subjective, or what Rahner calls "non-objective." Again, though rather thinly-veiled, Rahner is treading in the very territory that his *Heideggerian lens* attempts to deconstruct (*'destrukt'*).[67] Like Heidegger, Rahner is certainly aware of the inadequacies of subject-object relations and, as Jack Bonsor rightly observes:

> [. . .]each avoids the subject-object division of the Cartesian problematic by beginning with the human existent as always already involved in the world, with other entities. Subjectivity arises precisely through commerce with what is other. For [Heidegger and Rahner], the human existent becomes through involvement in the world and, thus, all knowledge is intrinsically existential.[68]

In light of Bonsor's point, "the human existent" is Rahner's concept of subjectivity.

By carefully using "non-objective" as a way to convey the orientation of transcendence "towards the holy mystery, the knowledge of God."

Knowledge of God as a "holy mystery" is crucial to conceptualizing the *experiential-existential*—it allows for the "experiential" to be *what is experienced* and the "existential" to be *what experience is*. Essentially, *what is experienced* is based on an epistemological situation and an abiding existential orientation. From both, human knowledge must grasp the "holy mystery" of God as a way of experiencing/knowing God and experiencing/knowing ourselves.[69] Rahner understands "holy mystery" as "something with which we are always familiar," and, though it may be initially incomprehensible, it is "self-evident in human life."[70] This self-evidence (*'Selbstverständlichen'*)[71] is grounded on a kind of knowledge that Rahner

67. See note 54.

68. Bonsor, *Rahner, Heidegger, and Truth: Karl Rahner's Notion of Christian Truth: The Influence of Heidegger*, 65.

69. I am using experiencing and knowing interchangeably, especially if it is possible to call experiencing a way of knowing and knowing a task tied to experiencing. But, moreover, I am connecting these two terms in relation to how John Calvin opens *Institutes of the Christian Religion*. See Calvin, *Institutes of the Christian Religion: Volume 1*, 35–39.

70. Rahner, *Foundations of Christian Faith: An Introduction to the Idea of Christianity*, 22.

71. Rahner, *Grundkurs des Glaubens: Einführung in den Begriff des Christentums*, 33.

calls "transcendental knowledge"—Rahner defines it as a "basic and original orientation towards absolute mystery, which constitutes [humankind's] fundamental experience of God, is a permanent existential of man as a spiritual subject."[72] Rahner's "permanent existential of man as a spiritual subject" (*'ein dauerndes Existential des Menschen al seines geistigen Subjektes ist'*)[73] is equivalent to what I have coined *experiential-existential*. I wish to make that connection clear, if my intent is to express what I believe to be Rahner's *experiential-existential* pathmarke. Like Rahner, I view the *experiential-existential* as permanently situated in the intersectionality of *what experience is* and primordiality of χάρις, when humanity encounters ἀλήθεια in the clearing.

The *experiential-existential* is constituted upon transcendental knowledge. What I mean, then, is that transcendental knowledge represents a fore-structure[74] upon which experience/knowledge of God and experience/knowledge of ourselves become *experiential-existential*. Transcendental knowledge, as such, is the extension of the pre-apprehension of ". . .all the individual movements and experiences [that] are borne by an ultimate and primordial movement."[75] That "ultimate and primordial movement," as Rahner describes, is a *Heideggerian pathmark* along the primordiality of experience as χάρις, on the way towards ἀλήθεια. In this sense, pre-apprehension is a compass that is calibrated by χάρις and guides transcendental knowledge in the direction of ἀλήθεια. In this way, when understanding the role that pre-apprehension plays in transcendental knowledge—what I have equated to experience/knowledge of God and experience/knowledge of ourselves, particularly as Rahner's argument in *Geist in Welt* suggests— Rahner describes transcendental knowledge in the following way:

> The concept 'God' is not a grasp of God by which a person masters the mystery, but it is letting oneself be grasped by the mystery

72. Rahner, *Foundations of Christian Faith: An Introduction to the Idea of Christianity*, 52.

73. Rahner, *Grundkurs des Glaubens: Einführung in den Begriff des Christentums*, 61.

74. This is Hans-Georg Gadamer's term to describe the "fore-understandings" or "fore-meanings" that undergird what can be known about the world around us. Speaking strictly in terms of hermeneutics, Gadamer is addressing, through Heidegger, is the "hermeneutical circle" problem of reading texts and how our "fore-structure" of understanding prevent us from delving any deeper than the ontical meaning of a text. Gadamer, *Truth and Method*, 235–240.

75. Rahner, *Foundations of Christian Faith: An Introduction to the Idea of Christianity*, 33.

which is present and yet ever distant. This mystery remains a mystery even though it reveals itself to [humankind] and thus continually grounds the possibility of [humankind] being a subject.[76]

What Rahner suggests is that transcendental knowledge is not just about "the concept God," but also the ability to "master the mystery" ('*Geheimnisses bemächtigt*')[77] of God's *Being*. On one level, transcendental knowledge is the extent to which human knowledge can conceptualize what God does epistemologically. However, on a deeper, existential level, human knowledge must connect to what God is. In effect, transcendental knowledge is a two-part knowledge of God: God as concept and God as mystery. In addition, that two-part knowledge of God as a "mystery" opens up the possibility of knowing ourselves, since, as Rahner argues, "[the mystery of God] reveals itself to [humankind]" and grounds humanity as "a subject." That is to say, humanity is a "transcendent subject" in the presence of the mystery of God.[78]

When experiencing the presence of the mystery of God, χάρις and ἀλήθεια "coincide in God."[79] If, as Bonsor further proposes in *Rahner, Heidegger, and Truth*, "God is the source of all finite beings and truths," then it is in that presence that humanity experiences in the finitude of the primordiality of experience as χάρις, on the way towards ἀλήθεια.

Though Bonsor believes that "this conception of truth, and being, is excluded by Heidegger in his understanding of the ontical distinction and fundamental ontology," I disagree with him.[80] From *Being and Time* forward, Heidegger constantly advances a concept of truth as ἀλήθεια and *being* by utilizing Brentano's "being in the sense of the true."[81] With this in mind, I also take issue with Bonsor's assertion that there are differences between Rahner and Heidegger concerning truth as ἀλήθεια, even if it is ac-

---

76. Ibid., 54.

77. Rahner, *Grundkurs des Glaubens: Einführung in den Begriff des Christentums*, 63.

78. Rahner, *Foundations of Christian Faith: An Introduction to the Idea of Christianity*, 42.

79. Bonsor, *Rahner, Heidegger, and Truth: Karl Rahner's Notion of Christian Truth: The Influence of Heidegger*, 65.

80. Ibid.

81. Brentano describes "being in the sense of the true" in the following manner: ". . .a thing that had no beginning and will always be, a thing that is continuously undergoing changes and producing changes in everything outside itself, thus making indirectly necessary the uniformity of the temporal process of things." Brentano, *The Theory of Categories*, 18; 21.

curate to suggest that there is a difference "in the task each sets for himself in his fundamental ontology and in the resulting conception of being."[82] I believe that Rahner's sense of truth as ἀλήθεια is aligned with Heidegger's. Though Heidegger's task is certainly different from Rahner's, both unquestionably adhere to a relatedness between ἀλήθεια and *being*—it is extent to which the latter conceals ἀλήθεια. This relational concept of "truth" and *being* is how Heidegger, as well as Rahner, differentiate "there-ness" from "is-ness," in order to divide *being* in its everydayness from ἀλήθεια.

In my view, Rahner's *Heideggerian lens* certainly appropriates Heidegger's conception of *primordial being* and "truth"—especially, as the primordiality of experience as χάρις and ἀλήθεια, respectively. Such an appropriation becomes even more apparent in Rahner's notion of the mystery of God as "a mystery which constantly reveals itself and at the same time conceals itself."[83] However, the means by which the mystery of God reveals (or *unconceals*) itself to humanity is how God communicates with humanity. This is precisely because, as Rahner contends, "God communicates [God's self] to [humankind] in his own reality [which] is the mystery and the fullness of grace."[84] There is an existential situatedness between humanity's "own reality" and "the mystery and fullness of grace." To this end, grace—in its most fundamental sense, as the primordiality of experience as χάρις—is God's self-communication.[85]

The primordiality of experience as χάρις, God's self-communication, and ἀλήθεια are all forms of transcendental knowledge that take humanity beyond *being* in its finite everydayness. These are entities of infinitude "about which we always know on account of the absolute range of the *Vorgriff.*"[86] Though there is a Husserlian intentionality[87] to '*Vorgriff*' or pre-apprehension, Rahner concludes that:

---

82. Bonsor, *Rahner, Heidegger, and Truth: Karl Rahner's Notion of Christian Truth: The Influence of Heidegger,* 65.

83. Rahner, *Foundations of Christian Faith: An Introduction to the Idea of Christianity,* , 42.

84. Rahner, *Nature and Grace: And Other Essays,* 21.

85. Kilby, *Karl Rahner: A Brief Introduction,* 21.

86. Rahner, *Hearer of the Word: Laying the Foundation for a Philosophy of Religion,* 59.

87. Husserl describes "intentionality" in the following manner: ". . .the world as it is for us becomes understandable as a structure of meaning formed out of elementary intentionalities. The being of these intentionalities themselves is nothing but one meaning-formation operating together with another, 'constituting' new meaning through

[. . .]in the present state of our knowledge, we cannot reach by
ourselves a positive knowledge of what is 'beyond' the domain of
the finite world, although the anticipation of this beyond is the
condition of our knowledge of things in the world. But this seems
to establish only a *de facto* hiddenness of the infinite being.[88]

What Rahner is describing is the relationship between the finite nature of
being and the infinitude of grace. To be exact, it is between the everydayness of human existence and the supernatural primordiality of experience
as χάρις. An existential understanding of the latter brings about an experiential understanding of the former, due to the *experiential-existential*
relatedness between the two.[89] Yet, as S. Paul Schilling notes in *Contemporary Continental Theologians*, ". . .though Rahner preserves the distinction
between nature and grace, he sees them as interpenetrating."[90] To this end,
with respect to "nature" and "grace," Rahner's negotiation between their
distinction and interpenetration is his *Heideggerian pathmark* and, subsequently, his *experiential-existential* pathmark.

synthesis." Husserl, *The Crisis of European Sciences and Transcendental Phenomenology:
An Introduction to Phenomenological Philosophy*, 168.

88. Rahner, *Hearer of the Word: Laying the Foundation for a Philosophy of Religion*,
60.

89. I call this "experiential relatedness" from Rahner's following explication: "For
the essence of man is such that it is experienced where "grace" is experienced, since
"grace" is only experienced where the spirit naturally is. And vice versa: where spirit is
experienced in the actual order of things, it is a supernaturally elevated spirit." Rahner,
"Nature and Grace," in *Theological Investigations Volume IV: More Recent Writings*, 184.

90. Schilling, *Contemporary Continental Theologians*, 212.

"Pathmarks" into the Incomplete
Being and Time

The "pathmarks" that Macquarrie, Bultmann, Tillich, and Rahner take in existential theology follows *Heideggerian pathmarks* towards the primordiality of *being* on the way to *unconcealment*, or ἀλήθεια. By way of each "venture," each existential theologian assumes a specific theological "stance" that utilizes an existential "lens"—while the former certainly grounds them fundamentally, the latter, by way of Heideggerian influences, allows them to "venture" beyond traditional theological framework with the use of philosophical propositions. In an effort at explaining the relationship between humanity and God, each existential theologian examines what it means to be human, not strictly in terms of theology, but as it is tied inextricably to an understanding of the philosophy of existence—the concept of *being*. In other words, *being* becomes the means by which each existential theologian theologizes from a philosophical point of view. To this end, *being* is a critical, hermeneutical component in the existential theologies of Macquarrie, Bultmann, Tillich, and Rahner—due to their respective Heideggerian influences, each of them is particularly invested in locating *primordial being* (*what being is*) and isolating "truth" (ἀλήθεια as *unconcealment*) in their respective meaning-making conceptualizations of scripture, tradition, reason, and experience.

Though it would be difficult to label Macquarrie, Bultmann, Tillich, or Rahner as "Heideggerians,"[1] especially since their chief interests are in

---

1. I use this term rather cautiously. The term itself is a bit problematic, since labeling any thinker a "Heideggerian" poses unavoidable problems. One problem, of course, is if a so-called "Heideggerian" is influenced by "early" or "later" Heidegger. With this in

"the theological" and Heidegger's are not, each still employs a distinctively *Heideggerian lens*. The degrees to which they each utilize Heidegger to *question of the meaning of God* do certainly vary in ideas and content, but there remains, in each of them, a purposeful manner of asking the question itself, which follows Heidegger's own approach in *Being and Time*. Like Heidegger, each is concerned with the relationship between *being* and God, as well as between philosophy and theology, especially since Macquarrie, Bultmann, Tillich, and Rahner alike consider Heidegger's question of the meaning of *Being* analogous to their *question of the meaning of God*.[2] It is possible, then, to consider each of them as "Heideggerian," if only in a general sense, because the term itself is likely an impossible label in the narrow sense.[3]

Nevertheless, in each of their respective cases, Heidegger plays a significant role in their theological thinking about the *question of the meaning of God*—for each of them, in light of Heidegger's projected task in *Being and Time*, it is important to "reawaken an understanding for the meaning of [the] question."[4] This is what I have called the *Heideggerian lens*. For each, this "lens" is situated mainly in terms of their individual exposure to *Being and Time*—how they understand *being*, primordiality, and *unconcealment* is rooted exclusively in "early Heidegger."[5] As a result, each approaches their own theological projects as philosophical-theological continuations of the incomplete philosophical project Heidegger began in *Being and Time*. If it can be argued that Heidegger's incomplete Part II was meant to be "the most theological part" of *Being and Time*, it is certainly possible to argue that Macquarrie, Bultmann, Tillich, and Rahner are each attempting to "venture" into that "incomplete" territory—this territory, as such, is an existential theology.

---

mind, another problem is if there is really an "early" or "later" Heidegger at all—I believe there is not. A third problem, particularly with respect to Macquarrie, Bultmann, Tillich, and Rahner is if any Heideggerianism found in their thinking is directly incommensurable with theology proper.

2. This analogy is especially important when taking into consideration Heidegger's own analogy between "being" and God and, in turn, the extent to Heidegger conceives of "being" in the same manner as the theologians/philosophers of the High Middle Ages. See note 56.

3. See note 323.

4. Heidegger, *Being and Time*, 1.

5. Heidegger is more explicit in writings and lectures after *Being and Time* about his meaning of "unconcealment."

To be clear, I argue that each "venture" made by Macquarrie, Bultmann, Tillich, and Rahner charts a different path into the "incomplete" territory of *Being and Time*. The different path each takes—that is to say, each "venture" made—is based on their own theological preoccupations and the extent to which those individual preoccupations can be thematically and hermeneutically buttressed to the incomplete Part II of *Being and Time*. Each finds in this incompleteness an opportunity go where Heidegger does not—because Heidegger refuses a theological voice, each never refuses theirs. By fully embracing their own theological voice, each existential theologian's "pathmark" undoubtedly "ventures" into a kind of territory that is parallel to the course Heidegger takes after *Being and Time*.

Consequently, each attempts a systematic theological work—Macquarrie's *Principles of Christian Theology*, Bultmann's *Theology of the New Testament*, Tillich's *Systematic Theology*, and Rahner's *Foundations of Christian Faith*—that is a summative expression of their theological understanding of primordiality and *unconcealment* through their respective *Heideggerian lens*. For all, a *Dasein*-like entity figures into how each perceives primordialty as a means to grasp *unconcealment*—Macquarrie's λογος, Bultmann's κηρυγμα, Tillich's καιρος, and Rahner's χάρις embody *Dasein*-like analytics towards the possibility of *primordial being* and άληθεια. Essentially, Macquarrie's *linguistical-existential* venture, Bultmann's *historical-existential* venture, Tillich's *rational-existential* venture, and Rahner's *experiential-existential* venture are all "pathmarks" into the incomplete Part II of *Being and Time*.

APPENDIX A

"λόγος"

As a term, λόγος appears in the New Testament a total of 330 times in various iterations—129 in the Gospels (33 in Matthew, 24 in Mark, 32 in Luke, 40 in John), 65 in Acts, 48 occurrences in the undisputed Pauline letters, and the remaining occurrences distributed among Colossians (7), Ephesians (4), 2 Thessalonians (5), Hebrews (12), the Pastorals (20), Revelation (18), James (5), First and Third John (7), and First and Second Peter (10), and only in Philemon, Second John, and Jude does "logos" not appear. Since λόγος has so many variants in the New Testament—not just between the Gospels and the Pauline letters, but between the Gospels themselves and among Pauline letters—the term can be defined as "word," "speech," "account," or "sermon."[1] Even still, depending upon its semantic context, λόγος might also be translated as the following: language, narrative, statement, pronouncement, question, report, teaching, call, and sense, all of which become hermeneutically contingent on either philological or theological grounds.[2] In recognizing this variety of meaning, it is important to be clear about how I wish to specifically present λόγος—that is, my intent is to focus narrowly on λόγος in its nominative case.

Let us begin by examining how λόγος is first presented in the Pauline letters. For example, in 1 Thessalonians 1:8, Paul presents λόγος as:

ἀφ._ὑμῶν_γὰρ_ἐξήχηται_ὁ_λόγος_τοῦ_
κυρίου_οὐ_μόνονἐντῇ_Μακεδονίᾳ_καὶ_[ἐντῇ]

1. Horst Balz and Gerhard Schneider, eds., *Exegetical Dictionary of the New Testament: Volume 2* (Grand Rapids, MI: William B. Eerdmans Publishing Company, 1991), 356.

2. Ibid., 357.

Ἀχαΐα,_ἀλλ._ἐν_παντὶ_τόπῳ_ἡ_πίστις·ὑμῶν_ἡ_πρὸς_τὸν_θεὸν_
ἐξελήλυθεν, ὥστε_μὴ_χρείαν_ἔχειν_ἡμᾶς_λαλεῖν_τι·[3]

Here, when Paul writes of the "ὁ λόγος τοῦ κυρίου," he means, literally, "the Word of the Lord." What this means is that Paul considers λόγος as more than just a speech, an account, or sermon. Those terms offer a relatively low hermeneutics of λόγος—they are simply representations of λόγος in its everydayness.[4] Instead, when Paul uses λόγος, he considers the term in a metaphysical manner, one that extends beyond its everyday usage. In saying "the Word of the Lord," it is an imperative to capitalize "Word," rather than use "word," since the latter is still an everyday usage. The "Word" denotes something different in God than in humankind—this difference is what Paul taps into, in order to suggest the transcendental power in "the Word of the Lord" over that of, for instance, "the word of humankind."

Like Paul's use of λόγος, the Gospel of John appropriates λόγος as "Word" similarly. Of course, λόγος appears in the Synoptics before it appears in John, since John is written later.[5] But, only John offers λόγος in its fullest Christological power and hermeneutical intent—John 1:1 offers the best example of how λόγος is used to denote the "absolute logos of the historical appearance of Jesus, the eternal and divine giver of life on earth."[6] Not only does John 1:1 provide an example of λόγος in the nominative case, but how it expresses "the Word of God" in a way that "stands out sharply" from all other aforementioned occurrences.[7] As a case in point, consider the following passage:

Ἐν_ἀρχῇ_ἦν_ὁ_λόγος, καὶ_ὁ_λόγος_ἦν_πρὸς_τὸν_θεόν,
καὶ_θεὸς_ἦν_ὁ_λόγος.[8]

3. *Novum Testamentum Graece*, Edited by Eberhard Nestle and Erwin Nestle (Stuttgart: Deutsche Bibelgesellschaft, 1979), 532.

4. See note 36.

5. Joseph B. Tyson, *The New Testament and Early Christianity* (New York, NY: Macmillan Publishing Company, 1984), 331.

6. Horst Balz and Gerhard Schneider, eds., *Exegetical Dictionary of the New Testament: Volume 2* (Grand Rapids, MI: William B. Eerdmans Publishing Company, 1991), 357.

7. Ibid.

8. *Novum Testamentum Graece*, Edited by Eberhard Nestle and Erwin Nestle (Stuttgart: Deutsche Bibelgesellschaft, 1979), 247.

Though it is a long sentence, in its entirely, this passage can be translated as "in the beginning was the Word, and the Word was with (the) God, and God was the Word."

In light of 1:1, the Gospel of John "opens with a hymn that celebrates God's revelation of himself to the world."[9] More importantly, the author of John suggests that God has existed alongside God's λόγος, and that λόγος is God's mind, as well as the purpose and the agent of God's self-disclosure.[10] From this eternal preexisting connection between God and λόγος, John proceeds to discuss λόγος as having an all-encompassing function in creation and, in turn, the specific function of identifying Christ himself as the personal λόγος.[11]

9. Charles M. Laymon, ed. *The Interpreter's One-Volume Commentary on the Bible* (Nashville, TN: Abingdon, 1982), 709.

10. Ibid.

11. Only John 1:1 discusses the "eternal preexistence" of λόγος with God. Subsequently, verses 2 through 5 describe the roles of λόγος in the creation and with identifying Christ's incarnation as "the historical coming of λόγος to the human world." Horst Balz and Gerhard Schneider, eds., *Exegetical Dictionary of the New Testament: Volume 2* (Grand Rapids, MI: William B. Eerdmans Publishing Company, 1991), 539.

APPENDIX B

"κηρυγμα"

In the New Testament canon, κηρυγμα appears as two alternate versions, both of which carry hermeneutical meanings and etymological roots: "keryx" and "kerysso"—while the former takes the pronoun form of "proclaimer," the latter assumes the verb form of "proclaim."[1] As a version of κηρυγμα, "kerysso" appears a total of 61 times in the New Testament: 9 in the Gospel of Matthew, 14 in the Gospel of Mark, 9 in the Gospel of Luke, 8 in the Book of Acts, 17 in the Pauline letters, 2 in Paul's Pastoral letters, and once each in First Peter 3:19 and Revelation 5:2.[2] However, the term κηρυγμα itself occurs only in Matthew 12:41, Luke 11:32, Mark 16:8 (with a shorter Markan ending), and has 4 occurrences in the following Pauline letters: Romans 16:25, the first Epistle to the Corinthians (1:21, 2:4, and 15:14), Second Timothy 4:17, and Titus 1:3.[3] In that nominative case, κηρυγμα holds the most significance, especially for Bultmann's existential theology. When translated as "proclamation," κηρυγμα, as a distinctly existential term, "corresponds to the faith that exudes achievement, in which the believer, who has been affected by the word that addresses him, becomes enlisted in the liberating service on the basis of the proclamation."[4] With

---

1. Holst Balz and Gerhard Schneider, eds., *Exegetical Dictionary of the New Testament: Volume 2* (Grand Rapids, MI: William B. Eerdmans Publishing Company, 1991), 288.

2. Ibid.

3. Ibid.

4. Ibid., 289.

this in mind, κήρυγμα denotes active participation between the proclaimer and the hearer, especially as described by Paul as the act of "proclaiming."[5]

In terms of its nominative case and the dating ascribed to Paul's corpus, κήρυγμα first appears in 1 Cor. 2:4 in the following:

καὶ_ὁ_λόγος_μου_καὶ_τὸ_κήρυγμά_
μουοὐκὲν_πειθοῖ[ς]_σοφίας_[λόγοις]_ἀλλ.
_ἐν_ἀποδείξει_πνεύματος_καὶ_δυνάμεως...[6]

Here, the segment "καὶ τὸ κήρυγμά μου" can be translated as either "and my preaching" or "and my proclamation."[7] There appears to be no significance difference between the two, since both are describing an act that, as aforementioned, require both a proclaimer and a hearer—"and my preaching" or "and my proclamation" are synonymous. In either case, Paul uses κήρυγμά to describe his "preaching" to the Corinthians, especially as a κήρυγμά that provides a kind of wisdom and instills a sort of power that cannot be accomplished by humankind.[8] But, more importantly, Paul sees his preaching as a "proclamation" of the mystery of God and Jesus Christ crucified.[9] This sentiment is repeated in Paul's Letter to the Romans, which is often dated after the Letter to the Corinthians.[10] Towards the end of the letter to the Romans, Paul discusses κήρυγμά in 16:25:

Τῷ_δὲ_δυναμένῳ_ὑμᾶς_στηρίξαι_κατὰ_τὸ_εὐαγγέλιόν_
μου_καὶ_τὸ_κήρυγμα_Ἰησοῦ_Χριστοῦ, κατὰ_ἀποκάλυψιν_
μυστηρίου_χρόνοις_αἰωνίοις_σεσιγημένου...[11]

Here, the segment "καὶ τὸ κήρυγμα Ἰησοῦ Χριστοῦ" is translated as "and the proclamation of Jesus Christ."[12] Clearly, Paul maintains the "proclamation"

---

5. Ibid.

6. *Novum Testamentum Graece*, Edited by Eberhard Nestle and Erwin Nestle (Stuttgart: Deutsche Bibelgesellschaft, 1979), 443.

7. The literal translation is closer to "preaching," but the NRSV assumes "proclamation."

8. Charles M. Laymon, ed. *The Interpreter's One-Volume Commentary on the Bible* (Nashville, TN: Abingdon, 1982), 797.

9. 1 Corinthians 2:1–2

10. Joseph B. Tyson, *The New Testament and Early Christianity* (New York, NY: Macmillan Publishing Company, 1984), 331.

11. *Novum Testamentum Graece*, Edited by Eberhard Nestle and Erwin Nestle (Stuttgart: Deutsche Bibelgesellschaft, 1979), 440.

12. In this verse, "proclamation" is both a literal translation and a translation in the NSRV.

meaning of κήρυγμα, even if, on occasion, he lends that meaning towards "preaching"—again, the two terms can be viewed synonymously, but a subtle difference can be offered when comparing use in Paul's letters to use in the Gospels.

If moving chronologically from Paul's letters to the Gospels, Matthew provides the earliest example of κήρυγμα in the Synoptics.[13] Matthew 12:41 expresses the following:

ἄνδρες_Νινευῖται_ἀναστήσονται_ἐν_τῇ_κρίσει_μετὰ_τῆς_
γενεᾶς_ταύτης_καὶ_κατακρινοῦσιν_αὐτήν,_ὅτι_μετενόησαν_
εἰς_τὸ_κήρυγμα_Ἰωνᾶ,_καὶ_ἰδοὺ_πλεῖον_Ἰωνᾶ_ὧδε.[14]

The segment "εἰς τὸ κήρυγμα Ἰωνᾶ" is literally translated as "into the preaching of Jonah," with the preposition "of" added for possessive clarity.[15] Of course, translating κήρυγμα as "preaching" makes sense, if Jonah is relating "his experience within the whale [where] his preaching [is] in response to which the people of Nineveh repented."[16] Though it is surely hermeneutically possible to substitute "proclamation" for "preaching" in Matthew 12:41, it appears that the author of Matthew intends to reserve the term "proclamation" for Jesus Christ, in order to differentiate between Christ's "preaching" and Jonah's "preaching." Only Christ can proclaim— that is, particularly if "proclaiming" points to Christology, more so than "preaching" does.

13. Not only is the Pauline corpus dated before the Gospels, but, within the Synoptics, Mark is the earliest followed by Matthew and Luke (which are often argued as being written in the same period of time, due to their similar content). See Joseph B. Tyson, *The New Testament and Early Christianity* (New York, NY: Macmillan Publishing Company, 1984), 158.

14. *Novum Testamentum Graece*, Edited by Eberhard Nestle and Erwin Nestle (Stuttgart: Deutsche Bibelgesellschaft, 1979), 32.

15. I have added "of" to denote a kind genitive use, even though κήρυγμα is in the nominative.

16. Charles M. Laymon, ed. *The Interpreter's One-Volume Commentary on the Bible* (Nashville, TN: Abingdon, 1982), 624.

APPENDIX C

"καιρος"

Καιρος has a total of 85 occurrences in the New Testament Canon in varying cases: 5 in Mark, 10 in Matthew, 13 in Luke, 3 in John, 9 in the Book of Acts, 17 in the undisputed Pauline letters, 6 in the disputed Pauline letters (Second Thessalonians, Ephesians, and Colossians), 7 in the Pastorals, 4 each in Hebrews and First Peter, and 7 in Revelation.[1] In the New Testament, the term καιρος is used as partial synonym of "chronos"— they are only partially synonyms, because "chronos" designates "a period of time" in the linear sense, while καιρος frequently refers to "eschatological filled time, time for decision."[2] The latter contains more hermeneutical meaning, not just the authors of the Gospels, but for Paul particularly.

If looking for where καιρος first occurs in the nominative in the New Testament, Paul's letters provide the first historical occurrence.[3] Paul's use of the term καιρος "has a wide spectrum of meaning," which varies greatly depending upon Paul's intended audience and the purpose of his letter.[4] This becomes especially apparent when Paul utilizes καιρος to refer to "the coming moment of judgment and/or parousia."[5] By conceptualizing

1. Horst Balz and Gerhard Schneider, eds., *Exegetical Dictionary of the New Testament: Volume 2* (Grand Rapids, MI: William B. Eerdmans Publishing Company, 1991), 232

2. Ibid.

3. Joseph B. Tyson, *The New Testament and Early Christianity* (New York, NY: Macmillan Publishing Company, 1984), 331.

4. Horst Balz and Gerhard Schneider, eds., *Exegetical Dictionary of the New Testament: Volume 2* (Grand Rapids, MI: William B. Eerdmans Publishing Company, 1991), 232.

5. Ibid., 233.

καιρος in this way, Paul, indeed, has an eschatological bent for the term, not just as "a time," but "the time"—for Paul, καιρος is certainly "the event." Therefore, Paul's first letter to the Corinthians contains Paul's eschatological understanding of καιρος. Consider 7:29 as an example:

τοῦτο_δέ_φημι,_ἀδελφοί, ὁ_καιρὸς_συνεσταλμένος_ἐστίν· τὸ_
λοιπὸν_ἵνα_καὶ_οἱ_ἔχοντες γυναῖκας_ὡς_μὴ_ἔχοντες_ὦσιν. . .[6]

Here, the segment "ὁ καιρὸς συνεσταλμένος ἐστίν" is translated literally as "the season straightened is." However, a more sensible construction would be "the season is straightened," since the segment's verb ἐστίν comes at the segment's end, rather than between καιρὸς (noun) and συνεσταλμένος (adjective). Nevertheless, for Paul, καιρὸς as "season" suggests that Paul recognizes the imminence of καιρὸς, especially as an eschatological event.

Like Paul's use in the first letter to the Corinthians, the Gospel of Mark uses καιρὸς similarly: it is not "time" in humanity's sense of the word, but a specific "eschatological time" in relation to God. For example, the author of Mark uses καιρὸς in the following from 1:15:

καὶ_λέγων,_ὅτι_πεπλήρωται_ὁ_καιρὸς_
καὶ_ἤγγικεν_ἡ_βασιλεία_τοῦ_θεοῦ·
μετανοεῖτε_καὶ_πιστεύετε_ἐν_τῷ_εὐαγγελίῳ.[7]

The segment that reads "καὶ λέγων, ὅτι πεπλήρωται ὁ καιρὸς καὶ ἤγγικεν ἡ βασιλεία τοῦ θεοῦ" can be literally translated as "and saying that has been fulfilled the time and has drawn near the kingdom of (the) God." This must be rearranged more sensibly as "and saying that the time has been fulfilled"—the time, then, is what "has drawn near the kingdom of God." Clearly, even when rearranged, the author of Mark shares Paul's eschatological concept of καιρὸς. But, with more muscular language, the author of Mark suggests that καιρὸς, when fulfilled, ushers in "the kingdom of God."

6. *Novum Testamentum Graece*, Edited by Eberhard Nestle and Erwin Nestle (Stuttgart: Deutsche Bibelgesellschaft, 1979), 452.

7 Ibid., 89.

APPENDIX D

"χάρις"

χάρις appears a total of 156 times in the New Testament in varying cases, carrying the meanings of "grace," "gratitude," or "esteem."[1] In the Gospels of Luke and John, χάρις occurs 8 and 4 times respectively, as well as 17 times in the Book of Acts.[2] But, χάρις can be found in its "highest frequency" in the Pauline letters: 24 in Romans, 10 in First Corinthians, 18 in Second Corinthians, 7 in Galatians, 3 in Philippians, 2 each in First Thessalonians and Philemon, in addition to 12 in Ephesians, 5 in Colossians, 13 in the Pastorals, 8 in Hebrews, and 10 in First Peter.[3] In each of these occurrences, χάρις is conceptualized as "the opening of access to God in the larger sense of precisely God himself."[4] What this means, then, is that χάρις makes it possible for God's existence to be accessed openly by human existence—it allows for the being-Being dialectic to the possible.[5] In this respect, χάρις can be conceptualized in the Aristotlean sense, since God's "Being" consists of a gratuitous nature, one that is bestowed upon humanity's "being."[6] Accordingly, "grace" as χάρις has a "special significance for Christian existence [to the extent that] existence in grace is...thought of as

1. Horst Balz and Gerhard Schneider, eds., *Exegetical Dictionary of the New Testament: Volume 3* (Grand Rapids, MI: William B. Eerdmans Publishing Company, 1993), 457.

2. Ibid.

3. Ibid.

4. Ibid., 458.

5. If considering the being-Being dialectic as the relatedness of humanity's "being" to God's "Being," then χάρις is what grounds that dialectic in existential relatedness.

6. See Aristotle, Rhetorics, 2.7.1385

a process of growth for which the initial proclamation has provided enduring standards in the form of doctrine."[7] To this end, χάρις is something that makes an encounter with God all the more experiential and existential— χάρις situates human existence as Christian existence in relation to God's existence and, in turn, edifies what it means to be human and have a connectedness to God.

In 1 Thessalonians 1:1, Paul presents the earliest nominative example[8] of χάρις as an "experiential-existential" encounter in the following passage:

Παῦλος_καὶ_Σιλουανὸς καὶ_Τιμόθεος_τῇ_ἐκκλησίᾳ_
Θεσσαλονικέωνἐν_θεῷ_πατρὶ_καὶ_κυρίῳ_Ἰησοῦ_Χριστῷ,_
χάρις_ὑμῖν_καὶ_εἰρήνη.[9]

The segment "χάρις ὑμῖν καὶ εἰρήνη" can be translated as "grace to you and peace." Though this segment is at the end of Paul's salutation to the Church of Thessalonia, Paul's notion of χάρις is connected to his notion of peace. That is, the possibility of "peace" comes from the actuality of χάρις. For Paul, χάρις is something that makes "peace" possible—and, for the budding Thessalonian Church, χάρις was assuredly an essential component of ensuring the survival of the church and the congregants. In this way, when Paul wishes χάρις to the audience of the first Thessalonian letter, he is wishing for God to grant that χάρις, since, once that χάρις is bestowed upon them, it will allow them to be at peace with God.

Like Paul, the Gospel of Luke presents χάρις as something that grants peace with God through the *experiential-existential*. Consider Luke 2:40 contains this earliest, nominative example of χάρις.[10] The author of Luke uses χάρις in the following:

7. Horst Balz and Gerhard Schneider, eds., *Exegetical Dictionary of the New Testament: Volume 3* (Grand Rapids, MI: William B. Eerdmans Publishing Company, 1993), 458.

8. The "earliest," since Paul's first letter to the Thessalonians is the earliest dated letter among the canonized Pauline letters (disputed or undisputed). Joseph B. Tyson, *The New Testament and Early Christianity* (New York, NY: Macmillan Publishing Company, 1984), 331.

9. *Novum Testamentum Graece*, Edited by Eberhard Nestle and Erwin Nestle (Stuttgart: Deutsche Bibelgesellschaft, 1979), 159.

10. It must be noted that there is, in fact, another example of "charis" within the Gospel of Luke that occurs earlier than 2:40. This case is in 1:30, but "charis" takes the accusative case, rather than the nominative.

Τὸ_δὲ_παιδίον_ηὔξανεν_καὶ_ἐκραταιοῦτο_πληρούμενον_
σοφίᾳ,_καὶ_χάρις_θεοῦ_ἦν_ἐπ_αὐτό.[11]-

When considering the segment "καὶ χάρις θεοῦ ἦν ἐπ αὐτό," the best translation would be "and (the) grace (of) God was upon him," when inserting
the article "the" and the preposition "of" in places for reading clarity.[12] Still,
in terms of meaning, the author of Luke believes χάρις to be something that
is placed "upon" humanity, through the experience humanity has with God.

---

11. *Novum Testamentum Graece*, Edited by Eberhard Nestle and Erwin Nestle (Stuttgart: Deutsche Bibelgesellschaft, 1979), 531.

12. The word θεοῦ is taking the genitive case, which warrants the preposition "of."

Bibliography

2012 Book of Discipline of the United Methodist Church. Nashville, TN: The United Methodist Publishing House, 2012.

Adams, James L. *Paul Tillich's Philosophy of Culture, Science, and Religion.* New York, NY: Schocken, 1970.

Aristotle. *Metaphysics.* Translated by Richard Hope. Ann Arbor, MI: The University of Michigan Press, 1960.

———. *Physics.* Translated by Richard Hope. Lincoln, NE: University of Nebraska Press, 1961.

Ashcraft, Morris. *Rudolf Bultmann.* Peabody, MA: Hendrickson, 1972.

Balz, Horst and Gerhard Schneider, eds. *Exegetical Dictionary of the New Testament: Volume 2.* Grand Rapids, MI: William B. Eerdmans, 1991.

———. *Exegetical Dictionary of the New Testament: Volume 3.* Grand Rapids, MI: William B. Eerdmans, 1993.

Barrett, William. *Irrational Man: A Study in Existential Philosophy.* Garden City, NY: Doubleday, 1958.

———. *What is Existentialism?* New York, NY: Grove, 1964.

Bauer, Walter. *A Greek-English Lexicon of the New Testament and Other Early Christian Literature.* Chicago, IL: The University Of Chicago Press, 1979.

Blackham, H. J., ed. *Reality, Man, and Existence: Essential Works of Existentialism.* New York, NY: Bantam, 1965.

Blackham, H. J. *Six Existentialist Thinkers.* New York, NY: Harper and Brothers, 1959.

Bonsor, Jack A. *Rahner, Heidegger, and Truth: Karl Rahner's Notion of Christian Truth: The Influence of Heidegger.* Lanham, MD: University Press of America, 1987.

Breisach, Ernst. *Introduction to Modern Existentialism.* New York, NY: Grove, 1962.

Brentano, Franz. *The Origin of the Knowledge of Right and Wrong,* Translated by Cecil Hague. London, UK: Archibald Constable and Company, Limited, 1902.

———. *The Theory of Categories.* Translated by Roderick M. Chisholm and Norbert Guterman. The Hague: Martinus Nijhoff, 1981.

Brown, Charles E. *The Self in Time: Retrieving Existential Theology and Freud.* New York, NY: University Press of America, 1997.

Bultmann, Rudolf. "The Historicity of Man and Faith." In *Existence and Faith: The Shorter Writings of Rudolf Bultmann.* Edited and Translated by Schubert M. Ogden. New York, NY: The World, 1966: 92–110.

———. *History and Eschatology: The Presence of Eternity: The Gifford Lectures 1955.* New York, NY: Harper and Row, 1957.

Bibliography

——. *The History of the Synoptic Tradition*. Translated by John Marsh. New York, NY: Harper and Row, 1968.

——. *Jesus and the Word*. Translated by Louise P. Smith and Erminie H. Lantero. London, UK: Charles Scribner's Son's, 1958.

——. *Jesus Christ and Mythology*. New York, NY: Charles Scribner's Sons, 1958.

——. "New Testament and Mythology." In *Kerygma and Myth: A Theological Debate*, Edited by Hans W. Bartsch. New York, NY: Harper and Row, 1961: 1–44.

——. *Primitive Christianity in its Contemporary Setting*. Translated by Reginald H. Fuller. Philadelphia, PA: Fortress, 1956.

——. "The Problem of a Theological Exegesis of the New Testament." In *Rudolf Bultmann: Interpreting Faith for the Modern Era*. Edited by Roger A. Johnson. San Francisco, CA: Collins San Francisco, 1987: 86–119.

——. *Theologie des Neuen Testaments*. Tübingen: J. C. B. Mohr, 1968.

——. *Theology of the New Testament Volume 1*. Translated by Kendrick Grobel. New York, NY: Charles Scribner's Sons, 1951.

——. *Theology of the New Testament Volume 2*. Translated by Kendrick Grobel. New York, NY: Charles Scribner's Sons, 1955.

Calvin, John. *Institutes of the Christian Religion: Volume 1*. Edited by John T. McNeill. Translated by Ford L. Battles. Philadelphia, PA: The Westminster, 1960.

Clayton, John P. "Questioning, Answering, and Tillich's Concept of Correlation." In *Kairos and Logos: Studies in the Roots and Implications of Tillich's Theology*. Edited by John J. Carey. Macon, GA: Mercer University Press, 1978: 121–140.

Collins, James. *The Existentialists: A Critical Study*. Chicago, IL: Henry Regnery, 1952.

Congdon, David. *The Mission of Demythologizing: Rudolf Bultmann's Dialectical Theology*. Minneapolis, MN: Fortress Press, 2015.

Deleuze, Gilles. *Pure Immanence: Essays on a Life*. Translated by Anne Boyman. New York, NY: Zone Books, 2001.

Dennison, William. *The Young Bultmann: Context for His Understanding of God, 1884–1925*. New York, NY: Peter Lang, 2008.

Di Giovanni, George, ed. "Preface." *Between Kant and Hegel: Texts in the Development of Post-Kantian Idealism*. Indianapolis, IN: Hackett Publishing Company, 2000.

Edie, James M. "The Absence of God." In *Christianity and Existentialism*. Evanston, IL: Northwestern University Press, 1963: 113–148.

Fritz, Peter J. *Karl Rahner's Theological Aesthetics*. Washington, D.C., The Catholic University of America Press, 2014.

Gadamer, Hans-Georg. *Truth and Method*. Translated by Garrett Barden and John Cumming. New York, NY: Crossroad, 1985.

Gall, Robert S. *Beyond Theism and Atheism: Heidegger's Significance for Religious Thinking*. Dordrecht, The Netherlands: Martinus Nijhoff, 1987.

Gilkey, Langdon. *Gilkey on Tillich*. New York, NY: Crossroad, 1990.

Grigg, Richard. *Symbol and Empowerment: Paul Tillich's Post-Theistic System*. Macon, GA: Mercer University Press, 1985.

Guignon, Charles, ed. *The Cambridge Companion to Heidegger*. New York, NY: Cambridge University Press, 1993.

Hammann, Konrad. *Rudolf Bultmann: A Biography*. Translated by Philip E. Devenish. Salem, OR: Polebridge Press, 2013

Harrelson, Walter J., Donald Senior, Abraham Smith, Phyllis Trible, and James C. VanderKam, eds. *The New Interpreter's Study Bible: New Revised Standard Version with the Apocrypha.* Nashville, TN: Abingdon, 2003.

Heidegger, Martin. *The Basic Problems of Phenomenology.* Translated by Albert Hofstadter. Bloomington, IN: Indiana University Press, 1982.

———. *Basic Questions of Philosophy: Selected "Problems" of "Logic."* Translated by Richard Rojcewicz and André Schuwer. Bloomington, IN: Indiana University Press, 1994.

———. *Being and Time.* Translated by John Macquarrie and Edward Robinson. San Francisco, CA: Harper San Francisco, 1962.

———. *Being and Truth.* Translated by Gregory Fried and Richard Polt. Bloomington, IN: Indiana University Press, 2010.

———. *Contributions to Philosophy (From Enowning).* Translated by Parvis Emad and Kenneth Maly. Bloomington, IN: Indiana University Press, 1999.

———. *Early Greek Thinking: The Dawn of Western Philosophy.* Translated by David F. Krell and Frank A. Capuzzi. New York, NY: Harper and Row Publishers, 1984.

———. "The End of Philosophy and the Task of Thinking." In *Basic Writings.* Edited by David F. Krell. San Francisco, CA: Harper San Francisco, 1992: 427–449.

———. *The Essence of Truth: On Plato's Cave Allegory and Theaetetus.* Translated by Ted Sadler. New York, NY: Continuum, 2002.

———. *The Event.* Translated by Richard Rojcewicz. Bloomington, IN: Indiana University Press, 2013.

———. *The Fundamental Concepts of Metaphysics: World, Finitude, Solitude.* Translated by William Mcneill and Nicholas Walker. Bloomington, IN: Indiana University Press, 1995.

———. *Hegel.* Translated by Joseph Arel and Niels Feuerhahn. Bloomington, IN: Indiana University Press, 2015.

———. *Hegel's Phenomenology of Spirit.* Translated by Parvis Emad and Kenneth Maly. Bloomington, IN: Indiana University Press, 1994.

———. *History of the Concept of Time: Prolegomena.* Translated by Theodore Kisiel. Bloomington, IN: Indiana University Press, 1985.

———. *An Introduction to Metaphysics.* Translated by Ralph Manheim. New haven, CT: Yale University Press, 1959.

———. *Introduction to Phenomenological Research.* Translated by Daniel O. Dahlstrom (Bloomington, IN: Indiana University Press, 2003.

———. *Kant and the Problem of Metaphysics.* Translated by Richard Taft. Bloomington, IN: Indiana University Press, 1997.

———. "Letter on Humanism." In *Basic Writings.* Edited by David F. Krell. San Francisco, CA: Harper San Francisco, 1992: 213–265.

———. *Logic: The Question of Truth.* Translated by Thomas Sheehan. Bloomington, IN: Indiana University Press, 2010.

———. *Logic as the Question Concerning the Essence of Language.* Translated by Wanda T. Gregory and Yvonne Unna. New York, NY: State University of New York Press, 2009.

———. *The Metaphysical Foundation of Logic.* Translated by Michael Heim. Bloomington, IN: Indiana University Press, 1984.

———. *Mindfulness.* Translated by Parvis Emad and Thomas Kalary. New York, NY: Continuum, 2006.

———. *Nietzsche: Volume 1: The Will to Power as Art*. Translated and Edited by David F. Krell. New York, NY: Harper and Row, 1979.

———. *Nietzsche: Volume 3: The Will to Power as Knowledge and as Metaphysics*. Edited by David F. Krell. New York, NY: Harper and Row Publishers, 1987.

———. *Off the Beaten Path*. Translated and Edited by Julian Young and Kenneth Haynes. New York, NY: Cambridge University Press, 2002.

———. "On the Essence of Truth." In *Basic Writings*. Edited by David F. Krell. San Francisco, CA: Harper San Francisco, 1992: 111–138.

———. *On the Way to Language*. Translated by Peter D. Hertz. Harper and Row, 1971.

———. *Ontology—The Hermeneutics of Facticity*. Translated by John van Buren. Bloomington, IN: Indiana University Press, 2008.

———. "Origin of the Work of Art." In *Poetry, Language, Thought*. Translated by Albert Hofstadter. New York, NY: Harper and Row, 1971: 15–87.

———. "Overcoming Metaphysics." In *The End of Philosophy*. Translated by Joan Stambaugh. Chicago, IL: The University of Chicago Press, 1973: 84–110.

———. *Parmenides*. Translated by André Schuwer and Richard Rojcewicz. Bloomington, IN: Indiana University Press, 1992.

———. "Phenomenology and Theology." In *The Piety of Thinking*. Translated by James G. Hart and John C. Maraldo. Bloomington, IN: Indiana University Press, 1976: 5–21.

———. *The Phenomenology of Religious Life*. Translated by Matthias Fritsch and Jennifer A. Gosetti-Ferencei. Bloomington, IN: Indiana University Press, 2010.

———. "Plato's Doctrine of Truth." In *Pathmarks*. Translated and Edited by William McNeill. New York, NY: Cambridge University Press, 1988: 155–182.

———. *Plato's Sophist*. Translated by Richard Rojcewicz and André Schuwer. Bloomington, IN: Indiana University Press, 1997.

———. "Preface to the German Edition." In *Pathmarks*. Translated and Edited by William McNeill. New York, NY: Cambridge University Press, 1998.

———. *The Principle of Reason*. Translated by Reginald Lilly. Bloomington, IN: Indiana University Press, 1996.

———. "The Problem of Sin in Luther." In *Supplements: From the Earliest Essays to Being and Time and Beyond*. Edited by John van Buren. New York, NY: SUNY Press, 2002.

———. *Schelling's Treatise on the Essence of Human Freedom*. Translated by Joan Stambaugh. Athens, OH: Ohio University Press, 1985.

———. *Sein und Zeit*. Tübingen: Max Niemeyer Verlag, 1967.

———. "The Self-Assertion of the German University." In *The Heidegger Controversy: A Critical Reader*. Edited by Richard Wolin. Cambridge, MA: The MIT Press, 1991.

———. *What is Called Thinking?* Translated by New York, NY: Harper Collins, 1976.

Hemming, Laurence P. *Heidegger's Atheism: The Refusal of a Theological Voice*. Notre Dame, IN: University of Notre Dame Press, 2002.

Herberg, Will, ed. *Four Existentialist Theologians: A Reader from the Works of Jacques Maritain, Nicolas Berdyaev, Martin Buber, and Paul Tillich*. Garden City, NY: Doubleday and Company Inc., 1958.

Husserl, Edmund. *The Crisis of European Sciences and Transcendental Phenomenology: An Introduction to Phenomenological Philosophy*. Translated by David Carr. Evanston, IL: Northwestern University Press, 1970.

———. *Ideas: General Introduction to Pure Phenomenology*. Translated by W. R. Gibson. New York, NY: Humanities, 1931.

Jenkins, David. *The Scope and Limits of John Macquarrie's Existential Theology*. Stockholm: Uppsala, 1987.

Jensen, G. M. A. *An Existential Approach to Theology*. Milwaukee, WI: The Bruce, 1966.

Jones, Scott J. *John Wesley's Conception and Use of Scripture*. Nashville, TN: Abingdon, 1995.

Kant, Immanuel. *Critique of Pure Reason*. Translated by Norman Kemp Smith. New York, NY: Cambridge University Press, 1993.

Kaufmann, Walter. *Critique of Religion and Philosophy*. Princeton, NJ: Princeton University Press, 1958.

Kegley, Charles W., ed. *The Theology of Paul Tillich*. New York, NY: The Pilgrim, 1982.

Kelly, Geffrey B. "Introduction." *Karl Rahner: Theologian of the Graced Search for Meaning*. Edited by Geffrey B. Kelly. Minneapolis, MN: Fortress, 1992.

Kierkegaard, Soren. *The Concept of Anxiety: A Simple Psychologically Orienting Deliberating on the Dogmatic Issue of Heredity Sin*. Translated by Reidar Thomte. Princeton, NJ: Princeton University Press, 1980.

Kilby, Karen. *Karl Rahner: A Brief Introduction*. New York, NY: The Crossroad, 2007.

Kisiel, Theodore. *The Genesis of Heidegger's Being and Time*. Berkeley, CA: University of California Press, 1993.

———. *Heidegger's Way of Thought: Critical and Interpretative Signposts*. New York, NY: Continuum, 2002.

Kovacs, George. *The Question of God in Heidegger's Phenomenology*. Evanston, IL: Northwestern University Press, 1990.

Kreeft, Peter, ed. *A Summa of the Summa: The Essential Philosophical Passages of St. Thomas Aquinas' Summa Theologica*. San Francisco, CA: Ignatius, 1990.

Künneth, Walter. "Bultmann's Philosophy and the Reality of Salvation." In *Kerygma and History: A Symposium on the Theology of Rudolf Bultmann*. Selected, Translated and Edited by Carl E. Braaten and Roy A, Harrisville. New York, NY: Abingdon, 1962: 86–119.

Laymon, Charles M., ed. *The Interpreter's One-Volume Commentary on the Bible* (Nashville, TN: Abingdon, 1982.

Leibniz, Gottfried. "The Principles of Philosophy, or the Monadology." In *Discourse on Metaphysics, Correspondence with Arnauld, and Monadology*. Translated by George R. Montgomery. La Salle, IL: The Open Court, 1968.

———. "The Principles of Philosophy, or the Monadology." In *Philosophical Essays*. Translated by Roger Ariew and Daniel Garber. Indianapolis, IN: Hackett, 1989.

Long, Eugene T. *Existence, Being, and God: An Introduction to the Philosophical Theology of John Macquarrie*. New York, NY: Paragon House, 1985

Macquarrie, John. *Existentialism*. New York, NY: World, 1972.

———. *An Existentialist Theology: A Comparison of Heidegger and Bultmann*. New York, NY: The Macmillan Company, 1955.

———. *God-Talk: An Examination of the Language and Logic of Theology*. New York, NY: The Seabury, 1979.

———. *In Search of Deity: An Essay in Dialectical Theism*. New York, NY: The Crossroad, 1984.

———. *In Search of Humanity: A Theological and Philosophical Approach*. New York, NY: The Crossroad, 1983.

———. *Martin Heidegger*. Richmond, VA: John Knox, 1969.

———. *On Being a Theologian*. Edited by John H. Morgan. London, UK: SCM, 1999.

———. "Pilgrimage in Theology." In *Being and Truth: Essays in Honor of John Macquarrie*. Edited by Alistair Kee and Eugene T. Long. London, UK: SCM Press, 1986.

———. *Principles of Christian Theology*. New York, NY: Charles Scribner's Sons, 1977.

———. *The Scope of Demythologizing: Bultmann and his Critics*. London, UK: SCM, 1960.

———. *Studies in Christian Existentialism*. Montreal: McGill University Press, 1965.

———. *Twentieth-Century Religious Thought: The Frontiers of Philosophy and Theology, 1900–1970*. London, UK: SCM, 1963.

Macquarrie. John, ed. *Contemporary Religious Thinkers: From Idealist Metaphysicians to Existential Theologian*. New York, NY: Harper and Row, 1968.

Martin, Bernard. *The Existentialist Theology of Paul Tillich*. New Haven, CT: College and University Press, 1963.

McKelway, Alexander J. *The Systematic Theology of Paul Tillich: A Review and Analysis*. Richmond, VA: John Knox, 1965.

McManus, Denis. *Heidegger and the Measure of Truth: Themes from His Early Philosophy*. Oxford, UK: Oxford University Press, 2012.

Novum Testamentum Graece. Edited by Eberhard Nestle and Erwin Nestle. Stuttgart: Deutsche Bibelgesellschaft, 1979.

O'Meara, Dominic J. "Introduction." In *Neoplatonism and Christian Thought*. Edited by Dominic J. O'Meara. Albany, NY: State University of New York, 1982.

Ott, Hugo. *Martin Heidegger: A Political Life*. Translated by Allan Blunden. New York, NY: Basic, 1993.

Outler, Albert C. "The Wesleyan Quadrilateral in John Wesley," in *Wesleyan Theological Journal* v. 20, n 1 (Spring 1985): 7–18.

Outler, Albert C., ed. *John Wesley*. New York, NY: Oxford University Press, 1964.

———. *The Works of John Wesley: Volume 1: Sermons I, 1–33*. Nashville, TN: Abingdon, 1984.

Plato. *The Republic*. Translated by Raymond Larson. Wheeling, IL: Harlan Davidson, Inc., 1979.

———. *Theaetetus*. Translated by M. J. Levett. Indianapolis, IN: Hackett, 1992.

Rahner, Karl. "Concerning the Relationship between Nature and Grace." In *Theological Investigations Volume 1: God, Christ, Mary, and Grace*. Translated by Cornelius Ernst. Baltimore, MD: Helicon, 1961: 297–317.

———. "Experience of Self and Experience of God." In *Theological Investigation Volume XIII: Theology, Anthropology, Christology*. Translated by David Bourke. New York, NY: The Seabury, 1975: 122–132.

———. *Foundations of Christian Faith: An Introduction to the Idea of Christianity*. Translated by William V. Dych. New York, NY: The Seabury, 1978.

———. *Grundkurs des Glaubens: Einführung in den Begriff des Christentums*. Freiburg: Herder, 1977.

———. *Hearer of the Word: Laying the Foundation for a Philosophy of Religion*. Translated by Joseph Donceel. New York, NY: Continuum, 1994.

———. "Nature and Grace." In *Theological Investigations Volume IV: More Recent Writings*. Translated by Kevin Smith. Baltimore, MD: Helicon, 1966: 165–188.

———. *Nature and Grace: And Other Essays*. New York, NY: Sheed and Ward, 1963.

———. "Philosophy and Philosophising in Theology" In *Theological Investigations Volume IX: Writings of 1965–1967*. Translated by Graham Harrison. New York, NY: Herder and Herder, 1972: 46–63.

Bibliography

———. "Philosophy and Theology" In *Theological Investigations Volume VI: Concerning the Vatican Council*. Translated by Karl-H and Boniface Kruger. Baltimore, MD: Helicon, 1969: 71–81.

———. "Possible Courses for the Theology of the Future." In *Theological Investigation Volume XIII: Theology, Anthropology, Christology*. Translated by David Bourke. New York, NY: The Seabury, 1975: 32–60.

———. "Reflections on the Experience of Grace." In *Theological Investigations Volume III: The Theology of the Spiritual Life*. Translated by Karl-H and Boniface Kruger. Baltimore, MD: Helicon, 1967: 86–90.

———. *Spirit in the World*. Translated by William Dych. New York, NY: Continuum, 1994.

Richardson, William J. *Heidegger: Through Phenomenology to Thought*. The Hague: Martinus Nijhoff, 1963.

Riceour, Paul. "Preface to Bultmann," in *Essays on Biblical Interpretation*. Translated and Edited by Lewis S. Mudge. Philadelphia, PA: Fortress, 1980: 49–72

Roberts, Robert C. *Rudolf Bultmann's Theology: A Critical Interpretation*. Grand Rapids, MI: William B. Eerdmans, 1976.

Saussure, Ferdinand de. *Course on General Linguistics*. Edited by Charles Bally and Albert Sechehaye. New York, NY: Philosophical Library, 1969.

Schalow, Frank and Alfred Denker, eds. *Historical Dictionary of Heidegger's Philosophy*. Lantham, MD: Scarecrow, 2010.

Schilling, S. Paul. *Contemporary Continental Theologians*. Nashville, TN: Abingdon, 1966.

Schleiermacher, Friedrich. *Hermeneutics: The Handwritten Manuscripts*. Translated by James Duke and Jack Forstman. Atlanta, GA: Scholars, 1997.

Sheehan, Thomas. *Karl Rahner: The Philosophical Foundations*. Athens, OH: Ohio University Press, 1987.

———. "Metaphysics and Bivalence: On Karl Rahner's *Geist in Welt*." *The Modern Schoolman*, no. 12 (1): 21–43 (1985).

Stone, Jerome A. "Tillich and Schelling's Later Philosophy." In *Kairos and Logos: Studies in the Roots and Implications of Tillich's Theology*. Edited by John J. Carey. Macon, GA: Mercer University Press, 1978: 3–35.

Taylor, Mark K. "Introduction: The Theological Development and Contribution of Paul Tillich." In *Paul Tillich: Theologian of the Boundaries*. Edited by Mark K. Taylor. San Francisco, CA: Collins, 1987: 11–34.

Thiselton, Anthony. *Two Horizons: New Testament Hermeneutics and Philosophical Description with Special Reference to Heidegger, Bultmann, Gadamer, and Wittgenstein*. Grand Rapids, MI: William B. Eerdmans, 1980.

Thomas, George F. "The Method and Structure of Tillich's Theology." In *The Theology of Paul Tillich*. Edited by Charles W Kegley. New York, NY: The Pilgrim, 1982: 86–107.

Thomas, J. Heywood. *Paul Tillich*. Richmond, VA: John Knox, 1966.

Tillich, Paul. *A History of Christian Thought: From Its Judaic and Hellenistic Origins to Existentialism*. Edited by Carl E. Braaten New York, NY: Simon and Schuster, 1968.

———. *Biblical Religion and the Search for Ultimate Reality*. Chicago, IL: The University of Chicago Press, 1955.

———. *The Courage to Be*. New Haven, CT: Yale University Press, 1952.

———. *The Eternal Now*. New York, NY: Charles Scribner's Sons, 1963.

———. *Mortality and Beyond*. New York, NY: Harper and Row, 1957.

———. *My Search for Absolutes*. New York, NY: Simon and Schuster, 1984.

―――. "The Problem of Theological Method." In *Four Existentialist Theologians: A reader from the Works of Jacques Maritain, Nicolas Berdyaev, Martin Buber, and Paul Tillich*. Selected by Will Herberg. Garden City, NY: Doubleday and Company, 1958: 163–182.

―――. *The Protestant Era*. Chicago, IL: The University of Chicago Press, 1957.

―――. *Systematic Theology Volume 1: Reason and Revelation, Being and God*. Chicago, IL: The University of Chicago Press, 1951.

―――. *Systematic Theology Volume 2: Existence and the Christ*. Chicago, IL: The University of Chicago Press, 1957.

―――. *The System of the Sciences: According to Objects and Methods*. Translated by Paul Wiebe. East Brunswick, NJ: Associated University Presses Inc., 1981.

―――. *Theology of Culture*. Edited by Robert C. Kimball. New York, NY: Oxford University Press, 1964.

―――. *What is Religion?* Translated by James L. Adams. New York, NY: Harper and Row, 1973.

Trench, Richard C. *Synonyms of the New Testament*. Grand Rapids, MI: William B. Eerdmans, 1880.

Tyson, Joseph B. *The New Testament and Early Christianity*. New York, NY: Macmillan, 1984.

Van Buren, John. *The Young Heidegger: Rumor of the Hidden King*. Bloomington, IN: Indiana University Press, 1994.

Warnock, Mary. *Existentialism*. New York, NY: Oxford University Press, 1970.

Weiss, Paul. *Modes of Being*. London, UK: Ferrer and Simons, Inc., 1958.

Wheat, Leonard F. *Paul Tillich's Dialectical Humanism: Unmasking the God above God*. Baltimore, MD: The Johns Hopkins Press, 1970.

Wittgenstein, Ludwig. *Tractatus Logico-Philosophicus*. Translated by C. K. Ogden. New York, NY: Harcourt, Brace, Company Inc., 1922.

Wolfe, Judith. *Heidegger and Theology*. New York, NY: Bloomsbury T&T Clark, 2014.

Young, Norman J. *History and Existential Theology: The Role of History in the Thought of Rudolf Bultmann*. Philadelphia, PA: The Westminster, 1969.

Index

Index

Index

Made in the USA
Lexington, KY
06 December 2018